Landscape and Labour

Landscape and Labour

Work, Place, and the Working Class in Eliot, Hardy, and Lawrence

Brian Elliott

ROWMAN & LITTLEFIELD
Lanham • Boulder • New York • London

Published by Rowman & Littlefield
An imprint of The Rowman & Littlefield Publishing Group, Inc.
4501 Forbes Boulevard, Suite 200, Lanham, Maryland 20706
www.rowman.com

86-90 Paul Street, London EC2A 4NE

Copyright © 2021 by Brian Elliott

All rights reserved. No part of this book may be reproduced in any form or by any electronic or mechanical means, including information storage and retrieval systems, without written permission from the publisher, except by a reviewer who may quote passages in a review.

British Library Cataloguing in Publication Information Available

Library of Congress Cataloging-in-Publication Data

Names: Elliott, Brian, 1941- author.
Title: Landscape and labour : work, place, and the working class in Eliot, Hardy, and Lawrence / Brian Elliott.
Description: Lanham : Rowman & Littlefield, [2021] | Includes bibliographical references and index.
Identifiers: LCCN 2021011646 (print) | LCCN 2021011647 (ebook) | ISBN 9781786609106 (cloth) | ISBN 9781786609113 (epub)
Subjects: LCSH: English fiction—19th century—History and criticism. | English fiction—20th century—History and criticism. | Working class in literature. | Eliot, George, 1819-1880—Criticism and interpretation. | Hardy, Thomas, 1840-1928—Criticism and interpretation. | Lawrence, D. H. (David Herbert), 1885-1930—Criticism and interpretation.
Classification: LCC PR868.L3 E45 2021 (print) | LCC PR868.L3 (ebook) | DDC 823/.8093553—dc23
LC record available at https://lccn.loc.gov/2021011646
LC ebook record available at https://lccn.loc.gov/2021011647

Contents

Introduction: The Political Economy of Work and Place	vii
The Rise of Cultural Studies: The British Working Class in the Academy	vii
Working-Class Culture and the Novel	xii
1 George Eliot and the Morality of Work	1
Adam Bede: The Artisan Takes the Stage	1
Silas Marner: Soulless Work and the Consolations of Community	8
The Mill on the Floss: Landscape, Loss, and Memory	15
Felix Holt and *Middlemarch*: The Retreat from Working-Class Lives	23
2 Thomas Hardy and the Living Landscape	33
Under the Greenwood Tree and *Far from the Madding Crowd*: The Pastoral Comedy	33
The Return of the Native, The Mayor of Casterbridge, and *The Woodlanders*: No Salvation through Work Alone	43
Tess of the D'Urbervilles and *Jude the Obscure*: A World without Ends	58
3 D. H. Lawrence and Vital Connection	71
Sons and Lovers: From Darkness to Light	71
The Rainbow: A Short History of Authentic Selfhood	81
Women in Love: The Crisis of Creative Life	91

4	New Land, New Labour	103
	Working the Land: The English Working Class and the Struggle for Social Value	103
	The Contemporary Problem of Work under Neoliberalism	114
	Visionary Landscapes of the Future	125
Conclusion: Neoliberalism and a New Working-Class Politics		135
	Labour Loses Its Voice	135
	Making Space for a Future Politics	141
Index		147

Introduction
The Political Economy of Work and Place

THE RISE OF CULTURAL STUDIES: THE BRITISH WORKING CLASS IN THE ACADEMY

From the late 1950s through to the early 1970s, Richard Hoggart and Raymond Williams helped found a new area of research and debate: cultural studies. Theirs was not a disinterested, scholarly pursuit, dedicated to founding a new university department or institute. Instead, cultural studies were at once an intensely personal and more political matter. These founding figures had each come from a working-class background and found themselves in a university environment whose core assumptions about society, values, and knowledge they did not share. For them, it was far from enough for modern Britain to admit a small proportion of 'bright' working-class youth; instead, it was a matter of staking claims for a working-class culture that had, until then, only ever been seen in terms of a social deficit. The working class were to be admitted to the universities in order to induct them into the ways of legitimate knowledge. Against this presumption, the original concern of cultural studies was to demonstrate that the working class had its own, just as legitimate, culture. Again, it was not enough to recognize that this working-class culture stood over and against the traditionally acknowledged 'high culture'. Rather, even in so-called high culture were to be found connections to working-class culture; connections which had been hitherto dismissed or downplayed.

The educational and cultural politics of contemporary Britain appear to have been ceding ground gained by the founders of cultural studies since the neoliberal counter-revolution of the 1980s. While there have never been more working-class people in universities and colleges, the social and cultural standing of the British working class has been in retreat for decades. An underlying hypothesis of this book is that the core reasons for this retreat are to be found, most crucially, in the social conditions of work. Britain's mature neoliberal economy has established a paradigm of work in terms of individualist entrepreneurialism. Under this paradigm, the pressures of individual self-improvement mount and the spectre of economic and social failure haunts all social and economic relations. These pressures fall particularly hard on members of the working class.

While Hoggart (1957) observed and described, over sixty years ago, a working class largely undisturbed by the neoliberal imperative of limitless self-improvement, by the early 1970s Sennett and Cobb (1972) discovered an American working class plagued by an unsatisfied craving for social recognition and personal dignity. What was also recorded by these American researchers was a curious mismatch between rising expectations for formal credentials and the actual relevance of those credentials to performing the tasks required on the job. Their explanation for this was simple but startling: educational (and, thereby, cultural) credentials were the most direct way to maintain the values of a social system based on a class hierarchy.

In contemporary political rhetoric on education in Britain one tends to hear the same message repeated, namely that the socially disadvantaged need to make more use of the educational resources put at their disposal in order to improve their lot. When I began university in the early 1990s, as a working-class student I was unburdened by tuition fees and was given a maintenance grant by my local education authority for four years. Nowadays, a similarly placed working-class school leaver will have to pay up to £9250 a year in tuition and may qualify for a maintenance loan to defray living expenses. Both will have to be paid back and, over three or four years, will see a young working-class graduate shackled to significant debt before they even have a chance to enter a profession of any kind.

In tandem, the terms of post-university work have changed, with the general expectation being that a graduate will have to accept a low-paid position or unpaid internship for a certain amount of time. Burdened by college debts and, almost certainly, with no parental funds available, a working-class graduate will be in no position to work for nothing. The chances are, then, that they will be more or less forced into casual work to pay the bills. If they wish to work in the 'creative industries', it is likely he or she will eke out a hand-to-mouth living for years if not decades. And all of this came about in a period of unprecedented wealth creation in the UK. It is in this unremittingly harsh context that working-class school leavers are being told to make the most of the educational opportunities presented to them. But the reality of these 'opportunities' is increasingly dawning on the current generation of British working-class school leavers.

As Foucault (2008) and others have pointed out, neoliberal governance is far from being simply an economic order that funnels increasing wealth to the '1 per cent'. It is that, of course; but it also entails, crucially, a certain distribution of social prestige. The early cultural theorists paid close attention to the growth in communications technologies in the nineteenth and twentieth centuries. As earlier thinkers, such as Walter Benjamin (2019 [1936]), had already noted, these technologies were founded on the new economic model of advertising. What Williams (2005) called the 'magical system', advertising first grew into a pervasive social reality thanks to advances in mechanical reproduction and photography. By the middle of the nineteenth century, one could identify in the great cities of Europe the beginnings of what came to be called the consumer society. The commodity in a historically specific sense came into being when images of the object of desire could precede and virtually replace the very object itself. This is the underlying logic of advertising: to unhinge social needs from their determinate and accustomed expression and thereby proliferate the socially acknowledged objects of desire.

Ironically enough, it was within the supremely bourgeois environment of commodity consumption that the typical Victorian concern for culture arose. For, in an everyday environment awash in desirable objects, how is one to select 'the best that has been thought and known'? The expression is from Matthew Arnold, whose *Culture and Anarchy* (1869) opposed the mob-rule degradation of democracy, in terms of 'doing what one wants', to the restraint of well-trained expert taste and formal education. It is worthwhile recalling that the political context in which the universal right to state education was established in Britain (through the Education Act of 1870) was deeply imbued with Arnold's concern to improve the unruly working-class masses. Here the working class is assumed to be intrinsically without culture, so that the task of education is essentially a matter of placing knowledge into empty vessels. What the educated worker hopefully comes to be is cultured; and, in order to arrive at this state, what the worker possesses in his unimproved state must be deemed essentially worthless. This is the original thesis of 'high culture', and its persistence, in our own times, is a primary concern of this inquiry.

In his ground-breaking work *The Uses of Literacy*, first published in 1957, Richard Hoggart splits his investigation into two quite distinct halves. The first half offers a portrait of northern English working-class life drawn from the author's first-hand experience. In this part of his book Hoggart refrains from making generalized judgements and attempts simply to record the typical expressions and habits of mind to be found in the working-class environment of Leeds he knew as a child and young man. The second half of the book is quite different. In it Hoggart offers a much broader critical analysis of contemporary developments that, in his view, largely work to undermine the authenticity and autonomy of working-class life. The sources of danger are essentially two: entertainment media and the pressures of the consumer society. Working-class culture, he fears, is being dangerously eroded by the insidious imposition of a bourgeois ideal of self-improvement. This threatens to undermine the cardinal virtues of working-class life in his eyes, namely communal solidarity and resistance to bureaucratic authority. If the social trends continue along the same path, he concludes, the British working-class will no longer recognize itself and be increasingly susceptible to all manner of cynical commercial and political manipulation.

Hoggart's analysis of working-class life was, in many ways, prescient. Even at the time, six decades ago, there was talk of the disappearance of the working class as British society unified around middle-class ideals and aspirations. This assumption was based on a rather crude economic analysis of social class, according to which the very existence of the working class was predicated on the industrialized workplace and great massing of workers into centres of manufacturing. The original project of cultural studies was dedicated to overthrowing this narrow view of class and establishing that working-class culture involved all kinds of nuances in behaviour and communication that could not be reduced to where and how one worked.

Behind the idea of the obsolescence of social class was the further presumption that once a minority of working-class people were admitted into the citadels of high culture the claims of social justice and mobility were more or less satisfied. Thus, the odd BBC documentary or high-profile drama was enough to show that there were, in fact, few or no remaining barriers to working-class equality of opportunity. This complacency brings with it an almost inevitable corollary: those in the working class who now fail to attain their desires for social improvement have only themselves to blame. This, in a nutshell, is what we find behind the social image of education in Britain today. But it retains the same patronizing presumptions voiced by Arnold in the 1860s: once society has made available to all the works of high culture nothing more can be rightly expected by the working class. Against this it must be argued that the real political task entailed by social democracy is not simply to absorb a pre-existing cultural sphere but to work towards a culture that is truly expressive of society as a whole.

A key aspect of the neoliberalization of British society since the late 1980s, therefore, has been an erosion and gradual reversal of working-class consciousness. Rarely if ever a vanguard institution of such consciousness, the British Labour party has, over the last three decades, witnessed a relentless drift toward a kind of gutless centrism that has worked to alienate large swathes of the British electorate. The rise and fall of Jeremy Corbyn, following two decades of Blairite dominance, now appears to be simply the latest in many symptoms of political disorientation within the British Left. The perennial question of whether political leaders lead or follow what gets euphemistically referred to as 'public opinion' loomed large in the media coverage of the Labour leader. At first dismissed by journalists across the political spectrum as an embarrassing throwback to the 1970s 'loony left', following the 2017 general election in Britain Corbyn was credited with revitalizing his party. His following among younger voters – always doomed to political apathy by popular media – was specifically highlighted. While Corbyn's political rhetoric did involve sharp criticism of neoliberalism, he largely avoided championing working-class interests, focusing instead on the rather banal and overgeneralized category of the economically marginalized. In the words of the former Conservative Prime Minister, Theresa May, this is the faceless class known as the 'just about managing'. Now that Labour has returned to a predictable centre-left stance under the leadership of Keir Starmer, it is to be expected that any new Labour government will more or less return the party to the highly successful but culturally vapid politics of a centrist 'Third-Way', putatively positioned 'beyond left and right'.

The deficit involved in this cross-party analysis of contemporary Britain is that it fails to acknowledge what the early cultural theorists saw only too well: namely, that the challenge of working-class politics is not, ultimately, reducible to a more equitable distribution of wealth. As important as this is to people's prestige and life chances, the historic working-class project is much more about social and political recognition. This is what was highlighted so brilliantly by the qualitative research conducted by Sennett and Cobb (1972) almost fifty years ago. Through extensive group and individual interviews with the white working class of Boston, they found their interviewees caught up in the agonizing double-binds of class in an advanced capitalist society. The principal function of class, as they see it, 'is that society injures human dignity in order to weaken people's ability to fight against the limits class imposes on their freedom' (p. 153). In other words, members of the working class see their own sense of self-worth in terms of a model of self-improvement that involves transcending their class position. Whether it is in the case of workers themselves or their children, this model of dignity and social regard brings with it a profound ambivalence to class position. If 'getting on' involves, for example, a transition out of blue-collar and into white-collar work, then the latter is often still viewed as 'not real work' at all.

A parallel ambiguity and ambivalence would appear to characterize contemporary workers' attitudes to the 'gig economy'. On the one hand, the optimistic neoliberal line on this is that truly innovative entrepreneurial types thrive as adaptable creatives. The idea of working for a large corporate or public-sector employer for years is portrayed as a personal deficit and supremely uncreative. As Angela McRobbie (2016) has recently argued, the 'creativity' label and its corollaries have forged a potent set of concepts that serves to cover over the harsh realities of work within the 'creative industries'. The conceptual history here is, of course, rich and long. Creativity has been, since the Romantic era, closely tied to the human power of imagination. In late eighteenth German philosophy and aesthetics, in particular, the idea that being truly human amounted to an active and creative imagination became something of a cultural cliché.

This can often be found in evidence today among prominent critics of the testing culture in contemporary education. Rather than drilling children on facts, we are admonished; their imaginative and creative powers should be cultivated. The problem, of course, is that neoliberalism, here as in countless other cases, has appropriated and refashioned the well-seasoned politics of imagination to its own ends. The iconic Steve Jobs-esque CEO now steps forward as the modern magician and role model for all aspiring young entrepreneurs, masking the basic economic fact that we live in an age of unparalleled capitalist consolidation in all economic areas, including, most crucially, media and entertainment. Ours is not, arguably, an era of go-getting capitalist enterprise where the outsider can suddenly emerge and rise to the top; rather, the game of neoliberal prestige and profit has never been more of a foregone conclusion.

The issue of rising economic disparity, which became briefly so fashionable with the publication of Thomas Piketty's *Capital in the 21st Century* (2014), is crucially important in debunking the myth that neoliberal capitalism has more or less successfully pedalled for three decades, namely that wealth production could only ever be good for all in society. But announcing a crisis of neoliberalism is of little use if there is no sense of a better way forward. As Fredric Jameson (2003) famously quipped, it can often seem easier to imagine the end of the world than the end of capitalism. What we can find in early British cultural theory is, however, precisely an act of political imagination that projects a society beyond capitalism.

WORKING-CLASS CULTURE AND THE NOVEL

In his early work Raymond Williams, pre-eminently among cultural theorists, looked to the British novel to reconstruct the historic emergence of working-class consciousness. Here I wish to retrace his steps; not simply in a spirit of homage but, more importantly, because I believe many of his observations can help us to retrieve the legacy of working-class politics in contemporary Britain. I am all too aware that this may seem a rather farfetched and academically dubious prospect. This book will likely displease most of its academic readership: it will not satisfy the literary theorists due to its sociological and political pretensions; nor will it please the social scientists, on account of its highly speculative form of analysis. And it will certainly not pass muster as philosophy, my own official academic specialization. Nevertheless, I hope it offers a stimulating and readable assessment of the authors and novels considered. Cultural studies came into existence as a transdisciplinary approach and it would be a curiously retrograde step to attempt to trammel its hybridity at this point.

So far, I have commented on the impetus and import of this book. We seem to be living through a generalized crisis that intertwines politics and work and this crisis can be diagnosed through the eclipse of the working class in Britain over the last four decades. But why focus on three British novelists from the mid-nineteenth century to pursue this task? This choice stems partly from the need any investigation has to identify a more specific context to advance an argument. E. P. Thompson's *The Making of the English Working Class* (1963) demonstrated the sheer complexity of the nineteenth-century British workers' movement, a complexity that involved uses of religion, advances in printing technology, self-organized education, and cooperative societies, in addition to the more overt acts of workplace resistance and militancy. Similarly, in their novels Eliot, Hardy, and Lawrence were, from a certain distance, working through, interpreting, and reimagining this rise of working-class consciousness and culture.

None of these authors can be straightforwardly described as a champion of the working class. Eliot, in particular, shares the typical mid-Victorian alarm at potential 'mob rule' in the face of working-class agitation (found also in the likes of Gaskell and Dickens). For his part, Hardy is clearly more interested in the tragedies of individual fate rather than collective class politics. Finally, Lawrence's overt position is one that largely disavows the ultimate reality of social class and looks forward to a kind of classless utopia. Nevertheless, the novels of these three writers can be credibly interpreted as offering something like a continuous narrative on the emergence of the English working class into political and cultural consciousness.

In staking this claim it is vitally important to acknowledge a further fact that unites these authors: their own class origins. All three came from either a lower-middle-class (Eliot and Hardy) or a working-class background (Lawrence). As writers, therefore, they had to struggle to find social validation for what they were doing. As Williams (1973) points out, the British literary establishment was prone to patronizing writers such as Eliot, Hardy, and Lawrence as 'self-taught'. We still see this kind of description in contemporary editions of their works. The fact is, they all received exceptionally high levels of formal education relative to their contemporaries. Thus, 'self-taught' really amounts to not attending one of a few prestigious 'public' schools and then one of the ancient English universities. In Eliot's case, she was, additionally, patronized as a woman having intellectual pretensions.

Despite their success as novelists, therefore, these writers had to fight a near-constant rear-guard action to prove their legitimacy as intellectual and cultural figures. A certain tendency to marginalization or outright exile is present in each of their lives. Thus, one key strand of our investigation will be to reconsider these writers' class position and how it interacted with their art and its contemporary reception. This concern will be closely allied with the related one of how work and the working class are portrayed in their novels. While the Victorian middle and upper classes were clearly concerned with the social ills that beset the British working class, these concerns were generally directed toward various schemes to improve them. What the novels we will examine offer, at their best, is a sympathetic portrayal of working-class lives in their own right and not simply as a deficit relative to middle-class virtues.

In a recent article, the late philosopher Roger Scruton (2012) advanced the following argument: 'A high culture is the self-consciousness of a society. It contains the works of art, literature, scholarship, and philosophy that establish a shared frame of reference among educated people. High culture is a precarious achievement, and endures only if it is underpinned by a sense of tradition, and by a broad endorsement of the surrounding social norms.' These words were written, clearly, as a self-conscious echo of Matthew Arnold's response to worker agitation in London's Hyde Park in 1866. In one sense, it is remarkable that Scruton can adopt this stance a century and a half later. In another sense, however, it reflects the sheer tenacity of the 'high culture' concept. The continued pull of this concept in educational policy is a case in point. Arguments about the literary 'canon', fought over in particular within English departments when postmodernism was reaching its voguish heights in the 1980s, recur with predictable regularity.

Recently, an initiative dedicated to 'decolonizing' the English curriculum has been advanced at Cambridge University. Cambridge was Williams' academic home immediately following and during the time he made his name as a cultural and literary theorist. His first major works of theory – *Culture and Society* (1958) and *The Long Revolution* (1961) – established the idea that culture was not reducible to the accustomed idea of 'high culture', but was also, more broadly, a matter of the everyday 'structures of feeling' that inform social relations. At this time, as a crucial adjunct to his appreciations and criticism of English literature, he published two novels of his own, *Border Country* (1960) and *Second Generation* (1964). In these creative contexts, Williams is preoccupied with two themes: the relations between country life and the industrial economy and the experience of growing up in a working-class family and making one's way, later in life, in a quite distinct, academic milieu. Drawing on his own experience directly, Williams saw reform of public education as a crucial goal of social democracy. Eschewing an orthodox Marxist (economy first, culture second) approach to politics, Williams saw the economic and the cultural as mutually reinforcing domains, each reflecting the general power distribution in society in distinct ways.

The main difficulty of today's 'culture wars' is that they typically oppose two positions, both of which are arguably too narrow in outlook to offer a way forward for contemporary democratic culture. On the one hand, the kind of cultural conservatism adopted by Scruton lacks inner dynamism and tends towards the parochial and patronizing. His idea of 'educated people' is self-validating, in the sense that he makes the same presumptions made by Arnold, namely that the possession of a genuine education is guaranteed by attending the 'right' institutions and studying the 'right' cultural artefacts. But this definition is not only conservative, it is circular and unchallengeable. The cultural progressives, by contrast, generally occupy a largely oppositional stance. The curriculum that needs to be 'decolonized' essentially needs to include a lesser proportion of dead white males. This creates its own circularity of argument, insofar as the supposed reason for their inclusion is a generally held ideology of 'white privilege' and patriarchy. While this is undoubtedly true, the binary oppositions typically generated tend to gloss over precisely the kind of historical social complexities illuminated by a work such as Thompson's (1963) *The Making of the English Working Class*.

The positive goal of such decolonizing curricular reform is usually identified as inclusion or diversity. There may also be an argument for the canon to be representative, at different scales: of modern Britain, a globalized world, and so forth. There is certainly an appeal here, whether explicitly state or not, to a kind of democratic representativeness: the content studied should draw on writing from a diverse body of artists and theoreticians. This concern is paralleled by one relating to the make-up of the student body and institution, in particular university teachers. Once again, we can trace an appeal here to a kind of democratic representativeness principle: namely, that the diversity of faculty should mirror the diversity of the student body. However, any appeal to 'diversity' begs the question of what kinds of diversity count. Race and ethnicity dominate these discussions in the academy, but this tends to obscure questions about social class. Identity politics tend to give precedence to markers of personal identity such as race, ethnicity, and sexual orientation; and these aspects of personal identity are further subject to the psychological process of identification. In other words, to a great extent, what I *am* is a matter of what I *feel* myself to be. Needless to say, cultural conservatives can have a field day with this kind of social subjectivism.

While these entrenched positions in the culture wars will not be an explicit concern in what follows, the intractable nature of this conflict does furnish a further justification for the approach adopted in this book. While Eliot, Hardy, and Lawrence are all firmly established in the canon of English literature, their internal marginality, so to speak, should not be overlooked. When one considers Hardy, for example, it is clear that he found much readier acceptance by the general reading public than by the British cultural elite of his time. Fortunately, he lived long enough to achieve establishment recognition, although by then he had ceased to publish novels decades before and turned his attention to poetic projects.

Another thing that is noticeable about controversies surrounding literary figures is how insular they are. Academics work within their own highly specialized and often isolated milieu and, while they enjoy conspicuous cultural prestige, they tend to be relatively blind to the broader social and political context of formal education. The academic as worker is a kind of highly skilled craftsperson, whose sense of worth is closely connected to their autonomy from other workers and members of their institution. This 'academic freedom' is an important institutionalized right to free speech and should be questioned only with other important social values in mind. But it raises the question: what are the social functions of teaching literature? In this study, my answer to that question is that one such function involves reading literature as testimony to the history of class consciousness.

In adopting this position there is, to my mind, a further dichotomy to be avoided. This is that the authors chosen were either fully conscious and deliberate mouthpieces of class politics or else utterly indifferent to such politics. Neither position would be suited to our case studies. This follows from the notion of class adopted in this work, namely that social class is *not* an aspect of personal identity or, at least, not reducible to this. Thompson (1963) captures this well when he rejects class as a category or structure and, instead, affirms class as 'something which in fact happens in human relationships' (p. 9). We will, similarly, read the novels of our authors as documents in which 'class happens' in human relationships. This may be in the form of intra- or inter-class relationships. Social class is, necessarily, an oppositional reality: friction and animosity, as well as intrigue and fascination, arise across class boundaries.

For the authors themselves, their success as artists brought class ascension, a process they more or less desired or accepted in each case. Given the material requirements connected to being an author – long periods of solitary reflection and writing – their social identity is likely to be something complex in the first place. The extent to which success and recognition bring about dramatic shifts in an author's social standing can only add to this complexity. There is an obvious incongruousness between the creation of literature and its reception, between its private and public life as it were. On one level, the novel will be to the author a quite intimate record of experiences and thoughts; but, on another, a novelist is no less a social animal than anyone else. One of the least helpful aspects of the romantic aesthetic ideology is its insistence on the radical social isolation of the artist. Taken to an extreme, this perspective reduces all literary work to a more or less elaborate form of private confession.

There is a further complication, allied to this romantic isolation thesis. This is what might be termed the hermeneutic challenge. Every author has a different stance on self-interpretation. This can range from total refusal to comment, on the basis that the work 'speaks for itself', to an almost manic desire to control the 'message' of one's works. Eliot, Hardy, and Lawrence all commented on their own work to varying degrees. Lawrence stands out among the three for his constant attempt to articulate a detailed worldview or metaphysic, fragments of which are to be found in all of his novels. Lawrence clearly did not view his efforts to construct a worldview as detrimental to the creative process. But the weight to be attached to an author's self-interpretation in any study of their work is a central aspect of what I am calling the hermeneutic challenge. Any act of interpretation – including that of the author themselves – places the work in a certain light, but it can never capture the meaning of the work as such. This leaves us with the problem of how to weigh an author's self-interpretation relative to other sources of interpretation.

In this book, I endeavour to pay close attention to the writer's self-commentary. This is because the author's own sense of their writing is a key part of their work. Equally, however, the author cannot know all there is to be known about their writing. This is another aspect of the hermeneutic situation: that the work 'says more' than the writer can bring explicitly to the reader's attention. This is not a sign of epistemic failure, but rather a structural limitation within which all expression takes place. Equally, the interpretation advanced here is not undertaken on the premise that I know better than the author about their own work. It is rather a question of knowing the work differently, due to my own social experience and interpretive purposes.

So far, I have commented on reasons for reading Eliot, Hardy, and Lawrence with reference to class relations. My general sense is that the current crisis of democratic culture and wave of populism (clearly a phenomenon not restricted to Britain) require us to reconsider the social history of the working class. The novels of our selected authors can help us to do this. But this book's title refers to labour *and landscape*. What of the theme of landscape? 'Landscape', as a word, has its own, quite particular, conceptual history. It is connected, above all, with a mode of painting within the historical development of the fine arts. It is, therefore, primarily an aesthetic concept. Traditional landscape art focuses on the natural environment and not on the human figure. Such figures may indeed be placed in the landscape by the artist, but normally they are not predominant. In the case of our chosen novelists, the narrative and action of the protagonists is constructed with constant reference to and close observation of the natural setting: the seasons, climate, botany, geology, and topography are all essential elements of the novel's warp and woof. Hardy's evocation of Egdon Heath at the beginning of *The*

Return of the Native is an excellent example. The harsh work and life that the heath permits serves as much more than a picturesque backdrop to the characters' actions. It is, instead, a presence of such power that it imposes a kind of fate upon the protagonists.

Of course, this elevation of landscape, both figuratively and literally, is also a key aspect of the Romantic heritage. The idea that character is formed by the place of nurturing, for good or ill, is the central conceit of much Romantic poetry. Wordsworth's poem 'Michael' is paradigmatic in this regard. What is arguably liberating about this perspective is that it raises the subjective elements of a narrated person's life to a grander, less purely psychological status. If the person is made by the place, but the place itself has a reality that transcends the psychological limitations of individual personality, then the writer can find a way to capture a shared cultural context through evocations of landscape. In addition, localized place also offers a powerful medium through which to capture the historic changes wrought by the developments of the capitalist economy.

While the novels of Eliot and Hardy are often seen to evince nostalgia for a simpler agrarian mode of existence, it is arguably more plausible to read them as documenting phases in the social transformation brought about in England by nineteenth-century capitalism. Marxist critique of capitalism can often seem implausible on account of its high level of generality; even the reality of the all-encompassing phenomenon 'capitalism' can appear doubtful. Through the medium of local landscape, however, such generalities can be given much more particular and concrete form. The point here, however, is not to extract a theory of capitalist critique from the novels selected. Rather, it is a matter of attempting to reconstruct how specific manners of cultural life are inflected by the industrializing capitalist economy.

I also wish to explore the connections our authors make between landscape and work. Much contemporary theory on work is preoccupied with globalization and automation. These processes may be celebrated or bemoaned, but they are generally assumed to be inevitable. What often gets covered over by this dominant narrative, however, is a clear contemporary trend towards 'relocalization'. By this I mean an explicit celebration of small-scale local manufacturing in supposedly deindustrialized economies. Urban sociologists, in particular, are attempting to explain what this reassertion of the local amounts to. My own take on it is that the value of work is intimately tied to a sense of local place. Taking pride in work and taking pride in the place of work are two sides of the same coin. We will explore this theme of work and place as a catalyst of social connection is the works of Richard Sennett (2006, 2008, 2012).

This attraction to the local does not, on the whole, reflect a concern for the exploitation of a global labour market, which makes cheap consumer goods from poorer countries available to the relatively affluent. Rather, my sense is that it stems predominantly from a desire to dignify work with the aura of cultural achievement. As Sennett and Cobb (1972) noted almost half a century ago, changing patterns of work are primarily challenging to the working class not only or even primarily because they involve the obsolescence of skills. Rather, changing work conditions make it less likely than one will gain general social recognition for one's labour. A settled culture of place, such as is depicted in the novels of Eliot, Hardy, and Lawrence, affords this kind of social recognition. Thus, landscape and labour are closely intertwined throughout our study and this interconnection will offer a constant point of reference.

My final observation in his introduction is a personal one. I noted above that this study will not pass muster as philosophy or literary theory. My personal itinerary into and through academia parallels, in certain respects at least, that of the authors chosen. This book is ultimately driven by a personal motivation: I want to understand what it means, in my own case, for someone to grow up in a working-class environment and make the transition to the domain of intellectual 'high culture'. Much sociological and psychological research has been conducted into the experience of so-called non-traditional students, but here I look for clues to the process of educational defamiliarization in the novels of the writers selected.

When I began as a student of English and philosophy at Edinburgh University in 1990, I had no label or any concrete expectations for how I related to my peers, teachers, and the academic milieu more generally. My first shock related to the seeming complacency of the predominantly upper-middle-class students I encountered. They didn't seem to be trying and appeared to treat the university as little more than a convenient context for socializing. Above all, they seemed to lack a sense of purpose. I, by contrast, arrived in Edinburgh with what I now suppose would be the typically overzealous earnestness of an intellectually ambitious working-class student (like Hardy's Jude in Christminster) who found it a great privilege to find oneself at an 'elite' university. The few fellow working-class students I encountered seemed deeply alienated, out of place and uncertain about how to fit in socially. By the end of my four years at Edinburgh I reached the conclusion that I had, in fact, not yet found an authentic academic environment. My doctoral work, to be conducted in another ancient university in Freiburg, Germany, would finally provide me, as I thought at the time, with an environment worthy of my intellectual ambitions.

It is now more than two decades since I completed my doctorate in philosophy and literature, and yet my sense of displacement within academia has, if anything, only increased. The discipline to which I supposed myself to be apprenticed is not something with which I identify. The institution of the university is, to my mind, even more alienating. It appears to be driven by bureaucratic imperatives and initiatives that have little if any relevance to what originally drew me into my studies. Within this context, and especially since moving to the United States over a decade ago, I am constantly confronted with the reality that, for working-class students, passage through college means mounting debt and, in many cases, a problematic consolation for the meaninglessness of their work life. All these aspects of my personal experience are deeply interwoven with my motivation for writing this book. Twenty years ago, the thought of personalizing an academic project in this way would have been quite unacceptable to me. Now, by contrast, I can find no other valid reason for writing at all. Belatedly, it would appear, I have accepted the proposition that my love of knowledge ultimately stems from a highly personal desire to understand myself and the world I have known since childhood.

Chapter 1

George Eliot and the Morality of Work

ADAM BEDE: THE ARTISAN TAKES THE STAGE

George Eliot's early novels, in particular *Adam Bede* and *Silas Marner*, feature the effects of work on character in a profound and thematically central manner. In the case of Adam Bede, the eponymous protagonist is depicted in a highly dignified and noble light in conjunction with his work. As a skilled craftsman and woodworker, Adam's moral character is put into relief in contrast to both his father and his master, the young squire Arthur Donnithorne. While the former is ruined by drink, the latter is corrupted by idleness. In the first chapter of her first full-length novel, Eliot begins with a depiction of Adam Bede singing hymns in his workshop:

> Such a voice could only come from a broad chest, and the broad chest belonged to a large-boned muscular man nearly six feet high, with a back so flat and a head so well poised that when he drew himself up to take a more distant survey of his work, he had the air of a soldier standing at ease. The sleeve rolled up at the elbow showed an arm that was likely to win the prize for feats of strength; yet the long supple hand, with its broad finger-tips, looked ready for works of skill. [. . .] The face was large and roughly hewn, and when in repose had no other beauty than such as belongs to an expression of good-humoured honest intelligence. (Eliot 2008a, p. 6)

Having establishing Adam Bede in the reader's mind through a description that is at once exalted and down to earth, the reader is made aware, in the context of a lively and familiar conversation between the men in the workshop, of Adam's theological justification for the kind of life he leads:

> But what does the Bible say? Why, it says as God put his sperrit into the workman as built the tabernacle, to make him do all the carved work and things as wanted a nice hand. And that is my way of looking at it: there's the sperrit of God in all things and all times – weekday as well as Sunday – and i' the great works and inventions, and i' the figuring and the mechanics. (Eliot 2008a, p. 9)

Adam's polemical point in this passage is largely against his brother, Seth, a young and ardent Methodist, closely associated with the female Methodist preacher, Dinah Morris. In a nutshell, Adam's philosophy preaches the holiness and redemptive capacity of everyday, practical work. Theologically speaking, one might say that Adam borders on hubris here, insofar as he elevates human work over the redemptive power of God's grace. In fact, one way of reading the overall arch of the moral development of Adam Bede is to see his transformation from a state of self-satisfied belief in his autonomous powers of labour to a condition where he recognizes, through prolonged personal suffering, the necessity of sympathetic acceptance of impotence and limitation in human agency. Adam's excessive sense of self-reliance through work, which comes into conflict with his largely unrecognized dependence on others, is something he is ultimately forced to acknowledge and accept.

The young Methodist preacher, Dinah Morris, possesses a kind of autonomy and purposiveness at once akin and yet quite distinct from that evinced by Adam. Dinah is, if anything, more driven than Adam, but her work as a charismatic Evangelical preacher is viewed as something derived from the Holy Spirit and so ultimately not of her own doing. In more humanistic terms, Dinah's preeminent work is the act of sympathy. But such work embodies a kind of paradox when viewed through the lens of Adam's self-guided craftsmanship. In the unforgiving scorn he displays towards the shortcoming of his parent, Adam seemingly forgets that his craft was handed over to him by his father, Thias Bede. While the death of the father, early on in the novel, does give rise to certain pangs of conscience in the son, Adam's attitude towards his father continues to be harshly judgemental. More generally, Adam's inability to feel sympathy for the failings of others colours all his relationships in the novel: with his parents and brother, with his master, Arthur Donnithorne, with his fiancée, Hetty Sorrel, and ultimately with himself. The only character Adam finds no fault with is the woman he marries at the end of the narrative, Dinah Morris, the implicit message of this culminating union being that Adam's pride in his work has finally been tempered by the sympathetic acceptance of reliance of others.

When considering the distinct work done by Adam and Dinah, it is worthwhile attending to how Eliot is careful to imbue Dinah's physical characteristics with her moral dispositions. Thus, when we first encounter Dinah preaching to the rural community of Hayslope, she is described as having eyes that 'seemed rather to be shedding love than making observations; they had the liquid look which tells that the mind is full of what it has to give out, rather than impressed by external objects' (Eliot 2008a, p. 21). This description immediately accentuates the contrast with Adam, to whom is attributed the very 'keen glance of the dark eyes' prominently absent in Dinah. We thus note a series of oppositions between the two characters: Adam's attention to external objects and detail, his tendency to weigh, measure, and judge; and Dinah's opposed spiritual inwardness, her tendency to suffer the pains of others, rather than calculate and judge their failings. In this way, Eliot embodies in her two protagonists the complexity of a dialectical opposition, the tensions and eventual resolution of which constitutes the overarching structure of the novel's drama. In the climactic marriage of Adam and Dinah a kind of synthesis is achieved, whereby Dinah accepts the necessity of union with a particular person and Adam absorbs the lessons of a broader sympathy for human suffering. The work of the hand and the work of the heart are thus emblematically unified at the close of the novel.

Having set out the general structure, let us turn to the detail of Eliot's depiction of work in *Adam Bede*. The first chapter, entitled 'The Workshop', not only displays the eponymous protagonist at work from the first moment we encounter him, it also brings home to the reader Adam's place within an immediate community of workers. His younger brother, Seth, is cast as a more congenial and sympathetic character, one that is free of the rather austere sense of self-respect and dignity that so strongly imbues Adam. Seth is rather slavishly devoted to Dinah and shares her Methodist pietism. He courts Dinah in a mode of adoration, as one looks to an unreachable idol rather than to another flesh and blood individual. In opposition to his brother's otherworldliness, Adam insists on grasping the modern industrial reality unfolding around them, 'the canals, an' th' aqueducts, an' the coal-pit engines, and Arkwright's mills' (Eliot 2008a, p. 9). We also see, in the first chapter, how the brothers' fellow craftsmen view them with respect to their character and community standing. Thus, Wiry Ben, who teases Seth in the first chapter for his attachment to Dinah, defends his eligibility as a potential husband to Dinah in the second chapter when the pub landlord, Mr Casson, insist that Dinah's 'kin wouldn't like to demean herself to a common carpenter' (p. 20).

In this manner, the broader context of community-standing relative to occupation is brought into focus. The exchange between Ben and Casson points to another social opposition that became acute in the period of early industrial development, namely that been fixed and liquid assets. While the Bede family can take pride in their independence as artisanal workers, they lack the standing of property owners. Dinah belongs to the Poyser family at the Hall Farm, who, while they are tenants of the Donnithorne estate, still enjoy a higher class standing due to owning their own livestock. While the

Bede household is chiefly dignified by its cleanliness, it is the possessions on display and held in store that lends the Hall Farm its social respectability. This motif of prestige through ownership is most pronounced in Eliot's follow-up novel, *The Mill on the Floss*. Here the fate of Bessy Tulliver's household possessions, in the face of her husband's bankruptcy, is emblematic of the family's social opprobrium: 'The disgrace is, for one o' the family to ha' married a man as has brought her to beggary. The disgrace is, as they're to be sold up' (Eliot 2015, p. 198).

It is worthwhile, in this connection, of considering Eliot's standing as an intellectual and cultural producer. The writer herself comes from the middle-class milieu of clerical life depicted in her first forays into literary creation. Her choice, relatively late in life, to earn her living as a popular writer places her in a peculiar position vis-à-vis socio-economic status. It was only in the Victorian period that such a choice even became viable for the likes of Eliot. While it is set two generations back in time at the end of the eighteenth century, one can appreciate a certain parallelism between Eliot the writer and Adam Bede the small-scale craftsman. As Tim Dolan (2009) notes:

> For [Eliot], the artisan embodied the ideal of a responsible, progressive worker, whose independence safeguarded him from the corruptions of class, that corporate form of self-interest which blinded its members to their responsibilities and capacities to pursue social relations independently and clear-sightedly. (p. 122)

In the overtly revolutionary period of post-1848 Europe, the class position of Eliot as writer and social commentator is a pressing matter. One way to elide if not obviate this concern is precisely to depict social relations in a past that is not so much dim and distant as familiar and reasonably reassuring. As becomes much more explicit when she publishes *Felix Holt: The Radical* in 1866 and then 'The address to working men, by Felix Holt' in 1868, Eliot is 'wary of class: wary that the struggles of competing economic groups should underpin all social description, and wary of the language of social description itself, which is a calculated intervention in society' (Dolin 2009, p. 119). Again, this raises a question not simply of personal background and conviction on the part of Eliot, but also of where the popular writer stands in the predominant order of production. This latter question becomes particularly acute in the case of Eliot as she embraces, in very forthright terms, the Romantic aesthetic of lending literary dignity to the commonplace lives of the working class.

The rise of the popular novel rests on a whole complex of technological and material innovations in the first half of the nineteenth century. Along with these goes, to an equal or even greater extent, a set of social preconditions, not least of which is the overtly political struggle for freedom of the press in England from the 1790s on. In this particular dimension of social history, we find a crucial intertwining between the class of artisanal craftsmen and freedom of expression. As E. P. Thompson (1968 [1963]) remarks: 'In the contest between 1792 and 1836 the artisans and workers made this tradition [of the 'freeborn Englishman'] peculiarly their own, adding to the claim for free speech and thought their own claim for untrammelled propagation, in the cheapest possible form, of the products of this thought.' The very mode of existence made possible to Eliot is, then, to some degree a legacy of a radical working-class heritage to which she stands, in sentiment at least, fundamentally opposed. This contradiction is, however, unsurprising, given the gap that separates the subjects depicted (the 'common' workers) and the anticipated readership (the educated middle class).

We should also bear in mind the generalized anxiety that gripped the British cultural elite in the years immediately preceding the 1867 Reform Act, which significantly extended the enfranchisement of working-class men. As a prominent statement of this anxiety at the time, Matthew Arnold's (1993 [1869]) *Culture and Anarchy* occupies an archetypal status. The underlying purpose of 'culture', for Arnold, is gradual human self-perfection, a project endangered by aristocratic indifference on the part of 'barbarians', the belief in purely materialistic industrial progress held by 'philistines' and, lastly, in the 'doing what one likes' anarchism of a rising 'populace'. For Arnold, the working-class was largely divided between the latter two groups but was not necessarily excluded from the propagation of what he considered true culture. The immediate background of Arnold, whose occupation was inspector of schools, was pedagogy and the social impacts of schooling. Like his fellow social commentator and social theorist John Stuart Mill, Arnold was convinced that the rise of popular enfranchisement, if it were not to prove disastrous, must be antedated by a rigorous programme of public education. In the 1860s middle-class commentators such as Arnold and Mill were highly alarmed that the British working class were increasingly willing to take matters into their own hands when seeking to advance their class interests.

Against this backdrop of social and cultural critique, it is striking that Adam Bede is suitably deferential to his master, Arthur Donnithorne. In a rather Hegelian twist, however, the young squire's sense of himself as a worthy successor to his grandfather is dependent on Adam's good opinion of him. In Arnold's terms, Arthur is certainly a 'philistine', deprecating the Latin he has learned as useless and professing: 'But I don't think a knowledge of the classics is a pressing want to a country gentleman; as far as I can see, he'd much better have a knowledge of manures' (Eliot 2008a, p. 154). Despite Arthur's self-aggrandizing schemes for improving the estate and the lives of the workers who live on it, it is his weakness of will that Eliot accentuates. The young squire is portrayed as essentially adrift and, to a great extent, a victim of gentlemanly idleness. It is clearly this idleness that leads him into a flirtatious and eventually disastrous relationship with the milkmaid Hetty Sorel, who happens to be Adam's love interest. And it is the contest of Arthur and Adam in relation to Hetty that allows Eliot to place the character of the two men side by side and show Arthur severely wanting.

The theme of the lowly female who is, one way or another, preyed upon by a dashing male of superior social status is a stock feature of Victorian novels and one that also looms large in the novels of Hardy. In Adam Bede, the pathos of Arthur's relationship to Hetty is largely generated by the squire's resources of self-delusion. He does not set out to ruin Hetty's social reputation and subsequent chances of a happy marriage, though Adam makes clear to him, in almost brutal terms, that this can be the only result of his conduct. Arthur's leading passion, ironically enough, is to be admired by the local working-class community as a well-meaning and beneficent landowner. But this very desire blinds him to the standards whereby this community assesses its own worth. For her part, Hetty wallows in her own delusions, which are, in a manner analogous to Arthur's, predicated on disconnection from the duties of work. When the reader first encounters her, in the dairy of the Hall Farm, Eliot is at pains to accentuate the disturbing contrast between surface appearance and true character. Likening her to the animals she works with, we are offered the following moral assessment:

> Hetty's was a spring-tide beauty; it was the beauty of young frisking things, round-limbed, gambolling, circumventing you by a false air of innocence – the innocence of a young star-browed calf, for example, that, being inclined for a promenade out of bounds, leads you a severe steeple-chase over hedge and ditch, and only comes to a stand in the middle of a bog. (Eliot 2008a, p. 77)

The danger that lurks beneath Hetty's seeming innocence works to place a doubt in the reader's mind vis-à-vis Arthur's romanticized perspective of the young milkmaid. The parallel between Arthur and Hetty – what makes them at once akin and yet a disastrous match – rests on their self-conceit and vanity. Both are afflicted by a particularly striking degree of amour-propre, such that they are largely blind to the consequences of their actions to others. And in both cases Eliot juxtaposes characters of the same sex to invite the reader to take their relative moral measure. Accordingly, Arthur's failings are put into relief by Adam's exemplary virtues, just as Hetty's pettiness and injudiciousness are highlighted by Dinah's almost superhuman sagacity and self-denial.

The point I wish to accentuate at this point is how Eliot uses occupation and work as the milieu in which to present these comparisons of moral character. As related, the reader is first presented with the upright figure of Adam in the midst of the carpentry workshop, an initial context in which Adam is able to present his doctrine of redemption of character through the steadfast and painstaking work of the hand. Due to his father's negligence, in the first chapters of the novel we see Adam essentially working a day and a half at his carpentry without rest. Dinah is similarly committed to her work, in this case with even more overt dedication to a vocation. In contrast, while Arthur is presented as a dashing captain of the Loamshire militia, he is also depicted very much as a man awaiting his proper role in life. Interestingly, an earlier childhood relationship between Adam and Arthur casts the carpenter as the captain's mentor. Analogously, between the two orphaned nieces, Dinah offers herself as a kind of moral guide to the young milkmaid. One feature that makes for a striking commonality between all four characters is an absence of parental guidance. Both young women lack biological parents of any kind, while Arthur chiefly looks to his godfather, the curate Mr Irwine, for perspective and a sense of direction. Adam, finally, is put into the strange position of acting as parent to his own father and mother. As the former dies at the start of the narrative, it is a mark of Adam's fortitude and resilience that he is able to maintain and even enhance his strengths of character while being severely tested by the vicissitudes he experiences in the course of in the novel.

In the chapter entitled 'A Vocation', Dinah is questioned by the Church of England rector, Mr Irwine, about the origins and nature of her vocation as a preacher. There is no condescension in the exchange, but rather a kind of wonder that a young woman such as Dinah could find the courage to address gatherings of strangers without even knowing what she is to say to them. One aspect of Dinah's account of her work is particularly striking, namely the inverse relationship between the gentleness of the environment and the religious fervour of those who inhabit it. In Dinah's words:

> But I've noticed, that in these villages where the people lead a quiet life among the green pastures and the still waters, tilling the ground and tending the cattle, there's a strange deadness to the Word, as different as can be from the great towns, like Leeds, where I once went to visit a holy woman who preaches there. It's wonderful how rich is the harvest of souls up those high-walled streets, where you seem to walk as in a prison-yard, and the ear is deafened with the sounds of worldly toil. I think maybe it is because the promise is sweeter when this life is so dark and weary, and the soul gets more hungry when the body is ill at ease. (Eliot 2008a, p. 84)

Dinah, we learn, works in a cotton-mill in 'Stonyshire', a region constantly contrasted with 'Loamshire' in which the village of Hayslope is located. Mrs Poyser's regular appeal to Dinah that she remains at the Hall Farm is rejected by Dinah on the basis that her work lies elsewhere, in the harder milieu of Stonyshire. By contrast, Eliot makes clear that the softer country of Loamshire is well suited to the time-honoured traditions and moderation of the established Church of England. These latter qualities are embodied by the generous and magnanimous Mr Irwine who, as the drama of Hetty and his godson, Arthur, ensues, acts as the main agent of good to right the wrongs committed by the young pair of lovers. While it is largely hinted at rather than spelled out, the persistent subtext of Eliot's narrative is that the underlying stability of social relations in Hayslope is sufficient to maintain people in their right and proper place. In his unassuming way, Mr Irwine acts as a kind of moral paradigm of sympathy tempered with fair judgement who is able to take the measure of character and deed and bring events to a suitably reassuring resolution.

In Eliot's case, she had herself traversed the distance from English Evangelicalism to humanistic agnosticism in early adulthood. But her move away from the former clearly did not make her averse to portraying it in a sympathetic light. Compared, in particular, to the callous vanity and thoughtlessness of Hetty, Dinah's moral attributes are brought to light with great emphasis. For all that, Dinah's self-possession is ultimately portrayed as a kind of unnatural disposition, one that certainly puts her at odds with the traditional order of things observed in Hayslope. Having rejected marriage and the comforts of domestic life as a tempting indulgence throughout most of the novel, it is only after accepting that she has been mistaken in her ultimate calling that Dinah finally agrees to marry Adam. In the penultimate and surprisingly brief chapter of the novel, 'Marriage Bells', Eliot summons all the characters of the narrative back onto the stage for one last curtain call, thereby making clear the resolution and restoration of order represented by this culminating union.

SILAS MARNER: SOULLESS WORK AND THE CONSOLATIONS OF COMMUNITY

In her first full-length novel Eliot places the characters of Adam and Dinah at the centre of her portrayal of English village life between the years 1799 and 1807, thereby emphasizing the creed, uttered by Adam after the death of his father: 'There's nothing but what's bearable as long as a man can work' (Eliot 2008a, p. 105). Setting aside, for the time being, her intervening novel, *The Mill on the Floss*, Eliot's unusually short book *Silas Marner* portrays an eponymous protagonist whose life seemingly contradicts Adam's tenet. Historically, the novel is set in the same time period as *Adam Bede*, as the narrator informs us, 'the early years on this century' (Eliot 2008b, p. 4).

The setting of Silas' early life is just the type of fervent urban Evangelical community we can suppose Dinah to have resided within during her days in Stonyshire. Wrongly accused of stealing by his closest friend, Silas is cast out of his close-knit religious community and seeks an exile of anonymity in the rural village of Raveloe. As in *Adam Bede*, Eliot accentuates the impression of contrast of town and country made on Silas as a result of his move:

> Nothing could be more unlike his native town, set within sight of the widespread hillsides, than this low, wooded region, where he felt hidden even from the heavens by the screening trees and hedgerows. There was nothing here, when he rose in the deep morning quiet and looked out on the dewy brambles and rank tufted grass, that seemed to have any relation with that life centring in Lantern Yard, which had once been to him the altar-place of high dispensations. (Eliot 2008b, p. 14)

Eliot goes on to evoke an archaic period in human development when 'it was believed that each territory was inhabited and ruled by its own divinities, so that a man could cross the bordering heights and be out of the reach of his native gods' (p. 15). While removing himself from his native place serves to place him beyond the troubling presence of his former community. Silas makes little to no effort in his first decade and a half there to integrate himself into his new community of Raveloe. Instead, he turns to his work of weaving at his loom. Such work, however, is quite other in its effect than the salutary, cleansing labour Adam praises when confronted with the family tragedy of losing his father. It is mechanical and so bereft of mind, soul and sentiment. It is labour done for its own sake, merely to fill the time now that Silas' vital connections to his fellow human beings have been severed by the acts of betrayal at the hands of his closest friend and of exile at the behest of his religious community. As a consequence, Eliot depicts Silas reduced to the state of a mindless insect:

> He seemed to weave, like the spider, from pure impulse, without reflection. Every man's work, pursued steadily, tends in this way to become an end in itself. Silas's hand satisfied itself with throwing the shuttle, and his eye with seeing the little squares in the cloth complete themselves under his effort. Then there were the calls of hunger; and Silas, in his solitude, had to provide his own breakfast, dinner, and supper, to fetch his own water from the well, and put his own kettle on the fire, and all these immediate promptings helped, along with the weaving, to reduce his life to the unquestioning activity of a spinning insect. (Eliot 2008b, p. 15)

At this point in the narrative, Eliot is accentuating the one key fact: that Silas has lost touch with the earlier phase of his life but has manifestly failed to transform that traumatic rending out of a native milieu into any kind of new life in community. He lives among but is resolutely not connected to the residents of Raveloe. It is worthwhile drawing attention here to Eliot's earlier intense work (in the 1840s and 50s) on German philosophy and literature. In the German romantic tradition, especially that stemming from Friedrich Schiller's (2016 [1795]) *On the Aesthetic Education of Man*, the notions of sensibility (*Sinnlichkeit*) and especially imagination (*Einbildungskraft*) played a pivotal role in staking out a highly influential philosophical anthropology. In light of this, we can say that Eliot depicts Silas as having lost the power of both of these key human faculties, which have become all the more attenuated thanks to the daily practice of his mechanical work of weaving. Schiller's aesthetics put centre stage the notion of the moral imagination, understood as the ability to place oneself at will in the shoes of another. Considered from the vantage point of her own literary practice, this power is precisely the one Eliot must claim for herself, particularly when she portrays the life and works of characters very different to her own and to that of her educated and refined middle-class readers.

In *Adam Bede*, the redemptive power of work is portrayed in the context of a problematic relationship with what cannot be achieved by the individual worker on his or her own terms. While, in simple terms, Adam's flaw is to put too much stock in his autonomy as a worker, Dinah places too much blind faith in the promptings and power of the divine spirit. This bears direct comparison with the ancient debate on human freewill and divine grace, central to Christian theology since the time of Saint Augustine in the fifth century CE. For Eliot, the key mediating term is the human community. Both Adam and Dinah, in distinct ways, rather hubristically raise themselves up out of fellowship and equality with their working communities. Such alienation is depicted to an extreme degree in Eliot's later novel through the figure of Silas Marner, though in this case this condition is the result of antecedent trauma and extreme humiliation brought on by the actions of others.

The extremity in which Silas finds himself is brought home to the reader by the obsessive, repetitive, and mechanical manner in which he works. Here, work has a narcotic and sedative effect, and the gold coins which he avariciously hordes become an object of love in the absence of any real affection for or from a fellow human being. Silas is not an evil character in the sense of harbouring ill-will towards others in the village. He was ill-served by his closest friend and by the broader religious community at Lantern Yard, but he eschewed revenge and does not seek the misery of others as a palliative for his own distress. In so refraining from vengeance Silas remains ripe for redemption. This comes in the form of an 'angelic visitation' that is redolent of the Biblical nativity story. The key passage, relating the appearance of an unknown child following the disappearance of Silas' gold, is arresting in its fable-like vividness:

> He felt his heart begin to beat violently, and for a few moments he was unable to stretch out his hand and grasp the restored treasure. The heap of gold seemed to glow and get larger beneath his agitated gaze. He leaned forward at last, and stretched forth his hand; but instead of the hard coin with the familiar resisting outline, his fingers encountered soft warm curls. In utter amazement, Silas feel on his knees and bent his head low to examine the marvel: it was a sleeping child – a round, fair thing, with soft yellow rings all over its head. (Eliot 2008b, p. 109)

The fact that Eliot sets this scene on a bitter winter's night on New Year's Eve heightens the sense of fateful transition in Silas' encounter with the young child he will go on to call Eppie, after his mother and a sister who died in early youth. The weaver has again, as at the opening of the narrative, been tricked, but this time by an anonymous beneficent force that acts to restore his cold coins in the form of a child offering the warmth of meaningful human attachment. The young child's instinctive reliance on the old man to feed and protect her is sufficient to override Silas' habitual mistrust of others. Eliot is careful to signal that the encounter is a matter of moral reawakening and miraculous restitution of character:

> [I]t stirred fibres that had never been moved in Raveloe – old quiverings of tenderness – old impressions of awe at the presentiment of some Power presiding over his life; for his imagination had not yet extricated itself from the sense of mystery in the child's sudden presence, and had formed no conjectures of ordinary natural means by which the event could have been brought about. (Eliot 2008b, p. 109)

Juxtaposed to the tale of Silas' fall and redemption is the story of two brothers, Godfrey and Dunstan Cass, sons of the local squire. Having conducted a clandestine affair with a woman (the mother of the child found by Silas), Godfrey is tormented by his malicious younger brother who threatens to reveal the matter to their father. This would spoil Godfrey's chances with the local beauty, Nancy Lammeter, whom Godfrey is expected to marry. As was the case with Arthur Donnithorne in *Adam Bede*, the squire's two sons are depicted as suffering moral weakness on account of idleness. While Dunstan is the real malefactor, who steals Silas' horde of coins to pay his debts, Godfrey is caught up in his own intrigues due to lack of fortitude and purpose. Eliot also accentuates the point that the Cass household has slipped into a kind of desuetude thanks to the absence of a presiding female, the squire's wife having died many years before the narrative begins. Thus, the main source of wrongdoing in the novel is implicitly ascribed by Eliot to the various ways the central characters fail to pursue worthwhile, character-building work.

Godfrey is portrayed by Eliot as suffering from a constitutional 'irresolution and moral cowardice' (Eliot 2008b, p. 26), which gives rise to his choice to endure blackmail at the hands of his younger brother rather than face the prospect of admitting his affair to his father and disinheritance, a condition that would threaten to render him 'almost as helpless as an uprooted tree' (p. 27). The disastrous pact Godfrey makes with his brother to allow him to sell his horse to pay off debts he has also concealed from his father, unwittingly leads to his redemption through marriage to Nancy Lammeter. The price he pays, according to the fairy-tale logic of the book, is to be granted no children in this marriage and to remain estranged from his one biological child, Eppie, throughout her childhood and youth. In both the case of Silas and of Godfrey, what gives firm roots to character is the gracious love of nurturing females. In this, Eliot is one of the key English Victorian novelists who shape the literary trope of the mother-figure as the presiding, beneficent deity of the good and happy home.

By way of example, we can point to the lowly but pivotal character of Dolly Winthrop whose help to Silas, as a lonely middle-aged man with no experience of childrearing, is crucial to his success as a novice parent who is effectively cut off from his local community. It is Dolly who insists, against Silas' bemused resistance, that the child should be christened, a sacrament the man is unfamiliar with. Eventually, Silas submits to the necessity of baptism, going so far as to get christened himself. And it is this ritual act that begins, in an overt manner, Silas' true induction into the village community:

> He had no distinct idea about the baptism and the church-going, except that Dolly had said it was for the good of the child; and in this way, as the weeks grew to months, the child created fresh and fresh links between his life and the lives from which he had hitherto shrunk continually into narrower isolation.

In this process of sympathetic awakening, beautifully evoked by Eliot in the passages following Eppie's early development, Silas attains to a new life that overcomes the deadening effect of the trauma he suffered in Lantern Yard. His obsessive, repetitive work at the loom is now willingly interrupted for the sake of a higher vocation – that of childrearing. Bringing up Eppie constitutes a kind of work that is radically redemptive for Silas and remains a matter of wonder given her miraculous and unbidden appearance in the man's life. The images Eliot uses to evoke this process of restitution are predominantly organic, alluding to plants and flowers drawn upwards by the light and warmth of the sun. This is linked to the plant lore Silas learned from his mother, to which he now tentatively returns as the child also reawakens his susceptibility to the surrounding natural world:

> Sitting on the banks in this way, Silas began to look for the once familiar herbs again, and as the leaves, with their unchanged outline and markings, lay on his palm, there was a sense of crowding remembrances from which he turned away timidly, taking refuge in Eppie's little world, that lay lightly on his enfeebled spirit. As the child's mind was growing into knowledge, his mind was growing into memory: as her life unfolded, his soul, long stupefied in a cold narrow prison, was unfolding too, and trembling gradually into full consciousness. (p. 124)

This passage and others relating the process of veritable rebirth experienced by Silas thanks to the miraculous advent of Eppie into his life, marks Eliot's elaboration of the epigraph which stands at the entrance to the novel. The lines are from Wordsworth's poem from Lyrical Ballads, 'Michael': 'A child, more than all other gifts/That earth can offer to declining man, / Brings hope with it, and forward-looking thoughts' (p. 1). The salutary effects to the adult of recollecting one's own childhood are also lauded by Wordsworth. In fact, such a process of reflective retrieval is identified as the very medium in which great poetry is conceived.

The same process of personal redemption and restitution can be expressed in terms of reintegration. In the case of Silas this process has two complementary aspects to it. On the one hand, Silas stands at odds with his immediate environment – both human and natural – in Raveloe. He lives a physically isolated life in his solitary cottage and limits his interactions to the bare minimum. On the other hand, the traumatic nature of his expulsion from the severely religious community of Lantern Yard has led him to suppress all memories of his earlier life upon arrival at the rural village. By rights, Silas should have lived out the remainder of his days toiling at his barren work of weaving, have died a lonely miser whose life passed without provoking the slightest concern of others. True work, for Eliot, mends such dissolution of character and effects a lasting bond between the individual and their community. But it also binds together the phases of an individual's life. While the purpose of Silas' weaving was the mere hoarding of wealth, the gold of new human life bestowed upon him removes the false god of money in favour of the true god of human warmth and sympathy.

As is apparent to a more pronounced and explicit degree in *Adam Bede*, Eliot is also dealing with the ghosts of her own past in Silas Marner in the form of a reckoning with her youthful attachment to austere Evangelicalism. While Eliot presents the Methodist preacher Dinah Morris in a sympathetic and arguably idealizing fashion, the non-conformist sect to which Silas belonged are depicted largely as superstitious bigots given to harsh and capricious moralizing. Again, in common with her earlier novel, in *Silas Marner* the spontaneous warmth and moderation of rural Anglicanism is sharply contrasted with the fanaticism of the forms of religion that proliferate in the urban environments where the social impacts of early industrialization were felt with greatest force. A key point here is that nowhere in the novel does Eliot engage with the heritage of social and political struggle that emerged from this period of English history. This is noteworthy for a Victorian writer who was intimately familiar with the philosophical and theological debates that intersected with the political clashes that marked the first two decades of her life in the 1820s and 30s.

Of course, it can be readily said that Eliot is going about the business of writing successful novels and making a living from this practice, rather than penning polemical essays and social critiques on the issues of the day. This might suffice as a response, were it not for the social commentary that we do actually find interspersed, with increasing regularity, in her novels. In fact, as Raymond Williams (1983) eloquently notes, the oscillation between narrative description and authorial commentary is a salient feature of Eliot's writing, something that points to a certain internal tension if not contradiction in the development of the nineteenth-century novel. As Williams sees it, the issue resolves into one of capturing everyday life through the voices and speech patterns of the people themselves as opposed to the elevated and removed voice of the authorial critic:

> This problem appears sometimes more acute in the later examples, as increasingly, from George Eliot's later novels onward, the form of fiction of this kind comes to be determined, overall, by analysis rather than by narrative. Then, related to this, there is the second development, which appears to work, at times, in quite other directions. This is the incorporation, in prose, of spoken as opposed to written rhythms and constructions. The most evident local example of this development is in the reported direct speech (what is still, in the critical power of the dramatic tradition, called the dialogue) of the novels. Here undoubtedly, in the period we are examining, there are important developments and discoveries. But this is only one aspect of a general movement, running through the nineteenth century and reaching a climax in our own, towards the restoration of speech rhythms as the normal basis for many different kinds of prose. (Williams 1983, pp. 79–80)

It is noteworthy, when following the arc of development in Eliot's novels, that the presence of the common labouring class gradually diminishes over time. While her first full-length novel, *Adam Bede*, has clear affinities with earlier novels of Elizabeth Gaskell such as *Mary Barton* and *North and South* (both works very much centred on the lives of the working-class), a decade on from this debut a novel such as *Middlemarch* is much more in tune with lives her readership could readily compare to their own. As her writing progresses, it is clear that the Wordsworthian edict of ennobling the everyday lives and language of working class ceases to be the animating principle of Eliot's vocation as a writer.

THE MILL ON THE FLOSS: LANDSCAPE, LOSS, AND MEMORY

The minutiae of social distinction among the lower middle class are an abiding preoccupation rather than a sidenote in Eliot's second full-length novel, *The Mill on the Floss*, originally published a year after *Adam Bede*, in 1860. While the disparities in educational provision extended to the siblings, Maggie and Tom Tulliver, take centre stage in the first two parts or 'books' of the novel, the middle sections focus on the ignominious downfall of the Tulliver family fortunes. Their removal from Dorlcote Mill and loss of precious domestic possessions serves as an object lesson in class-based humiliation, especially for the son, Tom Tulliver, who stands on the brink of adulthood determined to reclaim the family fortunes. As with the first two novels of her admired contemporary, Elizabeth Gaskell, in *The Mill on the Floss* Eliot follows the lead of her debut novel by maintaining narrative focus on characters of the working and lower middle class.

So far in this first chapter little has been said about our second overarching theme of landscape. In *The Mill on the Floss* the Wordsworthian appreciation of landscape in terms of the life-long affective legacy of a childhood lived out in a particular natural place is clearly in evidence. Much of the power of Eliot's second novel derives from her evocation of the childhood of Maggie and Tom in the early chapters. The freedom and joy the children experience exploring the outside world around the farm are sharply contrasted with the tension of adult expectations and strictures inside the mill, particularly when the children's aunts and uncles are visiting. Thus, the landscape is presented as a place of sheltering and nurturing, a milieu where the children are comparatively free to feel connected and vibrant, rather than trammelled by the edicts of an indoor adult world they little understand or empathize with. The affective connection between landscape and selfhood is emphasized through Eliot's identifying both her own narrative voice and the presumed sentiments of the reader with the experience of the children:

> Life did change for Tom and Maggie; and yet they were not wrong in believing that the thoughts and loves of those first years would always make part of their lives. We could never have loved the earth so well if we had had no childhood in it, – if it were not the earth where the same flowers came up again every spring that we used to gather with our tiny fingers as we sat lisping to ourselves on the grass – the same hips and haws on the autumn hedgerows – the same redbreasts that we used to call 'God's birds,' because they did no harm to the precious crops. What novelty is worth that sweet monotony where everything is known, and loved because it is known. (Eliot 2015, p. 39)

These remembered elements of the natural landscape, Eliot continues, make up 'the mother tongue of our imagination, the language that is laden with all the subtle inextricable associations the fleeting hours of our childhood left behind them' (pp. 39–40). Here, then, we have a full-blown enunciation of the Romantic veneration of nature and its beneficent influence on the character of the young child. Eliot's rhapsodic address in the passage cited was one familiar to her readers from contemporaries such as the art historian and social critic John Ruskin from his *Modern Painters*, which appeared in five volumes between 1843 and 1860. Like Eliot, Ruskin was brought up under the influence – in Ruskin's case via his Scottish mother – of a strict Evangelicalism that emphasized intimate knowledge of Biblical scripture. This influence was tempered, however, by the love of Romantic authors brought to the home-educated Ruskin by his father. When Ruskin suffered in early adulthood, as did Eliot, a crisis of faith in Christianity, his love of nature and art provided an abiding solace.

In the striking episode, early on in *The Mill on the Floss*, when Maggie brutally cuts off her long dark hair in protest at what she feels is the unfair treatment meted out to her by the adults in her life, this presages a future of self-destructive revolt against expectations of feminine decorum that is related in the rest of the narrative. The juxtaposition realized here is that between a natural environment allowing freedom and freely flowing sentiment and a domestic, human environment stopping up such sentiment under the severe strictures of class-based and gendered Victorian social norms. The mill itself – being lost by Maggie's father and reclaimed by her brother after her father's death – becomes emblematic, in this regard, of the ultimately futile effort to return to the distant glories of early childhood. As Eliot writes of Maggie and Tom at the end of the 'School-Time' section of the novel, following the news that Dorlcote mill will no longer remain the family's home: 'They had entered the thorny wilderness, and the golden gates of their childhood had for ever closed behind them' (Eliot 2015, p. 180).

Yet, while there may be a definitive transition out of childhood, Eliot also accentuates the lasting impact of childhood experience on the grown adult.

In the scene that immediately follows Maggie's self-administered haircut, her father's clemency and sympathy – opposed to the censure she meets with from her mother and aunts – is presented as permanently shaping the girl's affective constitution. While she initially attempts to brazen out the outrage and disapproval of the assembled women at her act of self-mutilation, a seemingly innocuous comment from her brother is enough for Maggie to succumb to bitter tears. In this context, it is only the father who expresses mildness and consolation to his 'little wench', only to be rebuked by a sister-in-law for 'spoiling' his daughter with such indulgent mildness. For Maggie, the experience of her father's sympathy is the crucial saving grace of the situation: 'Delicious words of tenderness! Maggie never forgot any of these moments when her father 'took her part;' she kept them in her heart, and thought of them long years after, when every one else said that her father had done very ill by his children' (Eliot 2015, p. 65).

Eliot's sensitivity towards topography and landscape is made clear in *The Mill on the Floss* through her evocation of the 'Red Deeps', and small tract of slightly elevated and wooded ground close to Dorlcote Mill. This the site where Maggie, having now entered young adulthood, meets with an older, more experienced Philip Wakem, the son of Lawyer Wakem who has vindictively ruined Maggie's father and taken ownership of the mill. At this stage of her life, when Maggie is desperately attempting to reconcile herself to an existence of pious renunciation and dull monotony, her sole consolations are book reading and solitary walks in the surrounding countryside. Amid her reflections, the Red Deeps constitutes a site of particularly romantic intensity:

> In her childish days Maggie held this place, called the Red Deeps, in very great awe, and needed all her confidence in Tom's bravery to reconcile her to an excursion thither – visions of robbers and fierce animals haunting every hollow. But now it had the charm for her which any broken ground, any mimic rock and ravine, have for the eyes that rest habitually on the level; especially in summer, when she could sit in a grassy hollow under the shadow of a branching ash, stooping aslant from the steep above her, and listen to the hum of insects, like tiniest bells on the garment of Silence, or see the sunlight piercing the distant boughs, as if to chase and drive home the truant heavenly blue of the wild hyacinths. (Eliot 2015, pp. 276–77)

This passage exemplifies, once again, the Romantic notion of the child's imaginative and affective connection to native place. Eliot accentuates the extremely limited extent of Maggie's world, limits which are natural to the psychological horizon of young childhood but trammelling to older youth. She also makes clear how childish apprehensions of the unknown are transformed into tender affection for the familiar in early adulthood. In this period when Maggie, forced to fight against her own inner drive for familial affection and acceptance, is attempting to inure her character to emotional deprivation, the novel's description suggests to the reader that the 'fierce animals' that haunted the Ref Deeps for the girl may reappear to the young women. Immediately following the passage quoted above, Maggie encounters Philip Wakem again for the first time in years, thereby setting in motion a tragic concatenation of events that will eventually lead to her death.

The fact that the Deeps represent a slight elevation in what is otherwise flat and level expanse of land also hints at something crucial to Maggie's existence, namely its unrelieved monotony following the fall of her father's fortunes. Unable to develop according to the promptings of her own nature, Maggie is obliged to measure her own worth by the affection she holds for the two key males in her life, her father and brother. While her brother had always exhibited ambivalence and censure towards her, following his bankruptcy, even Maggie's father fails to reciprocate the tenderness the girl ardently craves. As is accentuated throughout the book, Maggie's love of Philip Wakem is, in large part, driven by pity for his 'deformed figure'. Upon being startled by Philip's appearance, Eliot notes how Maggie is 'filled for the moment with nothing but the memory of her child's feelings – a memory that was always strong in her' (Eliot 2015, p. 278). While Eliot depicts, in such a scene, the child-like innocence of Maggie's thoughts and actions, this also serves to make clear to the reader the unnatural and unhealthy arresting of the girl's emotional and social development.

The tragedy of the relationship that develops between Maggie and Philip in the central sections of the book derives from the underlying desire for consolation that drives the young lovers together. Clearly, Maggie is drawn to Philip as a kind of pitiable alter-ego of herself. In maintaining her connection with Philip, despite the unabated hostility of her brother Tom, Maggie is indulging in an act of rebellion she knows will be fatal to her desire for love from her sibling. Thus, her love of Philip can be seen as a legacy of her childhood fight to preserve her self-image in the face of the criticisms of her brother, mother, and aunts. Only now Maggie is granted no consolation at the hands of her father, whose sympathetic tendency to 'take her part' has given way to the bitterness of an obsessive desire to worst his enemy, Lawyer Wakem. In this context, Maggie's love for Wakem's son can be considered at attempt to internalize and thereby transcend the break that separates her early childhood and young womanhood. Within the logic of the novel this attempt is doomed to failure. But the tragic logic is such that Maggie cannot, despite knowing the likely fruits of her affection for Philip, hold back from fostering the connection.

More or less forced, by circumstance, to remain morally in a child-like state, Maggie as a woman attaches to the only possible object of affection remaining to her. Having seemingly overcome her childhood fears of the 'fierce animals' that haunted the Red Deeps, she willingly embraces the greater danger of the pitiable and helpless animal, Philip Wakem. For his part, Philip recognizes the current of pity which vitiates Maggie's love for him, something which renders the young man a kind of fantasy replacement for the brother whose affection for his sister is always overpowered by moral disapproval. Maggie's image of Philip is too divorced from the reality of the young man and is, like the landscape around her, ultimately a trap of early childhood recollection rather than a viable conduit into adulthood for the lonely and humiliated young woman. As, at the end of the novel, her final flight from Philip and from the only landscape she has known ultimately attests, the freezing of Maggie's affective development in early youth ensures that the passage into settled adulthood is denied to her. In the final act, she must return to the mill, seemingly to rescue her brother and her reputation, but in fact only to be claimed, in death, by the landscape in which she was reared.

Eliot, in an authorial interjection, is keen to insist that Maggie's fate is not sealed by her character, but rather propelled in large part by circumstance and environment. Here she draws on the intimate knowledge of German letters and philosophy she had accrued in the decades before she started to write novels. Contesting Novalis' 'questionable aphorism' that 'character is destiny', Eliot professes: 'For the tragedy of our lives is not created entirely from within' (Eliot 2015, p. 371). This comment is made at a point in the novel when Maggie is being launched into polite society, as a young woman of strikingly 'passionate sensibility which belonged to her whole nature, and made her faults and virtues all merge into each other' (p. 371). To heighten the sense of impending tragedy, Eliot makes a point of emphasizing the ignorance – perhaps willed unknowing – of the protagonist: 'Maggie's destiny, then, is at present hidden, and we must wait for it to reveal itself like the course of an unmapped river: we only know that the river is full and rapid, and that for all rivers there is the same final home' (ibid.). What Maggie does not know, of course, is precisely being 'prefigured' here by the author, who menacingly hints at Maggie's ultimate death by drowning in the river Floss.

The river is, in fact, a constant presence in the novel. In the opening paragraph, it is addressed directly by the author in the mode of a poetic rhapsody: 'How lovely the little river is, with its dark, changing wavelets! It seems to me like a companion while I wander along the bank and listen to its low placid voice, as to the one who is deaf and loving' (Eliot 2015, p. 7). Towards the end of the narrative, on the fateful morning when Maggie finds herself alone with Stephen for the planned boat excursion, the river and its environs act as a kind of intoxicating incantation of forgetfulness to the young woman. The lovers, both in denial in certain ways of the consequences of their feelings for one another, are literally carried away by the forgetfulness wrought on them by the sweetness of a summer morning spent out on the river. Under this influence, the couple are suspended in a full moment of presence untroubled by the ties of the past or the consequences of the future. It is a moment of oblivious joy for which the river will exact the ultimate price from Maggie in the final scene of the book. But, for now, the young woman is content to sleepwalk into this final act of the tragedy:

> The breath of the young, unwearied day, the delicious rhythmic dip of the oars, the fragmentary song of a passing bird heard now and then, as if it were only the overflowing of brim-full gladness, the sweet solitude of a twofold consciousness that was mingled into one by that grave untiring gaze which need not be averted – what else could be in their minds for the first hour? Some low, subdued, languid exclamation of love came from Stephen from time to time, as he went on rowing idly, half automatically: otherwise, they spoke no word, for what could words have been but an inlet to thought? and thought did not belong to that enchanted haze in which they were enveloped – it belonged to the past and the future that lay outside the haze. (Eliot 2015, p. 430)

The harrowing remorse that Maggie feels, upon becoming fully aware of her semi-conscious elopement with Stephen, brings her back to her remaining family, to the mill, and to the river. In obvious contrast with the summer morning depicted in her outing with Stephen, the river is shown in its terrifying power in the consummating scene of the flood. The contradictions of Maggie's fate and feelings have become so knotted and insoluble that there seems no way out for her other than through untimely death. In depicting her death, Eliot offers a climactic moment of resolution and restitution that hearkens back to the very first scenes of the narrative. Maggie's desire for love, understanding, and recognition from her brother Tom is finally attained when he realizes her selfless sacrifice in rowing out to rescue him from the flooded mill. The culminating sentence evokes all the pathos of the Romantic belief in the sanctity of childhood love: 'The boat reappeared – but brother and sister had gone down in an embrace never to be parted: living through again in one supreme moment the days when they had clasped their little hands in love, and roamed the daisied fields together' (p. 483).

'Nature repairs her ravages – but not all', Eliot writes in her short, concluding chapter; and then elaborates: 'To the eyes that have dwelt on the past, there is no thorough repair' (ibid.). The resolution through death is thus incomplete. The forgetfulness of the landscape still bears traces – for those who know it at least – of the history of human sorrow. The seasons may return in a seemingly timeless cycle, but the lives of individuals are finite and unrepeatable. *The Mill on the Floss* is, in this light, above all a novel about the irretrievability and finality of childhood and youth. While it is obviously observant of the Romantic pieties of 'Nature,' it adds to these an irresistible current of personal tragedy predicated on the tension between personal happiness and the duties of orthodox morality. Maggie is, herself, the embodiment of this contradiction, being at turns led by natural generosity of sentiment and then by an overwrought sense of social responsibility for the sufferings of others. She bears within her an intense feeling for a Christian doctrine of personal renunciation brought to her by the reading of *The Imitation of Christ*, but is also borne down by a subterranean sense of resentment engendered by the continued pressure of remorseless self-denial. As we will see in Hardy's novels – particularly in the character of Sue in *Jude the Obscure* – the tension between personal happiness and religious renunciation is often acted out most directly on the bodies of female protagonists.

A further potential framing of the narrative structure in Eliot's second novel connects to the final lines of Wordsworth's (2008) short poem, 'My heart leaps up when I behold': 'The Child is father of the Man;/And I could wish my days to be/Bound each to each by natural piety' (p. 246). As noted, Maggie's peculiar tragedy is essentially a matter of thwarted development. Made to feel, from early childhood, that there is something wayward and recalcitrant in her nature, Maggie's youth and early womanhood oscillate between extreme self-abnegation and half-conscious self-indulgence. The psychic struggle she undergoes hinges on the fact that she at once feels but cannot understand that her sentiments and acts can be construed as anything other than pure and kind. From the first to the last scenes of the narrative it is the problematic love between Maggie and Tom that acts as the pivot for the sentimental and psychological aporia in which the female protagonist is entangled. Somewhat softening Maggie's almost constant mental anguish are the consolations offered by the local landscape. Even these consolations, however, are at best equivocal in the role they play in Maggie's destiny. When Maggie has vowed to live a simple and austere life, seeking to make her days 'bound each to each in natural piety', her childhood revolt against the social pressures that blunt her natural sensibility reaffirm themselves in early womanhood.

The consolations of nature and importance of native place are accentuated by Eliot from the very first words of the novel. Accordingly, the initial, short chapter of *The Mill on the Floss* amounts to a kind of poetic invocation of the Mill and its immediate landscape. The painterly qualities of the description are manifest, though there are also proto-cinematic elements in play. The description begins in a panoramic mode, with the river Floss hurrying 'on between its green banks to the sea, and the loving tide' (Eliot 2015, p. 7); but attention is soon brought, in the second sentence, to the more limited vista of the town of St Ogg's and its immediate environs. Unlike a painting, however, Eliot's description includes the presence of a guide, and it is soon clear that the scene is not going on in the present but rather in a personally recollected past: 'I remember those large dipping willows. I remember the stone bridge' (ibid.). This, then, is an act of poetic remembrance, a kind of invoking of the muse of memory. As the description of the idealized rural scene plays out, a startling identification occurs that places the narrator in the place and time of the depicted landscape: 'That little girl is watching [the mill wheel] too: she has been standing on just the same spot at the edge of the water ever since I paused on the bridge' (p. 8). A further paragraph on and the narrator is themselves now described, in a mode of peaceful recollection, 'dreaming that I was standing on the bridge in front of Dorlcote Mill, as it looked one February afternoon many years ago' (pp. 8–9). In this shifting of temporal perspectives, it is the landscape that provides, quite literally, the screen onto which the narrative continuity is projected. In these opening paragraphs of the novel, we are given a foretaste of the final verdict offered: 'Nature repairs her ravages – but not all. [. . .] To the eyes that have dwelt on the past, there is no thorough repair' (p. 483).

As we will explore in detail in the third chapter of this book, when engaged upon an uncompleted study of Hardy's novels D. H. Lawrence became convinced that, as a novelist, he needed a kind of metaphysical worldview in which to place convincing and authentic depictions of characters and events. The point here is not to produce imaginative narratives as some kind of illustration of a hard and fast theory of reality. Such a process is highly unlikely to yield engaging and satisfying novels. Rather, what Lawrence was getting at is that the author must be able to draw from some kind of fundamental experience of the human condition in order to freight their descriptions with the depth and weight of reality. In the case of *The Mill on the Floss* that experience has to do with the irrevocability of childhood memory. A way to capture the tragedy of Maggie would be to say that she remains too much in thrall to her childhood. Putting it is this way could lead us to a simple but false conclusion, namely, that Eliot's protagonist fails to grow up and remains in a 'regressive' infantile state. But this would amount, precisely, to missing the point of Eliot's 'metaphysic', which, if my supposition is correct, turns on the sense that childhood cannot – perhaps even should not – be something anyone seeks to overcome in any definitive fashion. While, in terms of their affective constitutions, Maggie and Tom appear to be poles apart, the brother is, albeit in a different way, thoroughly haunted by the past. Thus, Tom essentially devotes his later youth and early manhood to delivering his family from the social opprobrium brought upon it by his father's bankruptcy. To all appearances, he succeeds in wiping the slate clean, an act which, following Maggie's half-voluntary elopement with Stephen Guest, requires that he purify himself of all living ties with his sister. But again, as the scene of their shared death graphically depicts, he remains bound to his younger sister at the last, despite all his efforts to contradict this fundamental, living fact.

As with her recollections of her father's kindness in the face of generalized social disapproval and censure, Maggie's character is remarkable for the strength of her childhood sensibility which, ultimately, she can neither overcome nor repress. But the key to the dramatic tensions in *The Mill on the Floss* is realizing the strength Maggie demonstrates precisely in so refusing to pass beyond her state of childhood. The crucial question to pose here is: what is it that dooms to failure Maggie's attempted transition to adulthood? Her attempted mediation between childhood and adulthood is through the strict self-abnegation she finds in her reading of Thomas à Kempis's *The Imitation of Christ*. This, of course, recalls Eliot's own passage through the straight gate of Evangelicalism as a child and young woman, something that raises the question: Is Eliot herself the successful counterpart to Maggie's failed attempt to salvage the best of childhood into settled maturity? Otherwise put: Does Maggie's fate recount the counterfactual death of Eliot had she, the author, not found some manner of sufficiently repairing the 'ravages of the past' without succumbing to insensibility? Such a supposition stands starkly at odds with Eliot's depiction of the narrator, at the start of the novel, barely able to fend off drowsiness sufficiently to begin the tale: 'Before I dozed off, I was going to tell you . . .' (Eliot 2015, p. 9). For indeed, the novel proves to be anything other than a comforting fireside yarn told to while away a desolate winter's evening. It is essentially the tragedy of a young woman, who is at once too close to and yet too removed from the landscape in which she finds herself.

FELIX HOLT AND *MIDDLEMARCH*: THE RETREAT FROM WORKING-CLASS LIVES

The pivotal moment in Eliot's relative retreat from working-class lives had perhaps arrived with the publication of *Felix Holt: The Radical* in 1866 and the subsequent 'Address to Working Men, by Felix Holt' written at the behest of the Tory John Blackwood, who had published the novel. The latter writing was done explicitly in response to Blackwood's concerns about the Reform Act of 1867, which doubled enfranchisement from one to two million men. 'I am excessively anxious,' Blackwood wrote to Eliot in November 1867, 'that you should do an Address to Working Men as I am thoroughly convinced that no one could do it as well. When the new Reform Bill comes into operation the working man will be on his trial and if he misconducts himself it will go hard with the country, but at all events his class would be the greatest sufferers' (Eliot 1995, p. 483). Eliot's agreement to use her fictional character in order to influence the national mood and debate at a decisive period of political change is quite extraordinary in the history of the English novel.

The general stance voiced by Felix is one of social pacification and amelioration, with the task at hand depicted as managing progressive industrializing change in a way that maintains or even enhances the sense of social connectedness and mutual responsibility within the body politic of the nation as a whole. In the words of Felix's 'Address':

> What I mean is, that each class should be urged by the surrounding conditions to perform its particular work under the strong pressure of responsibility to the nation at large; that our public affairs should be got into a state in which there should be no impunity for foolish or faithless conduct. In this way, the public judgement should sift our incapability and dishonesty from posts of high charge, and even personal ambition would necessarily become of a worthier sort, since the desires of the most selfish men must be a good deal shaped by the opinions of those around them. (Eliot 1995, p. 491)

While the dramatic period represented in *Adam Bede* and *Silas Marner* placed it two generations before publication, *Felix Holt* is set just one generation earlier, at the time of the first Reform Act of 1832. This earlier Act abolished a large number of 'rotten boroughs' that were under the control of a powerful local landowner. In Britain the 1830s and 1840s were, by any measure, a period of extraordinary social and political upheaval. As E. P. Thompson (1968) makes clear in his meticulously detailed social history of the time, the period immediately before and after the 1832 Reform Act saw a veritable explosion of working-class pamphlets and fights over their free circulation: 'These small, closely printed weeklies carried news of the great struggle for General Unionism in these years, the lock-outs of 1834 and the protests at the Tolpuddle case, or searching debate and exposition of Socialist and trade union theory' (p. 800).

Felix Holt is certainly no Adam Bede. He does not speak with the common dialect and is rather given to speeches and intellectual self-improvement. He does practice a trade – he works with watches and clocks – and he believes in word, just as Adam did in deed, in the essential nature of honest work. But what is most striking is that Felix, from the first time we encounter him in an exchange with the local dissenting minister, Rufus Lyon, is a man to be channelled and tamed by others, rather than allowed his own scope of action and acknowledged as possessing an inherent ability for self-reform. Before the reader encounters him directly, his mother relates to the minister her son's recent history: 'giving up his 'prenticeship, and going off to study at Glasgow, and getting through all the bit of money his father saved for his bringing-up' (Eliot 1995, p. 56). To the minister's suggestion that, in view of his skills and education, Felix ought to 'seek some higher situation as clerk or assistant', his response points to a curious adherence to his father's class status:

> I'll take no employment that obliges me to prop up my chin with a high cravat, and wear straps, and pass the livelong day with a set of fellows who spend their spare money on shirt-pins. That sort of work is really lower than many handicrafts, it only happens to be paid out of proportion. That's why I set myself to learn the watchmaking trade. My father was a weaver first of all. It would have been better for him if he had remained a weaver. I came home through Lancashire and saw an uncle of mine who is a weaver still. I mean to stick to the class I belong to – people who don't follow the fashions. (Eliot 1995, pp. 63–64)

Here we encounter a problem that, as we will see in the next chapter, constitutes a central preoccupation in the works of Thomas Hardy. In Hardy, the theme finds its consummate expression in his final novel, *Jude the Obscure*, but is equally central in *The Return of the Native*. 'Why should I want to get into the middle class because I have some learning?' (Eliot 1995, p. 64) Felix asks of Rufus Lyon. The distance between *Adam Bede* and *Felix Holt* is most readily measured by the changed tenor of the times. The post-Napoleonic time is recognized as one of the most politically tumultuous in modern English history. In the imaginary coach-journey conjured up by Eliot in the 'Introduction' to Felix Holt, the reader is offered a meticulous verbal panorama of the Midlands, passing through a country of contrast and conflict. In her description, Eliot carefully depicts the effects industrialization had on the social context, one of which was the Radicalism represented by the eponymous protagonist of the novel:

> The breath of the manufacturing town, which made a cloudy day and a red gloom by night on the horizon, diffused itself over all the surrounding country, filling the air with eager unrest. Here was a population not convinced that old England was as good as possible; here were multitudinous men and women aware that their religion was not exactly the religion of their rulers, who might therefore be better than they were, and who, if better, might alter many things which now made the world perhaps more painful than it need be and certainly more sinful. (Eliot 1995, p. 6)

While Eliot had earlier depicted Adam and Arthur, in the late 1700s, as capable of intimate childhood friendship and mutual respect despite their clear difference of social rank, Felix professes a stringent sense of working-class loyalty and opposition to the conventional wisdom of middle-class superiority. Adam Bede shows no desire to question, let alone overturn, the given social order of things. His quarrel with Arthur Donnithorne rests exclusively on the morality of his conduct towards Hetty Sorel. While there is certainly a concern for propriety and the reputational vulnerability of a young woman of Hetty's social station, the point is that Adam does not judge Arthur negatively due to his superiority of social rank.

In *Felix Holt*, by contrast, Eliot takes on a period of Radicalism and unrest whose legacy, in the face of a lively national debate of further impending electoral reform, was very much in evidence in 1866 when the novel was published. What is striking about her handling of this period of English political history is Eliot's relative lack of success in using the character of Felix Holt to convey in a plausible and sympathetic manner the 'structure of feeling' at work among the working class during this period of political change. By centering the plot on the bewilderingly complex origins of Rufus Lyons's daughter, Esther, Eliot draws the reader into a kind of protracted legal intrigue worthy of Dickens' *Bleak House*. What is crucial about this, in the present context, is the seeming desire on Eliot's part to displace the centre of the reader's interest from the growth of working-class political consciousness to a question of upper-middle-class succession and inheritance.

To this extent, *Felix Holt* marks a distinct falling away from Eliot's earlier achievements – in *Adam Bede, The Mill on the Floss,* and *Silas Marner* – in presenting working-class lives in unprecedently vivid and sympathetic ways. According to Raymond Williams (1973), Eliot's tendency to present working-class generically and *en masse* was actually present from the outset:

> Another way of putting this would be to say that though Georg Eliot restores the real inhabitants of rural England to their places in what had been a socially selective landscape, she does not get much further than restoring them as a landscape. They begin to talk, as it were collectively, in which middle-class critics still foolishly call a kind of chorus, a 'ballad-element'. But as themselves they are still only socially present, and can emerge into personal consciousness only through externally formulated attitudes and ideas. (p. 168).

Stylistically, the problem Williams is identifying here can be articulated in terms of a tension between a novel alternating between narrative cohesion – particularly when this is achieved by means of direct speech – and reflective commentary. It would be a little facile to identify this as a tension between the inner and outer life of those captured in the prose of the novel. Rather, to Williams's thinking at least, it is more a question of how the writer acts as mediator between the forms of life depicted in the novel and the reader's reception of those forms and their attendant structures of feeling.

In his influential essay 'Base and Superstructure in Marxist Cultural Theory', Williams (2005) grasps Antonio Gramsci's notion of hegemony as 'a whole body of practices and expectations' and 'a sense of absolute because experienced reality beyond which it is very difficult for most members of the society to move, in most areas of their life' (p. 43). While this understanding suggests a certain notion of collective cognitive closure, Williams insists, in a direct and quite unambiguous way, on the revelatory capacity of literature vis-à-vis social understanding. The back and forth between social experience and literary expression constitutes, of course, nothing other than a rendering of Marxist materialism applied to a certain domain of production, in this case to novel writing. In Williams's (2005) words:

> It is always so, in the relation between literature and society: that the society determines, much more than we realize, and at deeper levels than we ordinarily admit, the writing of literature; but also that the society is not complete, not fully and immediately present, until the literature has been written, and that this literature, in prose as often as in any other form, can come through to stand as if on its own, with an intrinsic and permanent importance, so that we can see the rest of our living through it as well as it through the rest of our living. (p. 72)

This understanding of modern literature is also, arguably, consonant with the Aristotelian theory of art as imitation or mimesis. In the *Physics*, Aristotle (2008) argues that all artistic production – from carpentry to painting – is grasped as a human productive process that draws out potentialities of naturally occurring materials that cannot be realized in nature itself. Applied to Williams's theory of the novel, literature rests upon but is not limited to the nature of social experience. And this is why, for Williams, the development of the British novel is so crucial to modern society and politics: it acts, at its best, as a lens through which certain lineaments of contemporary social development can be seen more sharply and effectively. If, as Marx and Engels (1994) famously proclaimed in *The German Ideology*, the leading ideas stem from the leading class, then we can readily recognize the potential insurrectionary potentiality of the novelist of the mid-nineteenth century.

Certainly, by the time we reach the period of development that commences with the appearance of *Middlemarch* in 1871/2 it is fair to say that a much more stable and unproblematic parallel between the fictional protagonists and real readers has been attained in the development of Eliot's novel writing. While Eliot's penetrating power of character analysis is undoubtedly sharper than ever, the centre of interest remains fixed throughout on the mismatching of personalities in the disastrous unions of Dorothea Brooke and Mr Casaubon on the one hand and Rosamond Vincy and Dr Lydgate on the other. A third union, between Fred Vincy and Mary Garth revisits the theme of a childhood affection between people who, as adults, occupy distinct class positions, which was first explored in the relationship between Adam and

Arthur in *Adam Bede*. In *Middlemarch* Eliot draws attention to the nuances involved in social distinction in the social milieu portrayed:

> Even when Caleb Garth [Mary's father] was prosperous, the Vincys were on condescending terms with him and his wife, for there were nice distinctions of rank in Middlemarch; and though old manufacturers could not any more than dukes be connected with none but equals, they were conscious of an inherent social superiority which was defined with great nicety in practice, though hardly expressible in practice. (Eliot 2008c, p. 217)

When tackling more extreme contrasts of social status, in *Middlemarch* Eliot's underlying narrative bearing is one of sympathetic condescension towards working-class characters. What is striking above all is how Eliot tends to elide the social conflict between classes by pointing out the inevitable follies of an individual's limited perspective. This tends to render interactions between social classes rather farcical, as though the individual characters depicted were contrived puppets rather than fleshed-out human agents. This effect is partly achieved through the archness of action and dialogue and partly through direct appeals to the reader's indulgence and understanding.

A good example of this in *Middlemarch* is the rancorous encounter between Dagley, a tenant farmer, and Mr Brooke, his landlord. While Eliot makes clear, as she sets the scene, that the economic plight of farmers such as Dagley at the time depicted left much to be desired, she also castigates the corrosive influence of raised political consciousness brought about by working-class agitation in the run-up to the First Reform Bill of 1832. Thus, Dagley is made irascible not only by the state of the agricultural economy and by the fact he has been drinking, but also by indulging in political conversation about reform: 'He has also taken too much in the shape of muddy political talk, a stimulant dangerous disturbing to his farming conservatism, which consisted in holding that whatever is, is bad, and any change is likely to be worse' (Eliot 2008c, p. 370).

Mr Brooke has come, in a spirit of patrician beneficence, to inform him that his son has been caught poaching and to appeal to the father to take him in hand. Despite Brooke's mildness in his request, Dagley's response is sullen and defiant. In his drunkenness and rage, he assumes the landowner wants him to beat his son to teach him a lesson, an action the farmer is resolutely unwilling to carry out: 'No, I won't: I'll be dee'd if I'll leather my boy to please you or anybody else, not if you was twenty landlords istid o' one, and that a bad un' (p. 371). Certainly, the theme of intemperate male rage among the working-class is something of a constant in Eliot's novels, often connected to the maleficent effects of drinking. Also typical is the attempted intercession of a long-suffering wife or, in the case of Tulliver's beating of Lawyer Wakem in *The Mill on the Floss*, of a protective daughter.

In the scene in *Middlemarch*, however, it is the aggravation of working-class political ambition in the run-up to the Reform Bill that proves most fatal to Dagley's attitude towards the local landlord: 'An' you may do as you like now, for I'm none afeard on you. An' you'd better leave my boy aloan, an' look to yoursen, afore the Rinform has got upo' your back. That's what I'n got to say,' concluded Mr Dagley, striking his fork into the ground with a firmness which proved inconvenient as he tried to draw it up again' (p. 372). We note here how Eliot is unable to refrain from adding an element of ridicule to her portrait of the farmer, showing him struggling with the misuse of his own farming implement and thereby depicting him as an object of pastiche for her refined, middle-class readership.

Such a scene, I contend, stands in sharp contrast to the largely sympathetic renderings of working-class characters to be found in Eliot's earlier novels. This retreat from verisimilitude into a kind of pastoral pastiche seems often to hinge on the very real middle-class anxiety felt in Victorian Britain towards broadening political enfranchisement. To a great extent, Eliot could afford to be more generous towards the working-class characters of Adam Bede and Silas Marner thanks to the dramatic time in which the narratives are set. While the 1790s and early 1800s were politically determined by reactions to the French Revolution, the organization of the industrial working-class into a self-conscious political movement would not occur in Britain for another generation.

The fact that *Middlemarch* is set in the 1830s places it exactly in this period of heightened class-based political consciousness, organization, and agitation. And again, the period in which *Middlemarch* is written and published – the period the Second Reform Bill – was naturally regarded, one more generation on, as a recapitulation but also intensification of the politically charged times of the 1830s. In Dolin's (2009) view, the transition in political sensibility between *Adam Bede* and *Middlemarch* comes down to a difference between social rank and social class:

> Under the class system an individual's identity is not determined by his or her place in a fixed hierarchy of caste but within a particular class: it therefore introduced a notion of class interest, and of a society actually based on inequality, not on some preordained order. Class is a complicated term, in which interest groups, occupational groups, and sectional religious groups may overlap. Unlike rank, it presupposes the existence of conflict and tension between classes, and it stratifies and sectionalizes society along lines that are openly recognized as unequal: working and housing conditions, food and leisure pursuits, types of illnesses and lifespans. (p. 58)

It is, above all, class conflict that causes Eliot's narrative to slip from a sympathetic, if occasionally idealizing, portrayal of everyday working life, to a moralizing and often castigating depiction of such life. This development in Eliot's writing in no way negates the very real progress made in her early novels, progress which indeed allows the British working class to take the stage. Nor is it the case that the attenuation in Eliot's sympathy for lower-class characters finds no corresponding compensations in a certain complexifying of her depictions of the inner life of her middle-class protagonists. As we will see in the following chapters of this book, Eliot's discoveries and achievements in this regard were made lasting by the work done by later writers such as Hardy and Lawrence, who crucially inherited the earlier novelist's progress in capturing the everyday lives and landscapes of the English working class.

In this chapter, I have deliberately focused largely on Eliot's first three novels as they best illustrate the themes of labour and landscape as I wish to present them in this study. To recap, in *Adam Bede* Eliot offers a highly attractive and compelling depiction of skilled handicraft as a means to the sound development of character. Even in the character of Adam, however, Eliot raises a warning about the hubris that may arise from excessive self-reliance. Adam's female counterpart, Dinah, practices a very different kind of work, one that is both driven by and done on behalf of her care for others. Thus, Adam might possess practical intelligence to a remarkable degree and know everything's mechanical workings and measure, but he is apt to be harshly judgemental in the face of the moral failings of others. The narrative transformation of Adam accordingly rests on a journey towards the sentiment of kindness and forgiveness. The resolving synthesis of Eliot's first novel can thus be captured as a meeting of hand and heart. The crucible for this resolution is essentially the tightly woven agricultural community of Hayslope at a time before the effects of full economic industrialization had borne fruit with the working-class political organization that would so profoundly shape Britain from the 1830s on.

In *Silas Marner* Eliot depicts quite a different variant of the faith versus works dialectic first found in *Adam Bede*. Silas' exile from his close-knit urban non-conformist community results in a decade and a half of soulless labour in the rural village of Raveloe. In the case of Silas, his work of weaving acts as a salve for the bitterness he feels at the injustice meted out to him by those he loved. Its repetitive, mechanical nature does not build but rather corrodes character and reduces the protagonist's life to little more than a mindless pursuit of money. As with Adam, the essence of Silas' moral education lies in his largely involuntary realization that sympathy for others is the indispensable ingredient for well-rounded personal development. Silas' fortitude is demonstrated by the fact that the barren years of mindless work have not ultimately blunted his native capacity for fellow-feeling. The demands of unlooked-for parenthood displace his obsessive concern for hoarding wealth and allow Eliot to preach the lesson that work is only truly good to the extent it binds us to our neighbours. In other words, the individual's work alone is nothing; its sole moral purpose is to bring us into living contact with those around us.

Finally, as *The Mill on the Floss* makes most evident among Eliot's early novels, human community also shelters in a natural locale. In this regard, Eliot plainly inherits and adapts the Wordsworthian faith in the formative and healing power of local landscape. In relating the history of Maggie Tulliver, however, Eliot offers something very different to a sentimentalized depiction of some timeless English rural idyll. The central role granted to the river Floss offers a key metaphor for the dynamic nature of the landscape itself, which functions in the novel not as a static backdrop to human action, but rather as a changing, organic character in its own right. The dynamic fusion of character development and local landscape is the key theme I wish to develop in the next chapter, which turns to the novels of Thomas Hardy. Over two and a half decades of novel writing, from the early 1870s to the mid-1890s, Hardy not only inherited Eliot's achievements in rendering English rural life in the nineteenth century, he also went on to create a whole interconnected imaginary landscape of 'Wessex'. The role of place accordingly gains in significance in Hardy's novels, even as the social contradictions of full-blown economic industrialization in Britain reach a certain climax. This crisis can also be followed, as we will see, in Hardy's depiction of intensified complications between work and social development.

Chapter 2

Thomas Hardy and the Living Landscape

UNDER THE GREENWOOD TREE AND *FAR FROM THE MADDING CROWD*: THE PASTORAL COMEDY

Britain during the mid to late nineteenth century was caught up in an unprecedently rapid process of industrialization and urbanization. Between 1851 and 1901 the rural population dropped from nine to around seven and a half million, while the urban population rose from nine to twenty-eight million (Law 1967). This set the scene for an increasing sense of psychological distance from rural life, something that also lent itself to romanticizing nostalgia for the countryside and its modes of human existence. As we saw in the previous chapter, Eliot's depictions of rural England in the late eighteen and early nineteenth century certainly betray a certain indulgence of this idealizing impulse. In Eliot's novels it is above all the appeal to what Raymond Williams (1973) calls a 'knowable community' that attracts the author. When, towards the end of *Silas Marner*, Eliot has the weaver and his adopted daughter return to the urban setting of Lantern Yard, Silas is 'bewildered by the changes thirty years had brought to his native place' (Eliot 2008b, p. 171). More generally, in Eliot's early novels, urban centres of manufacturing tend to be present only as a hazy and rather sinister penumbra to the small-scale rural towns and villages in which the principal action takes place. It is not hard to appreciate that this focus on the distinctly limited context of the 'knowable community' of the English countryside constituted much of the attraction of the novels for her mid-Victorian readership.

As has also been noted, Eliot's pastoral descriptions quite evidently and self-consciously inherit the Wordsworthian valourizing of life in the countryside relative to urban existence. For all her travails and eventual downfall, the life of Maggie in *The Mill on the Floss* has a kind of glory and intensity to it that would have been difficult to render had she been the daughter of a struggling manufacturer or merchant in a northern industrial town. Of course, Eliot's landscape is very far from the sublimity of Wordsworth's native Cumbria: it is largely flat, relatively featureless, and made up of a network of market towns and villages found in close proximity. Hardy's topography is similar, though he does make use of the more awe-inspiring coastal landscapes. As we shall see in the next chapter, Lawrence's native landscape, situated at the border between Nottinghamshire and Derbyshire, can be readily compared to the rural literary settings of both Eliot and Hardy. This notion of a border country is, in the view of Williams (1973), the key to understanding the underlying character of Hardy's various depictions of Wessex life. In his interpretation of Hardy, Williams' chief polemical point is to counter the settled impression that his novels are motivated by an underlying desire to commemorate, in a nostalgic mode, the rural customs and settings of a rapidly disappearing way of life in rural England:

> But the real Hardy country, we soon come to see, is that border country so many of us have been living in: between custom and education, between work and ideas, between love of place and the experience of change. [. . .] There is always a great deal in [Hardy's novels] on an old rural world: old in custom and in memory, but also in a sense that belongs to the new times of conscious education, the oldness of history and indeed of prehistory: the educated consciousness of the facts of change. Within the major novels, in several different ways, the experience of change and of the difficulty of choice are central and even decisive. (Williams 1973, p. 197)

As Williams also observes, the crises of personal and social change become more evident in Hardy's narratives towards the end of his active novel-writing career. Although he would go on to live three more decades (Lawrence dies just two years after Hardy, in 1930), Hardy famously decided to write no more novels ostensibly due to the adverse response to the publication of *Jude the Obscure* in 1895. Certainly, the trajectory from an early narrative such as *Under the Greenwood Tree* (published in 1872) to the final two novels, *Tess of the D'Urbervilles* (1891) and *Jude the Obscure*, is remarkable for its complexification of character development and sense of contemporary social sensibility. When surveying this intense development over two and a half decades, it is difficult not to agree with Williams' claim that it is, above all, the experience of lived-through change that animates Hardy's novels at the most fundamental and decisive level. The somewhat tentative beginnings of Hardy's writing career, at a time when he is seemingly settled into a life as a junior architect, are quite understandable when one acknowledges his position as a young man without independent means and enjoying few personal connections with the cultural life of contemporary England.

Making a living as a novelist in Victorian Britain was largely about writing regular instalments for a periodic magazine, a mode of literary consumption that naturally lent itself to the picaresque and sensational in terms of plot and character development. Under these conditions, Hardy had first to make a name for himself as a popular writer before he could tackle anything as challenging as the themes of his final novels, which are tragic and almost epic in their literary tenor and psychological reach. Two early novels, *Desperate Remedies* (his first novel, published in 1871) and *A Pair of Blue Eyes* (published in 1873) are fast-moving romantic comedies with elements of a detective mystery designed to keep the reader engaged throughout the narrative. Between these two books, Hardy published *Under the Greenwood Tree*. While the narrative power of *A Pair of Blue Eyes* was drawn, to a not insignificant degree, by the unity of place granted by Hardy's evocative descriptions of a rugged, Cornish coastal landscape, the topographic unity of his second novel very much points the way towards what will go on to be the author's immediately recognizable native ground.

The full title of Hardy's second published novel is telling in this regard: *Under the Greenwood Tree; Or, The Mellstock Quire: A Rural Painting of the Dutch School*. The allusion to Dutch painting makes Hardy's landscape pretensions explicit as well as eliciting the expectation of painterly detail to the humble lives of everyday rural inhabitants. The tone of the narrative voice in *Under the Greenwood Tree* is distinctive Hardyesque from the first lines:

> To dwellers in a wood, almost every species of tree has its voice as well as its feature. At the passing of the breeze the fir-trees sob and moan no less distinctly than they rock: the holly whistles as it battles with itself; the ash hisses amid its quiverings; the beech rustles while its flat boughs rise and fall. And winter, which modifies the note of such trees as shed their leaves, does not destroy its individuality. (Hardy 2013, p. 11)

The setting of Christmastime a generation earlier immediately makes for a comforting sense of the familiar. Compared to the sophisticated and eloquent nature of characters portrayed in *Desperate Remedies* and *A Pair of Blue Eyes*, Hardy's rural cast for *Under the Greenwood Tree* are also reliably familiar and endearing. It is hard not to see shades of Shakespeare's 'mechanicals' in all such literary portraits of rustic village life and, indeed, the tale of Pyramus and Thisbe told by the rural troupe in *A Midsummer Night's Dream* is alluded to by Hardy in the course of the novel. Above all, the atmosphere of small-scale communal intimacy is everywhere apparent and this lends to the narrative a soothing sense of distance in time and space. The reader has the sense that this is a bounded world, whose outline is seemingly fixed by a consistency of families and customs of the inhabitants of the village of Mellstock over generations. All this lends itself to the sense of Hardy's narrative as a landscape painting bound within the contours of a distinct frame.

In his prefatory note from forty years after the novel's first appearance in 1872, Hardy remarked that *Under the Greenwood Tree* offers 'a fairly true picture, at first hand, of the personages, ways, and customs which were common among such orchestral bodies in the villages of fifty or sixty years ago' (Hardy 2013, p. 3). Surveying this production of his early years of novel writing, Hardy complains that his theme is treated 'farcically and flippantly at times,' but that 'circumstance would have rendered any aim at a deeper, more essential, more transcendent handling unadvisable at the date of writing' (p. 4). The ambivalence exhibited by Hardy with respect to his novel here is telling. On the one hand, he acknowledges the lasting value of recording for posterity certain features of English rural life, but, on the other, the superficiality of treatment is cause for regret. On the latter score, it is clear that by 'circumstance' Hardy is referring to the reality of his having to make a name for himself as a writer having attained a certain degree of popularity and renown. Given the self-consciously modest scope and documentary intent behind its composition, it is somewhat difficult to know what a 'more transcendent handling' of the theme of a village choir would amount to. One possibility would relate to the portrayal of the heroine, Fancy Day, who is the love interest that ostensibly represents the axis of the narrative. Based on how Hardy's novel writing developed, we can plausibly presume that any mature re-writing of *Under the Greenwood Tree* would have considerably heightened the pathos and sense of tragic fate connected to the female lead of Hardy's rural drama.

Not only is rural intimacy to the fore in *Under the Greenwood Tree*, so is the presence of natural cycles. The chapters of the short novel are divided into four parts: Winter, Spring, Summer, and Autumn and changes to the surrounding landscape of the village make a considerable impact on the overall atmosphere of Hardy's narrative. In fact, the sympathetic correspondence between the natural seasonal conditions and the mental atmosphere of characters is a stock feature of all three of the writers in this study. The alternation between meteorological phenomena and psychological mood is so naturalized in the composition of the novel that its effect upon the reader can be easily missed. Equally obvious but crucial to the impact of Hardy's narratives is the fact that he depicts a largely pedestrian form of life within the country. Hence, his characters are peculiarly exposed to the elements of the landscape. In the opening paragraphs of *Under the Greenwood Tree*, having alluded to the intimate knowledge of various tree species possessed by 'dwellers in a wood' he goes on to exemplify this knowledge in the figure of Dick Dewy, striding through the darkness of a winter's night under starlight:

The lonely lane he was following connected one of the hamlets of Mellstock parish with Upper Mellstock and Lewgate, and to his eyes, casually glancing upward, the silver and black-stemmed birches, with their characteristic tufts, the pale grey boughs of beech, the dark-creviced elm all appeared now as black and flat outlines upon the sky, wherein the white stars twinkled so vehemently that their flickering seemed like the flapping of wings. Within the woody pass, at a level anything lower than the horizon, all was dark as the grave. The copsewood forming the sides of the bower interlaced its branches so densely even at this season of the year that the draught from the north-east flew along the channel with scarcely an interruption from lateral breezes. (Hardy 2013, p. 11)

In Dick Dewey's tongue-tied pursuit of the beautiful if rather one-dimensional heroine of the story, Fancy Day, Hardy establishes a paradigm that will recur in his subsequent novels. In particular, portraying rival suitors to a woman tends to form the dramatic axis of most of the author's early productions and it is particularly to the fore in *Far from the Madding Crowd*, to which we will turn next. As the tragic pathos of his novels intensifies in the 1880s, this thematic crux gradually shifts to one of ill-judged unions and the difficulty or impossibility of overcoming them. In *Tess of the D'Urbervilles* and *Jude the Obscure*, the principal characters are relentlessly torn between rival partners, each of whom by turns respond to and elicits quite distinct features of the personality of the protagonist. Hardy tends to depict these struggles as a dynamic tension both within the individual themselves and deriving from opposed expectations from others. In the case of Tess, for example, Angel Clare's presumption that his wife has known no previous lovers and is immaculately untainted by such contact is transformed into horror and scorn when Tess finally confesses to her seduction and rape at the hands Alec d'Urberville.

At first glance *Far from the Madding Crowd* adopts the same basic plot structure of *Under the Greenwood Tree* (a number of male suitors pursuing one young, eligible woman) and complexifies it. The later novel is over twice the length of the earlier, but it is the qualitative changes in Hardy's portrayal of the relationships central to the novel that are most striking. The descriptions of rural work also gain in concreteness and solidity, as illustrated by the renderings of Oak's lambing during cold winter nights early on in the novel. Beside the meticulous details of the shepherd's hut and the necessary tasks of lambing season, Hardy invests the character of Oak with a natural dignity in his work and certain self-conscious contentment at his unmediated exposure to the natural settings and elemental forces:

Being a man not without a frequent consciousness that there was some charm in this life he led, he stood still after looking at the sky as a useful instrument, and regarded it in an appreciative spirit, as a work of art superlatively beautiful.

> For a moment he seemed impressed with the speaking loneliness of the scene, or rather with the complete abstraction from all its compass of the sights and sounds of man. Human shapes, interferences, troubles, and joys were all as if they were not, and there seemed to be on the shaded hemisphere of the globe no sentient being save himself: he could fancy them all gone round to the sunny side. (Hardy 2002, p. 18)

This evocative description encapsulates a certain poetics of solitude and a momentary dissolution into elemental features and forces, which lends an elevating and sublime backdrop to the human drama. There is a key element of dramatic irony to this description also, as the fixed contentment of Oak's life is about to be dispelled by the misfortune of losing a flock the sheep he has yet to pay for. As his name suggests, however, Oak's connection to the natural place, his commitment to hard if humble work, and his sensibility for the cosmic forces within which all human action takes place, means that he remains firmly rooted to the ground despite all vicissitudes he undergoes.

While the female love interest in *Under the Greenwood Tree,* Fancy Day, is little more than a cypher for an alluring if fickle object of desire, Bathsheba Everdene is presented as a full-blown character in her own right. In stark opposition to Oak, however, Bathsheba is presented as lacking any significant degree of steadfastness due to underlying vanity and fickleness. When fortune elevates her into property ownership, just as it had diminished Oak into being a common farm worker, she raises her sights in terms of matrimony and looks down on the plainness of the shepherd's lot. As we observed in the case of Eliot's early novels, seemingly small distinctions of economic and social standing loom large in Hardy's rural communities, where the sense of propriety and material advancement constantly brings strengths of character in conflict with the outer trappings of social value. Thus, just as Maggie's virtues in *The Mill on the Floss* are ultimately no safeguard against the contradictory forces of social expectation concerning a woman in her position, so Bathsheba's rise in fortune draws her into a disastrous union with the dashing but morally debased Sergeant Troy.

The figure of a beguiling but dissolute male is something of a stock character in the English Victorian novel. As we will see, Hardy's portrayal of his most famous tragic heroine in *Tess of the D'Urbervilles,* whose terrible downfall is initiated by her rape at the hands of Alec, brings this figure of the sensitive young woman's male nemesis to something of a logical conclusion. In the case of Bathsheba, the underlying mood of Hardy's narrative remains comedic rather than tragic. As the atmosphere of his novels darkens considerably, however, the aporias of mismatched unions became almost unbearable tensions lying at the heart of the narrative. In part, this development reflects changes in the economic, social, and political claims on behalf of women in the late nineteenth century. In this connection, a theme common to Eliot and Hardy is the growing consciousness that women's capabilities far outstrip their opportunities in Victorian Britain, at a time when marriage remains the seemingly inevitable mechanism for women to secure or advance their economic and social standing. For both Bathsheba Everdene and Maggie Tulliver their seeming vanity and capriciousness of character is just as much a reflection of social circumstance as it is of psychological constitution.

The fickleness of Bathsheba is given a foil by the resolute steadfastness of Gabriel Oak and this is reflected in the outward course of their economic and social progress. Having lost his sheep and thereby his chance of making his way in the world, Oak is taken on as a lowly shepherd by Bathsheba, whose fortunes have turned in an opposite direction to Oak's thanks to her inheriting a large farm from her uncle. Many of Hardy's novels portray failure, usually on the part of men, to gain social elevation through prolonged, deliberate effort in work. This theme in Hardy will reach its apogee in his final novel, *Jude the Obscure*. What is strongly indicated in such cases is the impotence of the individual to bend circumstances to their will. Sometimes, as is the case of Henchard's tendency towards irascibility in *The Mayor of Casterbridge*, the reversals of fortune are ascribed to a certain tragic flaw of character. More often, as when Oak loses his sheep due to an errant young sheep-dog, worldly plans are thwarted by something lying outside the character themselves in the form of pure bad luck. What is key to this process of reversals in fortune is its impact upon the character of the person affected. Hardy makes clear how this works in the case of Oak, a few months after the loss of his flock:

> Gabriel was paler now. His eyes were more meditative and his expression more sad. He had passed through an ordeal of wretchedness which had given him more than it had taken away. He had sunk from his modest elevation as pastoral king into the very slime-pits of Siddim; but there was left to him a dignified calm he had never known before and that indifference to fate which, though it often makes a villain of a man is the basis of his sublimity when it does not. And thus the abasement had been exultation and the loss gain. (Hardy 2002, p. 43)

In contrast to the Shepherd, Bathsheba's trials of character lie ahead. As Oak gains sublimity through suffering, the young woman's lack of resolution is exacerbated by her elevated fortune. Having scorned an offer of marriage from Oak, Bathsheba goes on to refuse a second offer, this time from the gentleman farmer, Boldwood. The external reason, as Hardy makes explicit, is that she has no need of the material possessions such a union would bring in light of her own independent fortune. However, having sent a capricious Valentine's letter to Boldwood containing her own offer of marriage, Bathsheba does have misgivings about refusing him as a potential husband.

In contrast to Oak's hard-won but ultimately constitutional resoluteness of character, Hardy explicates Bathsheba's striking weakness of will. In addition, Hardy intimates that Bathsheba has inherited this failing of character from her father. As is related through village gossip, when the farm workers (including Oak) gather at Warren's malthouse, Bathsheba's father was known to the villagers as 'one of the ficklest husbands alive . . . a' didn't want to be fickle, but he couldn't help it' (Hardy 2002, p. 64). Unlike a character such as Hetty Sorel in *Adam Bede*, however, Hardy makes of Bathsheba a more complex composite of dispositions:

> Bathsheba's was an impulsive nature under a deliberative aspect. An Elizabeth in brain and a Mary Stuart in spirit, she often performed actions of the greatest temerity with a manner of extreme discretion. Many of her thoughts were perfect syllogisms; unluckily they always remained thoughts: only a few were irrational assumptions; but unfortunately they were the ones which most frequently grew into deeds. (Hardy 2002, p. 131)

As was noted in the case of Eliot's early novels, wayward character is often portrayed in Hardy in conjunction with the absence of meaningful work. While Oak is strongly identified with the lowly but honest work of sheep-farming, Bathsheba's lack of fixed purpose or steadfast character is reflected in her vocational incapacity. This can hardly be blamed on her, as the very idea of an independent woman farmer is considered beyond the pale by the Wessex society in which she finds herself. While ostensibly possessing power over them, Bathsheba is doubly dependent on those who work her farm on her behalf: first, as a women with little to no practical knowledge of how to run a farm; and, secondly, as someone recently elevated to the position of proprietorship. Tricked by a dishonest and venial farm manager, Bathsheba turns to Oak as the one person she can trust with regard to the effective running of the farm and with respect to her personal life. But Oak's straightforward honesty, when admitting that he no longer harbours a desire to marry Bathsheba, proves too much for the young woman's vanity when she is told she has done wrong in misleading farmer Boldwood about her feelings towards him:

> A woman may be treated with a bitterness which is sweet to her, and with a rudeness which is not offensive. Bathsheba would have submitted to an indignant chastisement for her levity had Gabriel protested that he was loving her at the same time: the impetuosity of passion unrequited is bearable, even if it stings and anathematizes; there is a triumph in the humiliation and a tenderness in the strife. This is what she had been expecting, and what she had not got. To be lectured because the lecturer saw her in the cold morning light of open-shuttered disillusion was exasperating. (Hardy 2002, p. 134)

It is this insistence to be loved by all, at once innocent in its childishness and yet damning in its real-world consequences, that seals Bathsheba's fate in spurning the steadfast Farmer Boldwood in favour of the morally vacuous Sergeant Troy. While a union with the former would have been dictated by economic prudence, Bathsheba instead gives herself away to a superficially charming leech, who sees in her acquired wealth an escape from his own impecunious and dissolute ways.

Amid the main plotline following the vicissitudes of Bathsheba's three lovers, *Far from the Madding Crowd* is replete with details of the work of sheep farming. Many incidents related to such work form not only the backdrop but drive the action between characters. An example of this is the outbreak of bloat that affects Bathsheba's flock when they consume young clover a day after she has dismissed Oak as head shepherd following his frank expression of disapproval alluded to above. Hardy's description of Oak's treatment of the sheep is rigorously related in veterinarian detail. This exactness is typical of Hardy's scrupulously observed portrayal of agricultural work and integral to his mature novels. It is of a piece with his similarly punctilious observations relating to weather and landscape:

> Passing his hand over the sheep's left flank, and selecting the proper point, he punctured the skin and rumen with the lance as it stood in the tube; then he suddenly withdrew the lance, retaining the tube in its place. A current of air rushed up the tube forcible enough to have extinguished a candle held at the orifice. (Hardy 2002, p. 141)

Hardy marks time as well as action through recounting the seasonal work with the sheep: the washing of May gives way to the shearing of June. When describing the great Shearing Barn, Hardy descants on one of his habitual themes of rural continuity of place and lifestyle. Such passages seem to contradict directly Williams' claim that Hardy's underlying concern is with change. But this seeming contradiction is not borne out by closer scrutiny, as in fact Hardy signalizes elements of relative rural stasis in order to accentuate the fluidity of life and setting for his largely urban readership. Here we encounter self-consciousness on the part of Hardy the novelist that parallels Eliot's earlier authorial self-reflections. It is important to note, when reflecting on such seemingly parenthetical comments, that the author himself is implicated in this contrast between town and country life:

> The citizens' *Then* is the rustics' *Now*. In London twenty or thirty years ago are old times: in Paris ten years or five. In Weatherbury three- or four-score years were included in the mere present, and nothing less than a century set a mark on its face or tone. Five decades hardly modified the cut of a gaiter, the embroidery

of a smockfrock, by the breadth of a hair. Ten generations failed to alter the turn of a single phrase. In these Wessex nooks the busy outsider's ancient times are only old, his old times are still new; his present is futurity. (Hardy 2002, p. 144)

As the mood of Hardy's novels darkens through the 1880s, these allusions to the virtual lack of change in the Wessex countryside give way to acknowledgement of the realities of industrialized farming in England in the second half the nineteenth century. The description of the drudgery of field labouring in *Tess of the D'Urbervilles* is magnified into a collective horror when the labourers are forced to work in conjunction with a powerful contemporary harvesting and threshing machine. The sense of violation to the time-honoured practices of agricultural work as well as the stress placed on a finely tuned human sensibility by the machines of industrialized production, are themes that will be taken up and radicalized in the early novels of D. H. Lawrence, to whom we turn in the third chapter of this book. For Lawrence, unlike Hardy, access to the countryside, its natural rhythms and agricultural practices, is always overshadowed by the unavoidable despoliation of the land by the sights and sounds of coalmining. Indeed, the underlying tenor and pathos of Lawrence's literary world is that there are simply no rural refuges from the horrors of industrialization left to escape to.

But we should perhaps not overestimate the distance between Hardy and Lawrence. For Hardy too explicitly acknowledges the contrast of town and country and the loss of connection that typically characterized the life of the city dweller. Thus, the shear-shearers and wool gatherers are said to enjoy 'the superlative comfort derivable from the wool as it here exists new and pure' in a manner that is denied to 'persons unknown and far away' (Hardy 2002, p. 146). There is, of course, a certain irony involved in this contrast, when we reflect that just such unknown persons are likely to be enjoying this very description of rural life offered by the author. As we know from the early history of English urban planning, reforming the harsher aspects of industrialized urban existence by 'greening' the city was stock intervention. The same trend is highly visible in western cities today, in such movements as urban agriculture, community gardening, urban beekeeping, and so forth. It is important to recall that the training ground of such urban interventions and contemporary practices was constituted by literary portrayals of the relatively sound and healthy ways of traditional rural lifestyles.

The first phase of Hardy's novel writing, then, involves his discovery of 'Wessex' as an imaginary landscape in which to explore themes that pertain to labour and landscape. The two terms of our present study are woven together in Hardy novels in a far more consistent and radical manner than was the case in Eliot. While Eliot begins by embracing the Romantic mission to lend literary dignity to lowly and largely forgotten lives among the rural populace, in her mature phase of writing this is largely displaced by a focus on the cosmopolitan variety of her Victorian upper-middle- and upper-class contemporaries. But even in the first phase of his novel writing Hardy is very far from offering sentimentalized portraits of timeless rural life. Certainly, there is an antiquarian and preservationist strand and intention behind his descriptions. But these are leavened with many allusions to the contemporary realities of life and work in the English countryside. The novels which came to be seen as archetypally 'Hardyesque', however, are invested with a manner of metaphysical pessimism and tragedy that is largely absent in his books from the 1870s. Against this more tragic backdrop the trials of work and the consolations of landscape take on quite a different mode and modulation. This transition was a gradual process rather than a sudden leap, a process that we begin to trace by considering something of watershed novel, *The Return of the Native*.

THE RETURN OF THE NATIVE, *THE MAYOR OF CASTERBRIDGE*, AND *THE WOODLANDERS*: NO SALVATION THROUGH WORK ALONE

The first chapter of *The Return of the Native* depicts Hardy's most sustained literary landscapes. In it, Hardy depicts Egdon Heath as a veritable territory of prehistory, thereby evoking a sense of space and time beyond all possible human culture and conscious memory. It is, ultimately, less a landscape and more a presence of something thoroughly in- and pre-human, providing an intimation of the natural world as something immeasurably more profound and powerful than any settled human culture that rests upon it:

> Here at least were intelligible facts regarding landscape – far-reaching proofs productive of genuine satisfaction. The untameable, Ishmaelitish thing that Egdon now was it had always been.
> Civilization was its enemy [. . .] to know that everything around and underneath had been from prehistoric times as unaltered as the stars overhead, gave ballast to the mind adrift on change, and harassed by the irrepressible New. The great inviolate place had an ancient permanence which the sea cannot claim.
> (Hardy 2008d, pp. 11–12)

The allusion to Ishmael indicates that the heath finds itself in a position of involuntary exile, a condition that anticipates the situation of the protagonist of the novel, Clym Yeobright, the native who is set to return to this landscape. Hardy, we know, wrote and rewrote the novel over more than two years, in large part as he struggled to adapt to the distinct demands of serialized and whole-volume formats of publication (Hardy 2008d, p. xxviii). While the heath appears at the very beginning of the narrative, Hardy delays the entry of Clym until the reader is already a quarter of the way through the novel. When he does appear, the author offers a remarkable portrait of the protagonist, one that skilfully presages the tensions that will issue from Clym's ambivalence towards social advancement that reaches a point if crisis following his marriage to the ambitious Eustacia Vye. In this description, Hardy offers insights into character that only the most sensitively attuned observer would be likely to glean from an initial inspection. Indeed, the author explicitly offers up an appearance of Clym as something akin to a book to be read with great care and attention:

> Hence, people who began by beholding him ended by perusing him. His countenance was overlaid with legible meanings. Without being thought-worn he yet had certain marks derived from a perception of his surroundings, such as are not unfrequently found on men at the end of four or five years of endeavour which follow the close of placid pupillage. He already showed that thought is a disease of flesh, and indirectly bore evidence that ideal physical beauty is incompatible with growth of fellow-feeling and a full sense of the coil of things. Mental luminousness must be fed with the oil of life even though there is already a physical need for it; and the pitiful sight of two demands on one supply was just showing itself here. (Hardy 2008d, p. 135)

In Hardy's presentation of him, Yeobright is also a man stamped with the look of modernity and futurity. Hence, he is shown to appear pensive and to look on life 'as a thing to be put up with' (Hardy 2008d, p. 165) rather than enjoyed or even revelled in. We are here touching on the beginnings of Hardy's well-known pessimism or tragic sense of the human condition. In its full-blown articulations in the last novels – in *Tess* and *Jude* – the relentless logic of an individual's tragic fate is present throughout, and the reader is scarcely spared any horror that could conceivably befall the protagonists. Once again, Hardy's description of Yeobright depicts him as a book to be read rather than a portrait to be beheld: 'The observer's eye was arrested, not by his face as a picture, but by his face as a page; not by what it was, but by what it recorded' (ibid.).

But Hardy also takes pains to bring the character of Yeobright together with the brooding antiquity of the heath itself, thereby signalling to the reader that the young man's modernity is underlain by something sublimely old and certainly pre-modern: 'Clym had been so inwoven with the heath in his boyhood that hardly anybody could look upon it without thinking of him' (p. 166). He recounts the precocity of Clym as a child, shown in a series of achievements that brought him fame far beyond the expectations of regular childhood. In a way that anticipates his more strenuous and arguably more bitter depiction of the same theme in his last novel, *Jude the Obscure*, here Hardy alludes to the limited opportunities afforded an exceptionally talented boy who happens to be born into a humble social setting. There is even a certain strain of conscious self-ironizing in Hardy's predilection for narratives depicting an exceptional individual coming to grief with a time and place too narrow in sensibility and understanding to allow for genuine personal growth: 'So the subject recurred: if [Clym] were making a fortune and a name, so much the better for him; if he were making a tragical figure in the world, so much the better for a narrative' (Hardy 2008d, p. 166).

In his posthumously published study of Thomas Hardy – originally written in 1914 – D. H. Lawrence identified his main critical objection to Hardy's novels as the author's predisposition to insist on the inevitable tragedy that ensues when an individual's ideas and actions come into contact with societal norms and expectations. Figures such as Clym are labelled by Lawrence 'individualists': 'a man of distinct being, who must act in his own particular way to fulfil his own individual nature' (Steele 1985, p. 49). Thus, Lawrence places the axis of drama in Hardy's novel in the dialectic tensions, if not outright contradictions, between individual and community. For Lawrence, Hardy's instincts as an artist inherently make him side with the individual, whereas his sentimentality as a person makes him adhere to the greater good of the settled, known community. And it is this very tension Hardy lends, with increasing plangency, to the tragic undoing of the protagonists of his middle- and later-period novels. In these character portrayals, therefore, from Lawrence's perspective Hardy evinces a fatal ambivalence towards his own identity as a modern artist:

> This is obvious in Troy, Clym, Tess, and Jude. They have naturally distinct individuality, but, as it were, a weak life-flow, so that they cannot break away from the old adhesion, they cannot separate themselves from the mass which bore them, they cannot detach themselves from the common. Therefore they are pathetic rather than tragic figures. They have not the necessary strength: the question of their unfortunate end is begged at the beginning. (Steele 1985, p. 50)

Lawrence wrote these words at a point in his own life when he was precisely in the process of detaching himself 'from the common', by marrying Frieda Weekly, definitely establishing himself as a writer, and confronting a stalled self-exile made necessary by the outbreak of the Great War. In Lawrence's view, Hardy's novels are seriously vitiated by portraying the inevitable failure of an exceptional individual who tries but ultimately fails to break away from the community and context in which they were raised. For Lawrence, as we will explore in detail in the next chapter, this rupture was necessary, both on personal and on historic grounds. The mode of existence of the future, which Hardy hints at in his portrait of Clym Yeobright, had become an irresistible necessity of the present time for Lawrence.

Raymond Williams (1973), in *The Country and City*, recognizes the pivotal significance of *The Return of the Native* in Hardy's negotiation with the dialectical tensions between the growth of the individual's character and psyche and their place within the community. Williams, in turn, sees in the character of Clym an echo of his own personal history, which saw him move from a Welsh border community to Cambridge and eventually to the status of a university teacher and researcher writing books on English culture and literature. As we have seen, Williams rejects the common understanding that Hardy's primary intention as a novelist was to capture and preserve quaint customs of English rural life. He acknowledges, of course, the presence of this impulse. But he insists that below the surface of Hardy's carefully observed bucolic portraits lies something more fundamental: a subtlety articulated representation of the growing tensions between the individual's growth and the increasingly rapid transformation of a time-honoured collective rural way of life:

> [. . .] the more common pattern [in Hardy's fiction] is the relation between the changing nature of country living, determined as much by its own pressures as by pressures from 'outside', and one or more characters who have become in some degree separated from it yet remain by some tie of family inescapably involved. It is here that the social values are dramatized in a very complex way and it is here that most of the problems of Hardy's actual writing seem to arise. (Williams 1973, p. 200)

In the case of *The Return of the Native* it is Clym's rejection of his native community's expectation that he use his superior education and learning to further his social and economic interests that chiefly articulates the dramatic tension. As is revealed half way through the narrative, Clym's return to the place where he was raised is largely motivated by the conviction that has grown in him that his work selling jewellery in Paris is worthless. This is not simply because it makes too little use of his education; it is rather due to its lack of merit with regard to serving the core needs of society. There is, clearly, something of a Rousseauian hierarchy of social value at work in Clym's mind. This is mixed with an austerity of personal inclination and a quasi-religious fervour to place oneself, in a self-sacrificing way, at the service of the least fortunate in society. Thus, to Mrs Yeobright's protestation that she had 'always supposed you were going to push on as other men do – all who deserve the name – when they have been put in a good way of doing well' (Hardy 2008d, p. 173), Clym responds:

Talk about men who deserve the name, can any man deserving the name waste his time in that effeminate way, when he sees half the world going to ruin for want of somebody to buckle-to and teach 'em how to breast the misery they were born to. I get up every morning and see the whole of creation groaning and travailing in pain, as St Paul says, and yet there am I selling trinkets to women and fops, and pandering to the meanest vanities – I, who have health and strength enough for anything. I have been troubled in my mind about it all the year, and the end is that I cannot do it any more. (ibid.)

Between mother and son, between the one who has remained within the vicinity of the native place all her life and the other who has been educated and lived abroad, there are seemingly irreconcilable notions of 'doing well'. When asked by her son 'what is doing well?', Mrs Yeobright offers no answer, just as, Hardy adds, Socrates had no answer to the question 'what is wisdom?' and Jesus offered no response to Pilate's question 'what is truth?'. In other words, Clym is grappling with a fundamental and perhaps ultimately imponderable issue of what constitutes value in human life. The key thing to add, in the context of the present study, is that the field in which an implicit answer to this question is offered in Hardy's novel is that of work.

In his concrete response to the problem of social and personal value through work, Clym pursues a dual approach, driven partly by responsiveness to pressing social needs and partly by a desire to live simply on the heath. In a word, he desires to serve society and the land through a singular commitment to work considered not as a means to personal advancement but instead as a matter of vocational self-sacrifice. But Clym's attempted straight path towards this goal is dramatically obstructed by his ill-conceived choice of Eustacia Vye as his wife and prospective teacher at the local school he wishes to found. Eustacia's motivation in marrying is purely selfish in nature, as she fully expects Clym to return to a life of opulence and ease in Paris, allowing her to leave what she sees as the accursed limitations of Egdon Heath. She is disabused of this assumption soon after the marriage and gradually gravitates back to Damon Wildeve, despite the fact he is now married to Clym's cousin, Thomasin. When, at the end of the fifth book of the novel, Eustacia and Wildeve drown following a night-time assignation, Clym expresses, with profound hopelessness: 'I am getting used to the horror of my existence' (Hardy 2008d, p. 362). By the end of the book Hardy portrays Clym, with more than a touch of sardonic irony, as having reached his goal in a way far removed from his earlier idealistic fantasies of educator to the rural poor: 'Yeobright had, in fact, found his vocation in the career of an itinerant open-air preacher and lecturer on morally unimpeachable subjects' (p. 389).

By the time Hardy published *The Mayor of Casterbridge* – in 1886, eight years after *The Return of the Native* – the novelist's growing tendency to hinge his narrative on the relentless dissolution of one or more protagonists had reached a certain state of maturity. While Clym Yeobright – in common with Jude Farley in Hardy's last novel – represents an earnest young man of the working class who betters himself through education while lacking conventional social ambition, the eponymous mayor of Casterbridge, Michael Henchard, is dedicated to overcoming the failings of his early adulthood. Henchard's tragic flaw is his irascibility, which is exacerbated by alcohol on the fateful day he decides to sell his wife at a country fair. The oath of sobriety he then commits to is the precursor to a commitment to hard work and social respectability pursued in his new life in the market town of Casterbridge. As Eliot had tended to do in her early novels, Hardy sets the dramatic time of *The Mayor of Casterbridge* back in the 1830s, a period distant enough to feel unfamiliar to the reader but still within living memory. Hardy, as we have seen, professes a belief in the slowness of life and change in his imaged countryside of Wessex relative to the towns and cities imbued with rapidly changing fashions of thought, habit, and dress. This twofold distancing in time and space relative to his readership allows Hardy to render plausible if still shocking the tale of a man who sells his wife to a stranger for a small sum of money.

While Clym in *The Return of the Native* has elevated his social standing through education but then gone on to reject such status in favour of honest work, Henchard consciously courts high social standing to assuage the guilt he feels at his conduct as a young hay-trusser. Over two decades, he has built up a commanding place in the community of Casterbridge through sheer hard work and business acumen. In other words, he is the archetypal self-made man. What links Henchard to Yeobright is Hardy's insistence that neither man can extricate themselves from their respective past. The legacy of Henchard's earlier life is embodied for him with the return of his wife and what he initially takes to be his own daughter, Elizabeth-Jane. When he decides to trick the people of Casterbridge by carrying out a sham marriage to Susan rather than revealing the shameful manner in which they originally separated, the scene is set for a crucial revelation that is almost certain to ruin him. When Susan dies soon after their reunion, Henchard seeks to console himself by revealing to Elizabeth-Jane that she is not, as she supposes, the daughter of the sailor she grew up with but in fact Henchard's own. It is immediately after this, however, that Henchard reads the letter from his deceased wife informing him that his biological daughter died in infancy and the Elizabeth-Jane he now lives with was fathered by the man Henchard sold his wife to. The shock of this renewed dispossession is too much for the mayor and he reverts to the irascible coldness he habitually displayed towards his wife in their first years of marriage.

In a word, Henchard's sin is pride. He complains, in the first two chapters of the book, that his chances of making a good living for himself have been dashed by early marriage and fatherhood. Having dispensed of these impediments in order to make his fortune and establish his standing in Casterbridge, Henchard is haunted by loneliness. It is this that draws him to Donald Farfrae, a young Scotsman, who is presented by Hardy as something of an ideal alter-ego to Henchard in the novel. The implicit moral of the tale appears to be that there can be no personal salvation through work alone. But whereas the received doctrine of Christianity is that divine grace or the unearned beneficence of God is needed in addition to good works to achieve salvation, in Hardy's later novels it is more the case that a maleficent cosmic principle is in evidence, as an individual's limitations and character flaws are ruthlessly exploited to assure their downfall. Henchard is by no means an unsympathetic character. Certainly, using the foil of Farfrae allows Hardy to highlight the older man's roughness of temper and petty jealousies. But there is, equally, a tenderness and humaneness to Henchard that relatively preserves him from any valid claim of malignity or genuine viciousness of character. The combined blows of lost social standing, loss of his biological daughter, and supplanting at the hands of Farfrae and Newson, lead Henchard to end his days in utter penury and isolation. In the closing paragraph of the novel the sad wisdom of her step-father's fall is encapsulated in Elizabeth-Jane's realization that 'the doubtful honour of a brief transit through a sorry world hardly called for effusiveness, even when the path was suddenly irradiated at some half-way point by daybeams such as hers' (Hardy 2004, p. 310).

While Hardy's narrative requires a train of external events to represent the outward cause of the protagonist's dramatic rise and fall, *The Mayor of Casterbridge* is best understood as a character study. Although Henchard shows undoubted fortitude and practical wisdom when building himself up from a common journeyman to preeminent corn merchant of the market town where he resides, there is a pervasive melancholy about him that renders the maintenance of his position questionable. Henchard yearns for human connection but, at the same time, fears and resents the claims others make on him. He wants those he turns to for affection to love him spontaneously and generously, but is constantly on guard for any sign that their love for him is vitiated by negative judgement or reproof at his bearing and conduct. We might say, therefore, that Henchard is not prepared to do the 'work' of loving another. Instead, he wants such love to rest on an unshakeable foundation of radical acceptance of all he is.

One of the remarkable features of *The Mayor of Casterbridge* is the fact that Hardy identifies a concrete site in the town where collective melancholy is located. This speaks to Hardy's profoundly topographic literary imagination, whereby he grants 'a local habitation and name' to intergenerational grief and suffering. It is as though Henchard's intensely person fate can only become real in the narrative when it becomes situated in the landscape. Hardy describes a pair of bridges frequented by two distinct groups of outcasts and failures, one closer to the middle of the country town and a second on its outskirts. It is to the latter that Henchard eventually finds his way:

> The *misérables* who would pause on the remoter bridge were of a politer stamp. They included bankrupts, hypochondriacs, persons who were what is called 'out of a situation' from fault or lucklessness, the inefficient of the professional class [. . .]. While one in straits on the townward bridge did not mind who saw him so, and kept his back to the parapet to survey the passersby, one in straits on this never faced the road, never turned his head at coming footsteps, but, sensitive to his own condition, watched the current whenever a stranger approached, as if some strange fish interested him, though every finned thing had been poached out of the river years before. There and thus would they muse; if their grief were the grief of oppression they would wish themselves kings; if their grief were poverty, wish themselves millionaires; if sin, they would wish they were saints or angels; if despised love, that they were some much-courted Adonis of county fame. (Hardy 2004, p. 207)

The psychopathology of public space recurs in Hardy's novels and generates something of distinctively uncanny element in his narratives. Another example is found in *Jude the Obscure* where the Brown House situated on an elevated hill serves to localize tragic events in the life of Jude and his parents, and was previously the site of a gallows where people were put to death. In *The Mayor of Casterbridge* we learn nothing of Henchard's life prior to the opening scene where he sells his wife and yet a certain doom pervades the vicissitudes of his narrated development. The scene on the bridge has the odd effect of rendering his personal tragedy a phenomenon commonly shared. It is as though Hardy wishes to naturalize human suffering by describing a concrete place where, from time immemorial, people in suffering and shame have come to publicize their grief. Finally, there is the sense conveyed that Henchard's life-force is spent, burned out as he is by two decades of struggle to overcome the sins of youth in an effort that has seemingly come to nothing. He simply lacks the energy to build up his wealth and reputation again from nothing and, probably more importantly, no longer has anyone to whom he wishes to prove himself. Hence the plangent sentiments of his will, discovered by Elizabeth-Jane at the end of the novel, 'that no man remember me' (Hardy 2004, p. 309). It is this desired erasure, this will to disappear without trace, that increasingly inhabits the protagonists in Hardy's final decade of novel writing.

Of all Hardy's novels, it is *The Woodlanders* that offers his most scrupulously observed and meticulously detailed account of rural working life. Anticipated by the opening passages of *Under the Greenwood Tree*,

The Woodlanders centres on the community of Little Hintock where work revolves around knowledge of woodland crafts. As with the extended description of Egdon Heath, where Hardy evokes the peculiar isolation of the place in relation to the surrounding world, so too in the opening paragraphs of *The Woodlanders* does he accentuate the sublime feeling concentrated in the site of the narrative:

> It was one of those sequestered spots outside the gates of the world where may usually be found more meditation than action, and more listlessness than meditation, where reasoning proceeds on narrow premisses, and results in inferences wildly imaginative; yet where, from time to time, dramas of a grandeur and unity truly Sophoclean are enacted in the real, by virtue of the concentrated passions and closely knit interdependence of the lives therein. (Hardy 2005, pp. 7–8)

Hardy here immediately sets the tragic tone of the narrative but also points to a basic tension between isolation and intimacy, dissolution and connection, that plays out in the lives of his protagonists. We need to remain mindful of how this tension also relates back to the relationship between writer and reader. There is a documentary, even ethnographic intention that animates Hardy's efforts as a novelist to bring far-flung rural communities to the attention of sophisticated, urban-dwellers of the late nineteenth century. This brings with it all the problems and pitfalls of ethnography in terms of achieving closeness to 'subjects' while maintaining sufficient distance from them to translate their customs and behaviour into terms comprehensible to a general reading public. On one level, of course, this is a challenge for all creative writing: to trust that the commonality of a shared language will prove robust enough to allow the effective transmission of knowledge about things not known from first-hand experience. But Hardy's desired fidelity to documentary detail places him in a particularly difficult position, insofar as his only immediate work is one of writing and yet this must suffice as a surrogate for the quite other manners and modes of work he depicts. In *The Woodlanders* Hardy's way of meeting this challenge is to describe how the various tasks of woodland work shape the bodies of the local workers. He begins this process with his depiction of Marty South working through the night in her father's cottage:

> The young woman laid down the bill-hook for a moment, and examined the palm of her right hand, which unlike the other was ungloved, and showed little hardness or roughness about it. The palm was red and blistering, as if her present occupation were too recent to have subdued it to what it worked in. As with so many right hands born to manual labour, there was nothing in its fundamental

shape to bear out the physiological conventionalism that gradations of birth show themselves primarily in the form of this member. Nothing but a cast of the die of Destiny had decided that the girl should handle the tool; and the fingers which clasped the heavy ash haft might have skilfully guided the pencil or swept the string, had they only been set to do it in good time. (Hardy 2005, p. 10)

The mode of address in this passage is typical of Hardy's narrative voice, which possesses a certain sophisticated and knowing irony, at once bringing the reader near to the persons and places described while remaining vigilant for likely misconceptions based on incautious generalization. Above all, what is evident is Hardy's fellow-feeling and affection for what he describes. He thereby represents a continuation in English novel writing of Eliot's struggle to defend the act of representing the everyday lives of common rural communities to a largely upper-middle-class urban readership. In this connection it is telling that Hardy is not – unlike Eliot – prone to apologize for the presumption that his readers might condescend to be interested in the lives he depicts. Presumably this stems from both a change in the nature of English society and a difference of temperament between the two writers. One can say that the sensitivity to English rural life, work, and character pioneered by Eliot made Hardy's novels possible, both in the sense that they established a certain mode of writing and simultaneously created a susceptibility to it in their readership. Both writers combine the affecting beauty of pastoral landscape with the vividness of action and character, so that their novels can never be easily dismissed as escapism for an urban readership, though this element is undoubtedly present.

Whereas Eliot gradually distanced herself from the rural working class central to her early novels, Hardy only seems to get closer to them with time and to insist, with an increasingly emphatic tone, that their lives are of universal significance. This underlying tendency is captured well by Raymond Williams:

> The general structure of feeling in Hardy would be much less convincing if there were only the alienation, the frustration, the separation and isolation, the final catastrophes. What is defeated but not destroyed at the end of *The Woodlanders* or the end of *Tess* or the end of *Jude* is a warmth, a seriousness, an endurance in love and work that are the necessary definition of what Hardy knows and mourns as loss. [. . .] The losses are real and heartbreaking because the desires were real, the shared work was real, the unsatisfied impulses were real. Work and desire are very deeply connected in his whole imagination. (Williams 1973, p. 213)

In this passage Williams articulates, in simple but striking words, the pivotal meaning of Hardy's novels to the present study. The vital connection between work and desire is the key insight here. In Clym's wish to live simply on the heath and serve his community through founding a local school; and, similarly, in Henchard's desire to seek restitution from the sins of his past by building up a fortune in the corn-trading business, the failure of the project does not signify the nullity of the effort. Instead, the sense conveyed to the reader is something more profound than the depiction of merely personal failure. It is the insistence that, however the individual fares, our common fate is to seek meaning in and through work. In other words, a kind of philosophical anthropology animates Hardy's novel writing and lends to it an implicit, ever-active worldview. Not that Hardy, as a novel writer, offers the reader an argument to defend a certain interpretation of the human condition. His mode of writing is far too embedded in the intricacies of imagined scenes and acts for that to be the case. Nevertheless, it is hard to escape the impression that Hardy is writing out of anything other than a hard-won and unshakeable conviction that there is some underlying truth to the connection between 'work and desire' in human existence. As Williams insists, the generally acknowledged pessimism of Hardy's later novels in no way precludes a profound affirmation of the struggle for meaning and redemption through work so vividly depicted in his protagonists' lives.

Like Gabriel Oak in *Far from the Madding Crowd* or Diggory Venn in *The Return of the Native*, the central character of Giles Winterborne in *The Woodlanders* is raised to a certain pitch of reserved dignity by his knowledge of and dedication to his craft. It is seldom that such male characters meet their match in female counterparts, and their seriousness and steadfast sense of what is right are largely put into relief by Hardy by his juxtaposing them with rather frivolous and capricious women. *The Woodlanders* is somewhat exceptional in this regard, as Hardy makes clear from the beginning that Giles is naturally matched with Marty, though he remains in ignorance of this reality while he pursues the affections of the refined and educated Grace Melbury. In their first related exchange, after Marty has worked through the night to complete work expected of her sick father, Hardy accentuates the remote and solitary setting of their encounter in a way that expresses the author's tenderness towards his fictional setting and characters:

> They went out and walked together, the patterns of the airholes in the top of the lanterns rising now to the mist overhead, where they appeared of giant size, as if reaching the tent-shaped sky. They had no remarks to make to each other, and they uttered none. Hardly anything could be more isolated, or more self-contained, than the lives of these two walking here in the lonely hour before day, when grey shades, material and mental, are so very grey. And yet their lonely courses formed no detached design at all, but were part of the pattern in the great

web of human doings then weaving in both hemispheres, from the White Sea to Cape Horn. (Hardy 2005, p. 20)

In this passage, Hardy at once underscores the remoteness and intimacy of the narrated scene and yet reminds the reader of the broad, global context in which it is ultimately situated. It brings with it a curious sense of double consciousness, as if to invite the reader both to suspend their sense of the wider world beyond the story and yet to recall the realities of the global connectedness of all things. This serves to remind us – if such a reminder is needed – that Hardy's objective as a writer is something other and something more than simply inducing in the reader a wilful escapism achieved through immersing them in the perfect illusion of a self-contained rural location. Certainly, as we saw earlier in the case of the heath in *The Return of the Native*, Hardy does insist on the enduring qualities of a local landscape working in and through the habits and acts of its inhabitants. But Hardy's evocations of landscape are not trapped in the amber of a fixed nostalgia that keeps at bay any recognition of the breakneck social and material change that was sweeping Victorian England. Rather, as Williams insists, Hardy's images of the English landscape are truly constructed with self-conscious regard for deep-seated and irreversible change. It is precisely consciousness of change that lends to Hardy's depictions of landscape all the pathos of photographically captured moments of time that can never be repeated or regained.

Another salient contrast or tension particularly to the fore in *The Woodlanders* is that between social classes. While Marty South and Giles Winterborne constitute members of the local labouring class, the latter has been promised the hand in marriage of the daughter of the local timber merchant and landowner, Mr Melbury. His daughter, as noted, has been purposefully refined and educated so as to render her a fit bride and 'to make the gift as valuable a one as lay in his power to bestow' (p. 18). The problem is that this effort by Grace Melbury's father to work on his daughter to render her a more refined product has placed her perceived value beyond the proper reach of Winterborne. But this over-investing in his daughter, we learn early on in the novel, is the effect rather than cause of the underlying problem. For Melbury's desire to give his daughter way to the humble labourer stems from a trick he played on Winterborne's long-dead father to lure the woman who was to become Melbury's wife away from his then friend. Thus, we have a motive that bears direct comparison with that of Henchard in *The Mayor of Casterbridge*, namely to expiate one's guilt in early life by restoring to their proper place persons or families wantonly injured. The particular irony in the case of *The Woodlanders* is that Giles and Grace have a natural and spontaneous affection for one another that exists independently of the father's guilt-ridden desire to salve his conscience. It is only the fact that her father has sought to 'raise' the young woman that clouds this connection and so leads her to honour her father's change of mind and desire for her to make her rise in class permanent by marring Fitzpiers, the upper-class local doctor.

We have seen this manner of clashing class-based aspirations in Eliot in such cases as the disastrous flirtation of the local squire Arthur Donnithore with the lowly milkmaid Hetty Sorrel. On one level, it is possible to take away a simple lesson from these ill-matched unions, namely that it is always best to remain loyal to one's class and not disturb the given social order. But the dramatic presentation, common to Eliot and Hardy, is that the trouble really stems from idealization that blinds a person to the real nature of the object of desire. On each side of the social divide there is simply too little familiarity with the ways and manners of the opposed class to make mutual understanding and compatibility at all likely. It is also striking how the process of formal education is presented by Hardy and Eliot as compounding these kinds of class-based relationship issues.

In *The Mill on the Floss*, Tulliver takes much pride in the fact that he is giving his son Tom the education of a gentleman, even though his sister Maggie is constitutionally much better suited to profit from this undertaking. Analogously, in the *Woodlanders*, Hardy makes clear that Melbury's efforts to shape his daughter into a young lady of the higher classes have merely succeeded in alienating her from the rural locale and people to which she remains sentimentally and essentially attached. In both cases, an overbearing father intent on embracing an opportunity to raise the standing of his family in the eyes of others merely succeeds in making the way forward for his child less certain and rendering the grown man or woman painfully ambivalent towards the world they knew in childhood. In other words, in such efforts to cross the class divide by the means of formal education the result is a damaging fragmentation in the individual's sentimental attachment to formative people and places. This effort, therefore, represents work which can ultimately bring no resolution or restitution to the worker or to what is worked upon.

These currents of class conflict and contrast are channelled by Hardy's portrayal of Edred Fitzpiers, the ambitious young doctor who pursues and marries Grace Melbury but is immediately drawn away by the charms of the local aristocratic landowner, Felice Charmond. The doctor's dilemma centres on his vacillation between the novelty and variety of sophisticated upper-class existence and the homely solidity of country life known to the inhabitants of Hintock. While Hardy portrays Giles and Marty as his principal exemplars of lowly rural dignity through steadfast work and humility, Fitzpiers is shown to be incapable of anything beyond passing fancy and unfixed purpose. In this regard, his union with Grace is vitiated by the fact that he cannot appreciate the reality of the young woman enough to see her in her own right. Instead, he marries her on the basis of his superficial and sentimental desire to make his own the rustic simplicity of the village where he practices his profession. He perceives the virtues of standing fixed in one place all his days, but that place is not scored into his consciousness and habitual actions as it is for its long-term inhabitants. Consequently, Fitzpiers seeks distraction to alleviate the dullness of the cycle of life in the village, rather than willingly acquiescing with its predictable cyclical rhythms and patterns of close-knit community life:

> Winter in a solitary house in the country, without society, is tolerable, nay even enjoyable and delightful, given certain conditions; but these are not the conditions which attach to the life of a professional man who drops down into such a place by mere accident. They are present to the lives of Winterborne, Melbury, and Grace, but not to the doctor's. They are old association – an almost exhaustive biographical or historical acquaintance with every object, animate and inanimate, within the observer's horizon [. . .]. The spot may have beauty, grandeur, salubrity, convenience; but if it lack memories it will ultimately pall upon him who settles there without opportunity of intercourse with his kind. (Hardy 2005, p. 112)

Another way to capture the situation of Fitzpiers is to say that, in his case, there is a striking mismatch between landscape and labour. The word 'landscape', as we noted in the Introduction, is apt to carry the connotation of a contrived and artificial representation of people and place. In this sense, Hintock is precisely nothing more than a landscape to Fitzpiers, insofar as it is not scored into his very sense of self. The fact that Fitzpiers, after marrying Grace on the basis of his idealized appreciation of the simple and honest pastoral life he sees around him, prosecutes a disastrous affair with the local landowner, Felice Charmond, signals that his affective nature ultimately feels most at home elsewhere. It is ultimately a question of whether or not one accepts, willingly and gladly, the limitations of prospect imposed by one place. While he is attracted to an image of himself predicated on such an acceptance, it ultimately proves to be of insufficient force to constitute his fixed purpose in life. A scene in which he discovers Winterborne's woodland work shed illustrates this point very directly and movingly:

> A little shed had been constructed on the spot, of thatched hurdles and boughs, and in front of it was a fire, over which a kettle sang. Fitzpiers sat down inside the shelter and went on with his reading, except when he looked up to observe the scene and the actors. The thought that he might settle here and become welded in with this sylvan life by marrying Grace Melbury, crossed his mind for a moment. Why should he go further into the world than where he was? The secret of happiness lay in limiting the aspirations; these men's thoughts were

conterminous with the margin of the Hintock woodlands, and why should not his life be likewise limited, a small practice among the people around him being the bound of his desires? (Hardy 2005, p. 122–23)

Here we have an analogous dilemma to the one represented in the situation of Clym Yeobright in *The Return of the Native*, except, of course, that the place to which Clym returns is precisely the one known to him from childhood and youth. Clym's exceptional intellect has allowed him to break through to an outwardly successful life as a jewellery-seller in Paris. But he yearns for the heath and to put his talents to proper social use there. Fitzpiers, by contrast, comes to the woodland village seeking solitude to conduct his own scientific experiments and establish his medical practice. What he lacks to bind him permanently to Hintock is precisely that unquestioned familiarity borne of affective memory that, as Hardy relates, makes the uniformities of remote rural life a pleasure rather than a burden. Again, as with Eliot's portrayal of Arthur Donnithorne in *Adam Bede*, Hardy depicts Fitzpiers as a man whose ego needs the reinforcement provided by pursuing the adoration of a woman he idealizes and yet knows to be his social inferior. Accepting a recognized and settled place within the life of the rural village is impossible to Fitzpiers as his sense of self is unsettled, making it impossible for him to wed his professional ambitions to a fixed way of life. Put otherwise, in Fitzpiers Hardy offers a foil to make all the more evident the virtues, embodied above all by Winterborne and Marty South, of a settled way of life and steadfast work made possible by the established habits and traditions of a remote English village.

From the time of *A Pair of Blue Eyes* and *Far from the Madding Crowd*, works published in the first half of the 1870s, Hardy's novels feature variations on the theme of young men struggling to find their proper vocation in life. In *The Woodlanders*, Winterborne and Fitzpiers can be grasped as different aspects of one and the same fundamental problem: how to find personal redemption through a deliberately chosen mode of work. It is important to recognize that this is a fundamental problem of Hardy's novel writing and thus not something that ever finds a definitive resolution. It is readily observed that the motivation for dramatizing this problem stems from Hardy's early adulthood, a period when he was apprenticed to an architectural firm but laboured at poetry and, latterly, the writing of novels. On this level, the issue is more than simply a matter of choosing a viable career for oneself, though it is of course also this. It is a question of Hardy's class position, in a mid-Victorian Britain where accustomed social identities and customs were in flux as never before. As Williams often observes, Hardy was subjected, to an extraordinary degree, to a kind of patronizing indulgence by the cultural gatekeepers of the England of his day. This attitude stems, in turn, from a dialectic tension between education and social-cultural status that makes Hardy's novels something far more significant than sublimated biography. To Williams' mind, what Hardy is striving for is nothing less than the articulation of a new sense of common experience and relatedness to a shared world:

> [T]he educated observer, seeing nature, does not see the human being who is reaper; or, if he sees him, sees him only as a figure in a landscape. Hardy, in more extended and complicated ways, works through this complexity of choice. Without the insights of consciously learned history, and of the educated understanding of nature and behaviour, he cannot really observe at all, either with adequate precision or with an adequately extending human respect. But then the ordinary social model, the learned language, which includes these capacities, is, very clearly, in a divided culture, a form which includes an alienation. (Williams 1983, pp. 105–6)

Referring to the condescending connotation of the label 'autodidact' applied to Hardy (and later to Lawrence), Williams describes the author as a 'man caught by his personal history in the general crisis of the relation between education and class' (p. 106). Hardy was writing and publishing at a time when the valorized modes of education resulted in the alienation of the educated both from their own feelings and sense of self and from any grounded sense of fellow-feeling with others. It is in this context, Williams holds, that the English novel is attempting to find or invent a 'common language'. It is in Hardy's very last novels – *Tess of the D'Urbervilles* and *Jude the Obscure* – that the tensions engendered by the contemporary crisis 'between intelligence and fellow-feeling' and 'between education and class' reach an almost unbearable pitch. It is to this culminating phase of Hardy's novel writing that we now turn in the final section of this chapter.

TESS OF THE D'URBERVILLES AND *JUDE THE OBSCURE*: A WORLD WITHOUT ENDS

Anyone familiar with Hardy's novels cannot fail to be struck by the dramatic change in tone and tenor of his final two novels. It is not that the themes of *Tess of the D'Urbervilles* and *Jude the Obscure* had not been meticulously and repeatedly rehearsed by Hardy in the preceding two decades: the clash between social classes, ill-matched unions, and personal struggles to find a suitable vocation had long since become familiar elements of his narratives. But there is a more direct mode of address, a more relentless and unmitigated insistence on the undoing of the principal characters, and, above all, little to no sense of redemption in the denouement of the drama. Little wonder that, at the end of his novel writing career, Hardy's reputation as a novelist with a jarringly pessimistic worldview was established. The writer's concern that he has confronted readers with too austerely direct a depiction of contemporary social tensions is evident in the preface to both novels. Thus, whole recognizing that many critics had praised his handling of the delicate theme of a women's struggle to survive after being seduced by a man of socially superior status, Hardy's 1892 preface to *Tess*, which was originally published a year earlier, seeks to defend the novel against outrage on grounds of poetic licence: 'Nevertheless, though the novel was intended to be neither didactic nor aggressive, but in the scenic parts to be representative simply, and in the contemplative to be oftener charged with impressions than convictions, there have been objectors both to the matter and to the rendering' (Hardy 2005b, p. 4)

The preface that accompanied the first appearance of the novel strikes a rather different note and points to the central dilemma of a novel writer such as Hardy. Clearly, one of Hardy's underlying motives is to capture for his readers the realities of English country life. Both from first-hand experience and from more formal research, Hardy was a meticulous and painstaking observer of customs and character. Whereas his early Wessex novels go to great lengths to leaven the more tragic events of represented live with entertaining dialogue between minor characters, sketching of rural customs and beliefs, and vivid and arresting descriptions of his pastoral settings, in *Tess* there is a notable diminution in this effort to ameliorate the tragedy of the eponymous protagonist. From the first scene in which Tess is revealed to the reader, Hardy accentuates her child-like aspect of innocence, her proclivity for shame, and her readiness to be shamed by others. In the opening scene Tess is walking to the May-Day dance with a group of other young women, when they see her father, returning from a local tavern merry with drink and singing about his recently instilled sense of himself as the late issue of a local aristocratic family. Tess herself is described by Hardy as 'a mere vessel of emotion untinctured by experience' (Hardy 2005b, p. 21). He then elaborates on the youth and innocence of Tess:

> Phases of her childhood lurked in her aspect still. As she walked along to-day, for all her bouncing handsome womanliness, you could sometimes see her twelfth year in her cheeks, or her ninth sparkling from her eyes, and even her fifth would flit over the curves of her mouth now and then. Yet few knew and still fewer considered this. A small minority, mainly strangers, would look long at her in casually passing by, and grow momentarily fascinated by her freshness, and wonder if they would ever see her again; but to almost everybody she was a fine and picturesque country girl, and no more. (Hardy 2005, p. 21)

In other aspects of his initial descriptions of her, Hardy accentuates the modernity rather than the backwardness of Tess. This is brought out chiefly in contrast to the parents, especially the mother, who is steeped in the local customs and habits of mind and speech of traditional country life. The difference between mother and daughter is attributed to the formal education experienced by the latter, as Hardy makes clear in a parenthetical comment: 'Mrs Durbeyfield habitually spoke the dialect: her daughter, who had passed the sixth standard in the National school under a London-trained mistress, spoke two languages; the dialect at home, more or less; ordinary English abroad and to persons of quality' (p. 27). The rudimentary education enjoyed by Tess is enough to separate mother and daughter by veritable centuries:

> Between the mother, with her fast-perishing lumber of superstitions, folklore, dialect, and orally transmitted ballads, and the daughter, with her trained National teachings and Standard knowledge under an infinitely Revised Code, there was a gap of two hundred years as ordinarily understood. When they were together the Jacobean and the Victorian ages were juxtaposed. (p. 29)

Hardy's opening portrait of Tess is thus an intriguing amalgam of innocence and knowledge. She is also, like Maggie in *The Mill on the Floss*, given to feeling shame due to a heightened sense of vulnerability to the adverse judgement of others. We are first confronted with this emotional predisposition in two contexts: initially, when Tess is obliged to fetch her mother and father from a drinking spree at the local tavern; and then, immediately afterwards, when she is forced to transport beehives her father had been prevented from delivering as a result of his drinking the previous night. During that journey, which culminates in the accidental death of the family's draft horse, Tess gives voice to her view of the tragic nature of worldly existence, revealing to her younger brother her view that humanity suffers from the ill-fortune of inhabiting, among many happy and sound stars, 'a blighted one' (p. 37). The sense of an evil star guiding Tess's destiny is thus made evident from the outset. In more prosaic terms, it is the combination of her parents' feckless disposition and her own acute sense of shame at being responsible for the death of the household's horse that impels Tess to seek family recognition at the manor house of the d'Urbervilles. In this train of action, we see Hardy treating the familiar theme of relationships being forged across the divide of class distinctions. It is in part the hybrid nature of Tess as a local girl refined by formal education that adds to the complexity and pathos in her subsequent seduction and desertion at the hands of the manor's dissolute and idle son, Alec d'Urberville.

The contradictions alive in Tess are also expressed by Hardy in terms of her precocious physical attractions as opposed to her meekness and bashfulness of character. Tess also possesses a sense of pride and propriety, but this is generally trumped by her desire to be deferential to the wishes of others. It is this desire, allied with her lingering guilt over the death of the horse, that causes her to ignore her intimations of alarm when first encountering the superficial but winning charms of Alec d'Urberville. As we learn, Alec has cultivated a habit, well known to those who live and work around the manor house, of seducing young working-class women. To those whom Tess comes to know as a result of working at the house, this situation is taken to be a predictable and banal fact of life. Tess's natural reserve and modesty are taken as putting on airs of superiority by these others of her own class, and her unsullied beauty and unconsciousness about it give rise to envy and hostility in equal measure. Thus, when Tess is walking home from a country dance where much alcohol has been consumed by her companions, the local girls turn on Tess and she seeks solace in the attentions of Alec, even though she is aware of the danger he poses to her. Having already, following Tess's first encounter with Alec, pondered 'why she was doomed to be seen and coveted that day by the wrong man' (Hardy 2005, p. 48), Hardy elaborates on this interrogation immediately following Tess's seduction and rape:

> Why it was that upon this beautiful feminine tissue, sensitive as gossamer, and practically blank as snow as yet, there should have been traced such a coarse pattern as it was doomed to receive; why so often the coarse appropriates the finer thus, the wrong man the woman, the wrong woman the man, many thousand years of analytical philosophy have failed to explain to our sense of order. One may, indeed, admit the possibility of a retribution lurking in the present catastrophe. Doubtless some of Tess d'Urberville's mailed ancestors rollicking home from a fray had dealt the same measure even more ruthlessly towards the peasant girls of their time. But though to visit the sins of the fathers upon the children may be a morality good enough for divinities, it is scorned by average human nature; and it therefore does not mend the matter. (pp. 82–83)

Here we encounter the habitual theme of ill-matched unions, but it is now couched in the terms of what approximates to a universal principle of misfortune. There is certain bitterness of tone and an acrid pathos that brings home to the reader the acute sense that nothing precious and good can survive the malignity inherent in the course of human life. Having passed through an intermediary period of novel writing predicated on the sense that works alone are insufficient for personal salvation, Hardy's perspective now seems to have reached the point where it is true to say of his protagonists that they are ruled by a principle of unavoidable damnation. How, then, does this development in Hardy's 'metaphysic' reflect back on his representation of labour and landscape in his final two novels?

In outward terms, Tess's dilemma both before and after her initial seduction at the hands of Alec comes down to finding appropriate paying work. After her rape at the hands of Alec she immediately has to confront the reality that she is, in the eyes of her class, a 'fallen woman'. We recall that it was her parents' shiftlessness and, more particularly her father's inclination to drink and neglect his work duties that led Tess into the calamitous attempt to seek family recognition at the manor house. Tess has conceived a child to Alec and is therefore more or less obliged to secrete herself, following her return, in her childhood home. Her confinement there is broken only by night-time walks in the immediate vicinity. Describing these wanderings, Hardy accentuates Tess's correspondence with the place and with nature more generally:

> At times her whimsical fancy would intensify natural processes around her till they seemed a part of her own story. Rather they became part of it; for the world is only a psychological phenomenon, and what they seemed they were. The midnight airs and gusts, moaning amongst the tightly-wrapped buds and bark of the winter twigs, were formulae of bitter reproach. A wet day was the expression of irremediable grief at her weakness in the mind of some vague ethical being whom she could not class definitely as the God of her childhood, and could not comprehend as any other. (Hardy 2005, p. 97)

The dramatic tension, at this stage in the narrative, turns on Tess's vacillation between religiously informed moral terror at her transgression and natural revulsion that society should hold her, and not the knowing perpetrator, responsible for her plight. Hardy has been careful, in the early chapters of his novel, to drive home to the reader the peculiar mixture of pride and humility that characterizes his protagonist. Fundamentally, Tess is inept at finding a settled balance between her alternating concern and scorn for others' regard for her. Thus, on the one hand she rejects Alec's offer of material help before she leaves the manor, but on the other is acutely sensitive to any suggestion that people take a dim view of what happened to her at his hands. In one sense, Tess is simply caught up in the contradictions and hypocrisies of conventional social morality with its overlay of commonly received religious ethics. But it is the portrayal of Tess's inner struggle to reconcile the dictates of standard morality and religion with the burning conviction of its falsity and injustice in her own case that drives the drama of Hardy's narrative.

After the death of her son and the harrowing scene of her self-administered baptism of him with the name of 'Sorrow', several years following her return home from the manor Tess decides to leave her family home based on the recognition that her younger siblings 'would probably gain less good by her precepts than harm by her example' (Hardy 2005, p. 117). Tess makes her way to an adjacent region of large dairy farming, an area which has remained unfamiliar to her, 'and yet she felt akin to the landscape' (p. 113). Hardy offers a description of the new vista offered to Tess that makes an explicit allusion to certain Flemish masters who painted landscapes, city scenes, and devotional subjects:

> These myriads of cows stretching under her eyes from the far east to the far west outnumbered any she had ever seen at one glance before. The green lea was speckled as thickly with them as a canvas by Van Alsloot or Sallaert with burghers. The bright hues of the red and dun kine absorbed the evening sunlight, which the white-coated animals returned to the eye in rays almost dazzling, even at the distant elevation on which she stood. (Ibid.)

Tess's entry into this pastoral region and the immediate impact of the new landscape on her body and mind elicits a cheerfulness she has not known since her seduction at the hands of Alec d'Urberville. Her mother, we are told, was a humble milkmaid and it is in search of such work that Tess has undertaken her 'pilgrimage'. Tess is immediately hired by the dairy manager and accepted among the milkmaids as a welcome new addition. Hardy accentuates the honest and time-honoured traditional work methods of milking and, though he has some doubts about Tess's ability to do the work on account of the paleness of her face brought on by much domestic seclusion, dairyman Crick is assiduous in his efforts to smooth the way for Tess's integration into the workforce. Tess's stay at the dairy and her meeting and marrying of Angel Clare at this time constitute her happiest moments of adulthood. Tess has, for a short time at least, found a nurturing place that provides an intimate social circle which appreciates her qualities and acknowledges the unwonted refinement of her character. But this chapter of her life is destined to be relatively short-lived, as the long shadow of her past at the manor house comes to darken the brightness of her present pastoral landscape.

The second major blow to and decline in Tess's life, following the confession of her seduction by Alec to her new husband, Angel Clare, is made manifest by the decline in her fortunes in the workplace. From the kindness and seclusion of the Talbothays dairy, Tess is forced into the protracted itinerant existence of a casual farm labourer. She eventually reaches the nadir of this process at Flintcomb-Ash Farm working in the winter fields. At this juncture, Hardy takes the opportunity to paint one of his starkest pictures of the ongoing industrialization of English agriculture in depicting a coal-powered threshing machine. The description is at pains to stress how the machine bodies forth a violent and unnatural incursion of the urban world into the rural, something that is reflected in the mechanization both of labour and the workers themselves:

> By the engine stood a dark motionless being, a sooty and grimy embodiment of tallness, in a sort of trance, with a heap of coals by his side: it was the engine-man. The isolation of his manner and colour lent him the appearance of a creature from Tophet, who had strayed into the pellucid smokelessness of this region of yellow grain and pale soil, with which he had nothing in common, to amaze and to discompose is aborigines. What he looked he felt. He was in the agricultural world, but not of it. [. . .] He spoke in a strange northern accent, his thoughts being turned inwards upon himself, his eye on his iron charge; hardly perceiving the scenes around him, and caring for them not at all; holding only strictly necessary intercourse with the natives, as if some ancient doom compelled him to wander here against his will in the service of his Plutonic master. (Hardy 2005, pp. 345–46)

At the dairy, Tess had encountered the warmth of human companionship amid the daily rhythms of a pastoral life that appeared scarcely changed in centuries. The countryside was rich, soft, and mellow, and the pace of time measured by the natural waxing and waning of the seasons. At Flintcomb-Ash farm, by contrast, work is hard, badly paid, and, as we see from the passage quoted, dominated by the alien influence of the industrial technology stemming from the manufacturing cities and towns of northern England where the industrial revolution had begun a century earlier. Hardy's insistence on the stark contrast is, of course, a matter of poetic licence motivated by his desire to dramatize Tess's mental anguish and sense of radical alienation from the world around her which reaches its climax in the final sections of the novel. The point here, however, is that Hardy showcases the different faces of contemporary agricultural labour and landscape in order to represent the central drama of his narrative.

What could be regarded as, ultimately, no more than a stage-set upon which the action takes place is in fact integral to Hardy's literary presentation. As we saw in the case of Egdon Heath in *The Return of the Native*, the story of Tess only exists in and through representations of place-based labour. It would be no more plausible to remove Tess's life-narrative from the various places she inhabits and labours she enacts than it would be to place the drama of Clym's psychological development somewhere other than on the heath. It is, in fact, this indissoluble link between person, place and work that also amplifies the meaning of Hardy's novels such that their narrative becomes emblematic of much broader social, cultural, and political questions and contradictions of the time. This tendency of Hardy's work to drive the reader towards a direct confrontation with the central contemporary questions of social value reaches its apogee in his final novel, *Jude the Obscure*.

Such is the power of place in Hardy's last novel that its various parts are named after the places where the principal action occurs. Thus, the narrative begins in the rural hamlet of Marygreen, where Jude lives with his great-aunt, and depicts his upbringing from the age of eleven, his sensitive nature and intellectual ambitions, and, finally, his disastrous marriage to Arabella. The first chapters of the book contain many intimations of what awaits Jude in adulthood. The early episode where, out of sensitivity to their needs, he refuses to scare the rooks as required by Farmer Troutham, elicits the following dark presage: 'This weakness of character, as it may be called, suggested that he was the sort of man who was born to ache a good deal before the fall of the curtain on his unnecessary life should signify that all was well with him again' (Hardy 2002, p. 11). This echoes the sentiment expressed of his great Aunt, Drusilla, towards the orphaned Jude in the opening scene of the second chapter of the novel: 'It would ha' been a blessing if Goddy-mighty had took thee too wi' thy mother and father, poor useless boy' (p. 7). After conversing with a coal carter about his knowledge of Christminster, Jude definitively sets this place as his soul's destination in later life:

> It had been the yearning of his heart to find something to anchor on, to cling to; for some place which he could call admirable; should he find that place in this city if he could get there? Would it be a spot in which, without fear of farmers, or hindrance, or ridicule, he could watch and wait and set himself to some mighty undertaking like the men of old of whom he had heard? As the halo had been to his eyes when gazing at it a quarter of an hour earlier, so was the spot mentally to him as he pursued his dark way. (pp. 19–20)

Jude's painstaking efforts to gain mastery of Latin and ancient Greek, after he has obtained some outdated grammar books, mark his teenage years and cement his solitary and inward-looking mode of existence. He becomes apprenticed to a stonemason in the neighbouring town of Alfredston, but does this only as a means to making a living that will render his move to Christminster a credible possibility. What follows is Jude's fateful meeting with Arabella, at which point in the narrative the 'deadly war waged between flesh and spirit' (Hardy 2002, p. xlv) begins in earnest. Arabella's ruse of having Jude believe she is pregnant in order to force his hand into marrying her only leads to their mutual dissatisfaction. Arabella's decision, early on in the marriage, to leave Jude and accompany her parents who are emigrating to Australia, seemingly leaves the young man's path open to follow his dream of living and studying in Christminster. Jude's first entry into his 'New Jerusalem' is described in a remarkable passage where he becomes a living ghost communing with the dead of the ancient city:

> Knowing not a human being here Jude began to be impressed with the isolation of his own personality, as with a self-spectre, the sensation being that of

one who walked, but could not make himself seen or heard. He drew his breath pensively, and seeming thus almost his own ghost, gave his thoughts to the other ghostly presences with which the nooks were haunted. [. . .] The brushing of the wind against the angles, buttresses and door-jambs were as the passing of these only other inhabitants, the tappings of each ivy leaf were as the mutterings of their mournful souls, the shadows as their thin shapes in nervous movement, making him comrades in his solitude. In the gloom it was as if he ran against them without feeling their bodily frames. (Hardy 2002, pp. 73–74)

Hardy's description here is remarkable for its power to express the intensity of Jude's imaginative construction of the place for which he has yearned for a decade, since his first distant sight of the city aged eleven. Having traversed a distance which, dream-like, he felt he could never cross, Jude is now unable or unwilling to have the place participate in his own moment in time. Such an impression has his book-learning made upon him that the veritable psychic reality of Christminster renders it a city of ghosts. There is a terrible negation involved in this displacement in space and time, which involves a psychological mechanism whereby Jude's actual and desired reality can never coincide. This doubleness in Jude's experience is, at the same time, a reflection of the contingencies of his birth relative to the propensities of his character.

From the time of the incident relating his sympathy for the rooks in the farmer's field, it is impressed upon the reader how Jude's sensibilities are at odds with the practical wisdom and ingrained habits of the community he lives within. This mismatch between individual temperament and place is something we have encountered before, most notably in Hardy's presentation of Clym Yeobright in *The Return of the Native*. Jude seeks salvation by removing himself from the country to the city, while Clym attempts the reverse. In both cases, it is ultimately the entanglements of intimate human relationship that bring the irresolvable tensions to a tragic conclusion. However, while Hardy's motif of unhappy unions is the surface theme of these two novels, it is essential to note the much broader social-historical contradictions that underpin the narratives. These turn on the opposition between first-hand experience of a tight-knit rural community and the relatively placeless descriptions of experience made available through education and learning. The point is well expressed by Williams in *The Country and the City*:

> That real perception of tradition is available only to the man who has read about it, though what he then sees through it is his native country, to which he is already deeply bound by memory and experience of another kind: a family and a childhood; an intense association of people and places, which has been his own history. To see tradition in both ways is indeed Hardy's special gift: the native place and experience but also the education, the conscious inquiry.

Yet then to see living people, within this complicated sense of past and present, is another problem again. He sees as a participant who is also an observer; this is the source of the strain. For the process which allows him to observe is very clearly in Hardy's time one which includes, in its attachment to class feelings and class separations, a decisive alienation. (Williams 1973, p. 206)

There are many striking elements of Hardy's last novel that make of it not simply a continuation of settled themes and preoccupations evident in his earlier works, but rather something distinct in kind. What struck contemporary critics most forcefully, and to such an extent that Hardy decided to abandon novel-writing altogether, was the remorseless bleakness of the author's worldview. While the narrative of *Jude* is, at the surface level, a typical Hardy tale of ill-chosen marriages, it is the unmitigated sense of fissure between Jude and his social environment that makes the difference. Jude's affinity for and eventual marriage to Sue Bridehead brings this opposition to societal practices and norms into ever sharper relief. After widow Edlin relates to the young couple the story of the hanging of an ancestor of Jude and Sue near the Brown House where Jude had his first fateful sight of Christminter, Sue confesses her feeling that it is 'as if a tragic doom overhung our family, as it did the house of Atreus' (Hardy 2002, p. 273). What most offended late Victorian sensibilities about *Jude*, and still shocks, was the act whereby Father Time (the son the returned Arabella left with Jude, claiming it was his child) murders the two younger children of Sue and Jude. In the aftermath of this act, Hardy has Jude accounting for Father Time's action by giving voice to the bleak world view that clearly animates the narrative as a whole.

> It was his nature to do it. The doctor says there are such boys springing up amongst us – boys of a sort unknown in the last generation – the outcome of new views of life. They seem to see all its terrors before they are old enough to have staying power to resist them. He says it is the beginning of the coming universal wish not to live. He's an advanced man, the doctor; but he can give no consolation. (p. 326)

This perspective of universalized pessimism is immediately concentrated in Jude's particular case as he regards the face of the dead older boy, the product of his union with Arabella and the embodiment of all that union's terrible and bitter consequences: 'He was their nodal point, their focus, their expression in a single term' (ibid.). The overturning of the principle of self-preservation into its opposite anticipates Freud's conceptualization of the death drive, which similarly invests the human condition with an archaic thirst for annihilation. There are many intimations of the denouement of the novel in its earlier chapters, most obviously Jude's great-aunt cautioning Jude about the tragic history of his and Sue's parents and warning him not to marry. The tragic, traced back to its origins in ancient Greek drama, relates to an individual fate – known to the viewer but not the protagonist – that works on a level deeper than the capacity of individual human acts. On the psychological level, Hardy depicts Jude's fate in terms of his being, irremediably and irrevocably, out of place. When we first encounter him, as a boy of eleven, Jude is a displaced orphan tolerated but not particularly wanted by the great aunt he lives with. His dreams of Christminster and bookishness single him out, in the hamlet of Marygreen, as a quiet and queer boy and young man with aspirations to move to a city that has little to no living connection to the local inhabitants. Jude's otherworldliness blinds him to the machinations of Arabella, and, once he finally makes the journey to Christminster, he communes with ghosts rather than with its living inhabitants.

Jude resides in a crepuscular element, a twilight between an intolerable present and an impossible future. He lives as an outcast, moving from place to place throughout the narrative but never finding lasting contentment or a proper domain that would allow for the developments his yearns for. It is not only at Christminster that Jude finds himself among ghosts. His very attraction to his cousin, Sue Bridehead, involves his recognition of her as ghost-like entity, 'a phantasmal, bodiless creature' (Hardy 2002, p. 250). In his original preface to *Jude* Hardy writes of 'a deadly war waged between flesh and spirit' and this dualistic tension is apparent both in descriptions of the protagonists' thoughts and in their exchanges. While Hardy's prefatory formula, if read in isolation, could give rise to the suspicion of a static, rigid dichotomy pervading the narrative, in reality the tension between principles is very much fluid and dynamic. After she returns to Philottson, her former husband, Jude repines to the old widow Edlin about how Sue's grip on reality has been rendered phantasmal by her superstitious belief that her relationship with Jude was an act of sinful self-indulgence. Jude's final verdict on their tragedy is that both of them are ghosts, but ghosts of a future yet to be rather than revenants of a largely forgotten past:

> And now the ultimate horror has come – her giving herself like this to what she loathes, in her enslavement to forms! – she, so sensitive, so shrinking, that the very wind seemed to blow on her with a touch of reverence. [. . .] For Sue and me when we were at our own best, long ago – when our minds were clear, and our love of truth fearless – the time was not ripe for us! Our ideas are fifty years too soon to be any good for us. And so the resistance they met with brought reaction in her, and recklessness and ruin in me! (p. 388)

Christlike, Jude dies following his (re-)entry to the 'new Jerusalem', Christminster. Jude first comes to the city seemingly freed of his connections to Arabella, but dies unwillingly reunited with her and separated from Sue. Jude's hoarse dying speech, repeating the implacable outrage of Job's anger at an evil seemingly tolerated by a beneficent deity, also echoes Christ's bitter protest at God's abandonment of him in his agony on the cross. While Christ's words express the yearning of lost presence, Jude's are spoken in bitter renunciation: '*Let that day be darkness; let not God regard it from above, neither let the light shine upon it. Lo, let that night be solitary, let no joyful voice come therein*' (p. 392). With these words, coming at the end of Hardy's final novel, the dialectical balance between work and grace has reached a kind of negative culmination. Both, now, are revealed in their radical inefficacy with regard to human redemption and happiness. Jude's efforts, as a self-taught rural working-class orphan, have come to nothing.

The condescending advice of the college master he wrote to about his academic ambitions – to remain in his 'own sphere' and stick to 'your trade' – made clear his rejection from the community of scholars. His actually practised craft of stonemasonry might indeed, Hardy intimates have given Jude the solidity his life badly needed, but his fantastical desire to become a scholar made clear in him 'the modern vice of unrest' (p. 79). Jude's end is thus brought about by his lack of a proper place, both in the direct sense of a physical and social milieu where he can thrive according to his heart's desires; and by his failure to embrace his craft as a worthy vocation. While the tortured relations of Jude and Sue can scarcely be regarded as marginal to Hardy's final novel, they are clearly intended to be of much more generalized significance. The lesson of the tale seems to be something quite other than the hopelessness of social advance for the working class. It has much more to do with a search for conditions under which individuals are not forced to sacrifice being true to themselves in order to gain social recognition and acceptance. In other words, the question Hardy leaves us with concerns the struggle for individual self-realization in the face of social norms that make generalized dissatisfaction the price paid for social recognition. This question – of a possible space for the work of authentic selfhood – is the abiding central concern of the third and final novelist considered in this study, D. H. Lawrence.

Chapter 3

D. H. Lawrence and Vital Connection

SONS AND LOVERS: FROM DARKNESS TO LIGHT

In July 1914, a matter of weeks before he was married to Frieda Weekley in a London registry office and a matter of a month before Britain was at war with Germany, D. H. Lawrence was invited to write a study of Thomas Hardy (Steele 1985, p. xix). It was to be a short book, at 15,000 words, no more than an extended essay. Lawrence then wrote the study, in a manner typical of him in these years, in an intense period of creativity through September 1914. He reported in a letter: 'Out of sheer rage I've written my book about Thomas Hardy. It will be about anything but Thomas Hardy I am afraid – queer stuff – but not bad' (Steele 1985, p. xxii). Shortly after that, from November 1914 to March 1915, Lawrence completed a significant rewriting of *The Rainbow*. When we turn to that novel, we will be able to explore how the presence of Hardy can be felt in the handling of the material of *The Rainbow*. While the Hardy study was never published in Lawrence's lifetime, it offers a unique and invaluable explicit connection between two authors studied here.

While Hardy was born in 1840, forty-five years before Lawrence, he lived to within two years of Lawrence's early death in 1930. Thus, in a strange and rather disconcerting way, the two writers are contemporaries of a sort. Disconcerting, because the general tenor of Hardy's novel writing, the 'structure of feeling' (to use Raymond Williams's famous phrase), is quite distinct to what we find in Lawrence's books. Certainly, if we select one of the novels considered in the previous chapter, such as *Under the Greenwood Tree*, one comes away with the impression of a writer attempting to record, in gentle tones and fond revery, the quaint customs and modes of thinking and speech of a southern English agricultural community. Nothing could be further removed from the stark descriptions of northern English working-class industrial life, with its stifling and stultifying social environment, offered by Lawrence in his early novels and short stories. And yet, as we saw in the last chapter, Hardy's novels, in the space of little more than two decades, seem to span a genuinely epochal shift in social sensibility. The tale of Jude and Sue, of their struggles to live in a manner that is authentic in the face of relentless antagonism in the form of social, religious, and cultural orthodoxies, has something genuinely akin with Lawrence's literary atmosphere.

This theme of conflict is something with which Lawrence begins his study of Hardy: 'Man has made such a mighty struggle to feel at home on the face of the earth, without even yet succeeding' (Steele 1985, p. 7). As Lawrence begins to find his literary voice, this sense of general struggle becomes concentrated in the development of his central characters. While *The Rainbow*, to which we will turn in the next section of this chapter, depicts three successive generations of a family engaged in the effort 'to feel at home on the face of the earth', *Sons and Lovers* is much more limited in time and space and centred on a single protagonist, Paul Morel. The novel ends on an unresolved note: Paul's mother has died, he has wrested himself away from the living father and the family home, but the movement has been one relentless negation of what was. As such, it is a novel of rending, of the life and death effort to overcome, through an uncompromising effort, the environment into which a person is born. There is a stark beauty, almost reverence, in Lawrence's early writing about the environment in which he had grown to consciousness; but what underlies it, ultimately, is a will to overcome and to escape it. In a word, the concern is with finding a proper place and vocation suited to becoming what one truly is.

Lawrence finds something of an antithesis to his own efforts as a novelist in what he recognized as the underlying structure of Hardy's narratives. What he essentially reacts against in Hardy is what he sees as the inevitable undoing of any character who takes a principled stand against the values of the local community. Certainly, it is the case in Hardy's novels that those who chafe against societal expectations and dogmas (as with Henchard in the *Mayor of Casterbridge*, to take one example) meet with ruin and untimely death. The same is largely true of Eliot's novels also, as illustrated by the death of Maggie Tulliver at the end of *The Mill on the Floss*. Of course, to a great extent this is a staple of the romantic tradition, where the heightened sensibilities and idealized aspirations of a protagonist meet with stolid rejection by others around them and lead to the unhappiness and undoing of the one who will not reconcile themselves to social orthodoxy. Indeed, this dynamic is an essential ingredient of dramatic tension and development built into the structure of the central drama of the novel. Nevertheless, in *Study of Thomas Hardy*, Lawrence finds this stock line of narrative development intolerable:

This is the tragedy of Hardy, always the same: the tragedy of those who, more or less pioneers, have died in the wilderness whither they have escaped for free action, after having left the walled security, and the comparative imprisonment, of the established convention. This is the theme of novel after novel: remain quite within the convention, and you are good, safe, and happy in the long run, though you never have the vital pang of sympathy on your side; or, on the other hand, be passionate, individual, wilful, you will find the security of the convention a walled prison, you will escape, and you will die, either of your own lack of strength to bear the isolation and the exposure, or by direct revenge from the community, or from both. [. . .] The growth and development of this tragedy, the deeper and deeper realisation of this division and this problem, the coming towards some conclusion, is the one theme of the Wessex novels. (Steele 1985, pp. 22–23)

What preoccupies Lawrence in his study of Hardy is what he sees as the writer's insistence on the failure of the individual to wrest themselves successfully out of the milieu of the community and find their proper place as an individual. In the previous chapter, it was noted how Hardy hints at a possible path of contentment and happiness for Jude, had he been able to see his work as a stonemason as something more than a mere temporary means of survival while he pursued his unrealistic desire to become a student at the university. Hardy himself, we recall, was in his youth and early adulthood apprenticed to an architectural firm, an allied though more esteemed profession relative to stonemasonry. In accord with Jude's desire, Hardy fought through to being a successful writer and member of the cultural and intellectual class. Of course, Hardy had to compromise in his role as a writer in order to successfully navigate the contingencies of the Victorian publishing industry. The harshly critical response to the publication of *Jude*, ironically enough, led to Hardy's abandoning novel writing, though arguably he was able to make this decision after having made a living and name for himself as one of Britain's foremost novelists. Thus, the critical failure of *Jude* justifies Hardy in breaking his longstanding compact with the reading public; whereas the failure of Jude amounts to his being broken by a public that resolutely refuses to heed him and his heart's desires.

Along with the community, Lawrence identified work as one of the necessary mediations on the path towards true individual selfhood. Lawrence's *Study of Thomas Hardy* is an invaluable resource for understanding the Lawrence's developing worldview between the time of his breakthrough novel, *Sons and Lovers*, and his two subsequent major works, *The Rainbow* and *Women in Love*. Lawrence was raised in the Nottinghamshire town of Bestwood, situated in a coalmining district on the border with Derbyshire. His novels, short stories, and critical essays all reflect, in various ways, on the contrast between the natural landscape (especially flowers and birds) and the deadening effects of industrialized social conditions. The contrasts and conflicts contained within Lawrence's native place resonated strongly with the lived experience of Raymond Williams, who himself grew up in a border country (between South Wales and England), amid a countryside marked by industrialized coalmining. Williams reflects on Lawrence's position, both with regard to his native place and with respect to his attitude towards and hopes for social change:

> What Lawrence concentrated in his work was that unresolved complex of impulses and attachments of which, in the twentieth century, the relation of county and city, as states of mind and feeling, was the most evidently available form [. . .]. What Lawrence again and again rejects, though the fact that he is continually drawn to consider it is equally significant, is the idea and the practice of social agencies of change. Where Lawrence hesitates, always, is between the idea of regeneration and an idea of revolution. He stresses the future much more than the past, and the change is to be absolute, root and branch. But he sees available revolutionary movements as simply fights about property; he wants a different vision, a new sense of life, before he commits himself; otherwise it will be not regeneration but a final collapse. (Williams 1973, p. 268)

Lawrence's commitment to human regeneration is abundantly apparent in the narrative of *Sons and Lovers*, which can be rightly seen as the author's breakthrough novel. As it marks a kind of threshold in Lawrence's progress as a writer, it is tempting to see it purely in terms of necessary preparation for his literary work proper but of little value in and of itself. Representative of this perspective is F. R. Leavis: 'With *Sons and Lovers* Lawrence put something behind him. Not for nothing did he warn Edward Garnet [his editor] not to expect anything else of the same kind: "I shan't write in the same manner as *Sons and Lovers* again"' (Leavis 1955, p. 7). In my own view, this evaluation of *Sons and Lovers* is simplistic, predicated as it is on some fairly vague notion of what truly qualifies as 'great art'. Even if the novel constitutes a rite of passage, it does not follow that what makes the moment of transition can be looked back upon, in meditative tranquillity, as a mere relic of the man Lawrence was prior to becoming the artist he was destined to become. This point is crucial to the present study, insofar as the handling of the theme of landscape is intimately tied to the notion of a past that can never, definitively, be overcome.

As David Trotter points out in his editorial introduction to the novel: '*Sons and Lovers* is a *Bildungsroman*, and in *Bildungsromanen* nothing, including sexual "stimuli", is of interest unless it contributes to the hero's or heroine's education' (Lawrence 2009, p. xxviii). In the specific context, Trotter's point is that it is not a valid critique of the novel to observe that the women with whom the central protagonist, Paul Morel, has relationships are presented merely in terms of the man's character development. The whole purpose of the novel, in other words, is to present Paul's struggle to find himself in and through his interactions with others. *Sons and Lovers* begins, before the birth of Paul, with a depiction of his young mother questioning how she came to be in the position in which she finds herself, namely the poor wife of an unambitious miner, struggling to maintain a new home and bring up two young children. Her self-interrogation foreshadows the quest of her second son, yet to be born, that will constitute the chief burden of the narrative:

> 'What have *I* to do with it?' she said to herself. 'What have I to do with all this? Even the child I am going to have! It doesn't seem as if *I* were taken into account.'
>
> Sometimes life takes hold of one, carries the body along, accomplishes one's history, and yet is not real, but leaves oneself as it were slurred over
>
> 'I wait,' Mrs Morel said to herself – 'I wait, and what I wait for can never come.' (Lawrence 2009, p. 11)

What the mother expresses here, as we shall come to recognize, is a sentiment that is crucial to Lawrence's characters: a distinction between a life simply developing and maturing, according to some outwardly regarded and conventionally accepted view, and an individual's genuinely struggling through to a realization of their authentic self. This distinction is a subtle one, as it is not a question of a set of objective criteria that could be applied to a person in terms of their having achieved this or that. What can be said for certain is that, based on Lawrence's presentation of the process, a character's coming into authentic selfhood can only be achieved in and through their intimate relationships with another. To use the philosophical jargon, authenticity is for Lawrence 'dialectical'. That is, it arises through a series of oppositions between self and other, oppositions that do not diminish the self and other that stand opposed but rather enrich and complexify them. In *Sons and Lovers* the overall pathos of the narrative is one of a frustrated desire to escape the inauthentic. In this sense, it is only a rite of passage or *Bildungsroman* in the negative sense, namely insofar as Paul Morel has managed by the end to wrench himself free from the element in which his true self was lost.

One of the remarkable things about Lawrence as a writer is that he was, at the time of writing his early breakthrough novels, developing a fully-fledged 'metaphysic', a theory of reality which he also articulated in detail. The first recording of this we find in his *Study of Thomas Hardy*, which Lawrence freely conceded was largely about anything other than Hardy's works. That is an exaggeration – there is much in the way of valuable insight into

Hardy's novels – but it is certainly clear that Lawrence's major preoccupation in the *Study* is with the articulation of his vision of the true nature of things. Lawrence went on to develop what we might call his philosophy of life through the two short decades of his writing career, a period in which he produced critical essays and studies of American literature, of the notion of the unconscious, and, in his last major work, a starkly heterodox reading of the final book of the New Testament, *Apocalypse*. It is in his *Study*, however, that we are presented with a first delineation of precisely what Lawrence considered to be authentic individual selfhood:

> By individualist is meant, not a selfish or greedy person anxious to satisfy appetites, but a man of distinct being, who must act in his own particular way to fulfil his own individual nature. He is a man who, being beyond the average, chooses to rule his own life to his own completion, and as such is an aristocrat. (Steele 1985, p. 49)

Lawrence observes that, in his novels, Hardy 'is forced in the issue to stand with the community in condemnation of the aristocrat' and that, accordingly, 'he must select his individual with a definite weakness, a certain oldness of temper, inelastic, a certain inevitable and inconquerable adhesion to the community' (ibid.). As examples of this, Lawrence points to Clym, Tess, and Jude and observes: 'they cannot break away from the old adhesion, they cannot separate themselves from the mass which bore them, they cannot detach themselves from the common' (p. 50). In *Sons and Lovers* Lawrence depicts just this struggle, on the part of Paul Morel, to 'break away from the old adhesion'. On a superficial level, 'the common' in Paul's case is the Nottinghamshire mining town of Bestwood and its working-class social norms and mores. More profoundly, however, it is a matter of Paul's adhesion to the people, particularly the women, with and through which he strives to express himself. The key connection throughout the novel, as the title intimates, is that between Paul and his mother. By the time he has reached adolescence, with his older brother William gone to London, Paul constitutes his mother's primary object of interest:

> Mrs Morel clung now to Paul. He was quiet and not brilliant. But still he stuck to his painting, and still he stuck to his mother. Everything he did was for her. She waited for his coming home in the evening, and then she unburdened herself of all she had pondered, or of all that had occurred to her during the day. He sat and listened with his earnestness. The two shared lives. (Lawrence 1995, p. 133)

After the death of William, Paul succumbs to a protracted illness, whose severity is sufficient to draw the mother out of her stupor of mourning. Following this period, Paul gradually finds a new centre of interest in the Leivers family who work Willey farm in the countryside adjacent to Bestwood. The daughter of the family, Miriam, is set to become Paul's first love. The push and pull between Miriam and Paul's mother for a primary attachment to the young man's constitutes the core of the drama in the remaining two thirds of the novel. From the first, Lawrence accentuates Miriam's intensely romantic and inward religiosity:

> Her great companion was her mother. They were both brown-eyed, and inclined to be mystical, such women as treasure religion inside them, breath it in their nostrils, and see the whole of life in a mist thereof. So to Miriam, Christ and God made one great figure, which she loved tremblingly and passionately when a tremendous sunset burned out the western sky [. . .]. She madly wanted her little brother of four to let her swathe him and stifle him in her love; she went to church reverently, with bowed head, and quivered in anguish from the vulgarity of the other choir-girls and from the common-sounding voice of the curate. (pp. 165–66)

A more intimate relationship grows up between Paul and Miriam, one in which Miriam's intense inwardness meets with a confirming outward recognition in Paul. In his incipient artistic accomplishment, Paul in turn requires the presence of another, corresponding witness. This role is performed, in the first instance, by his mother; but slowly Miriam becomes Paul's preferred presence. In a key scene between the two young lovers, Miriam announces that she wants Paul to see a certain rose-bush she has discovered in a local wood. It is already late and the land is in twilight. While Miriam recognizes the beauty of the landscape, it cannot be realized in her until Paul has borne witness to it: 'Only he could make it her own, immortal' (p. 183). Amid the powerful scent of honeysuckle and the suggestive half-light of the darkening wood, Miriam cries out when the rose-bush comes into view:

> Paul and Miriam stood close together, silent, and watched. Point after point the steady roses shone out to them, seeming to kindle something in their souls. The dusk came like smoke around them, and still did not put out the roses.
> Paul looked into Miriam's eyes. She was pale and expectant with wonder, her lips were parted, and her dark eyes lay open to him. His look seemed to travel down into her. Her soul quivered. It was the communion she wanted. He turned aside, as if pained. He turned to the bush. (p. 184)

Throughout their courting, Lawrence interweaves beautifully observed scenes of the English countryside with the acts and exchanges between Paul and Miriam. The girl's rarefied sense of nature gives her a concrete context in which to maintain her sublimated attraction to Paul. Paul himself is depicted as torn between two worlds: on the one hand, the world of blood intimacy he knows from his family, with its physical closeness and matter-of-fact struggle with the exigencies of working-class life; on the other, the more refined world of book learning, art, and allegorical religious meaning. As the scene with the rose-bush makes clear, there is a fatal ambivalence – even repugnance – in Paul's reaction to the young woman's insistence on spiritualizing the natural world.

The dichotomy between the lovers could all too easily be represented and understood in terms of the overt distinctions between the working-class milieu of an industrial coalmining town as opposed to the relatively isolated life of a rural farmstead. Lawrence's portrayal of the conflict between Miriam and Paul does not allow itself to be so reduced. For one thing, Paul is portrayed from the outset as a fragile and sensitive individual, shrinking from the coarseness and simmering brutality of his father towards his more refined mother, who elicits and encourages her son's artistic bent. Equally, Paul's openness to nature is just as pronounced as Miriam's. What ultimately divides the young lovers is the degree to which Miriam must sublimate nature and human relations in order to acknowledge them as meaningful. The description of a decisive epiphany in Miriam's experience of Paul vividly exemplifies this point:

> Turning a corner in the lane, she came upon Paul, who stood bent over something, his mind fixed on it, working away steadily, patiently, a little hopelessly. She hesitated in her approach, to watch.
>
> He remained concentrated in the middle of the road. Beyond, one rift of rich gold in that colourless grey evening seemed to make him stand out in dark relief. She saw him, slender and firm, as if the setting sun had given him to her. A deep pain took hold of her, and she knew she must love him. And she had discovered him, discovered in him a rare potentiality, discovered his loneliness. Quivering as at some 'annunciation', she went slowly forward. (p. 191)

Rather bathetically, Miriam soon realizes that Paul had simply been attempting to fix his deceased brother's umbrella. Despite this, she tends the visionary experience to ensure its permanent meaning in her consciousness of Paul: 'She always regarded that sudden coming upon him in the lane as a revelation' (p. 192). While Miriam lives in the countryside, she is not marked by the physical conditions of farm work, but is rather alienated from them. Her alienation from the landscape is more subtle but related to her alienation from work. While Paul and Miriam draw together through their love of the natural landscape, they apprehend it in starkly different modes.

For Miriam, 'nature' offers an allegorical tapestry of spiritual, inner meaning. It is thereby rendered entirely psychological and its immemorial otherness with respect to human existence goes unrecognized. While Paul's family home is ostensibly situated in an industrial landscape further separated from the natural phenomena of the countryside, he is nevertheless able to apprehend the elemental forces in which all human striving appears as little more than infantile babbling. In the following scene, Lawrence seizes on the moon as the vehicle to express Paul's more profound relationship to the forces of nature:

> A corncrake in the hay-close called insistently. The moon slid quite quickly downwards, growing more flushed. Behind him the great flowers leaned as if they were calling. And then, like a shock, he caught another perfume, something raw and coarse. Hunting around, he found the purple iris, touched their fleshy throats and their dark, grasping hands. At any rate, he had found something. They stood stiff in the darkness. Their scent was brutal. The moon was melting down upon the crest of the hill. It was gone; all was dark. The corncrake called still. (p. 332)

To refer to the flower's scent as 'brutal' signals quite a different experience of the landscape to the one related in the scene describing Miriam's disclosure of the rose-bush to Paul. In Paul's experience, the natural landscape is something quite other that a screen for allegorical imaginings. Paul's landscape is inescapably beyond and before human consciousness, something primeval. Our only manner of genuine correspondence with such nature comes from within our own primal passions and drives. The failure of Miriam to assent to the physical, sexual dimension of her relationship with Paul is of a piece with their divergent experiences of nature. Paul descries something unfathomably ancient in the landscape and intuits in it an element of his own nature, something pre-civilized and 'brutal', that must find expression in his authentic sense. Ultimately, his search for authenticity through a seven-year relationship founders on Miriam's negation of this primeval human element, namely the sex-impulse. Hence, Paul must part from Miriam in recognition of this failure and of his ultimately unsatisfied drive to fulfil himself in all his various dimensions. Spiritualized love, he realizes, is the only modality acceptable to someone such as Miriam, and they must go their separate ways despite the very real development each has achieved in the context of their relationship.

There is little direct description of the primary work of the area around Bestwood in *Sons and Lovers*, namely coalmining. Certainly, the presence of mines is constantly alluded to and Walter Morel's habits and attitudes as a miner are a key ingredient of the narrative. Chiefly, though, the work of mining is something the novel looks around and away from and not at: *Sons and Lovers* is far from a twentieth-century sequel to Zola's *Germinal*. Paul is faced at the age of fourteen with the prospect of finding work and thereby making a contribution to the household income. His older brother, William, is already getting on in London; but Paul is a dreamy, introverted boy, who wants nothing more than to cultivate his painting, obtain an undemanding and quiet job, and live in a cottage near his mother. Typically for an adolescent, Paul is scoured by self-consciousness when he is obliged to go to the local library in order to consult the newspaper and copy out some job advertisements:

> Then he looked wistfully out of the window. Already he was a prisoner of industrialism. Large sunflowers stared over the old red wall of the garden opposite, looking in their jolly way down on the women who were hurrying with something for dinner. The valley was full of corn, brightening in the sun. Two collieries, among the fields, waved their small white plumes of steam. Far off were the woods of Aldersley, dark and fascinating. Already his heart went down. He was being taken into bondage. His freedom in the beloved home valley was going now. (p. 105)

This short passage highlights the two-sidedness that always manifests in Lawrence's descriptions of the area around Bestwood. *Sons and Lovers* begins with a brief synopsis of the history of coalmining in the region and how the town grew in response to the expansion of industrialization. Due to the central concern of the novel – the depiction of Paul's emergence into authentic self-awareness – the work that marks and makes the place is largely a scenic element in the narrative. It is quite other than a neutral backdrop, however, due to the psychological dynamic of the Morel family, according to which mother and children 'were peculiarly *against* their father' (p. 70). Nevertheless, the father's identification with work takes on a conciliatory and binding character when that work is performed at home in the presence of his children. At such times, the usual terror felt at the father's drinking and irascibility gives way to a warm appreciation of his skills and good humour:

> The only times when he entered again into the life of his own people was when he worked, and was happy at work. Sometimes, in the evening, he cobbled the boots or mended the kettle or his pit-bottle. Then he always wanted several attendants, and the children enjoyed it. They united with him in the work, in the actual doing of something, when he was his real self again.
>
> He was a good workman, dexterous, and one who, when he was in a good humour, always sang. He had whole periods, months, almost years, of friction and nasty temper. Then sometimes he was jolly again. It was nice to see him run with a piece of red-hot iron into the scullery, crying:
>
> 'Out of my road – out of my road!' (p. 76)

This passage and others like it show a quite different appreciation of work to that of the shadowy presence of the mines. As we shall see, in *The Rainbow* Lawrence also describes the binding and expressive virtues of work in the form of domestic handcraft. In that subsequent novel, a veritable gendered metaphysic places work on the side of the male polarity. This should be understood, I believe, as something other than a mere affirmation of gender stereotypes. It is not that female characters in Lawrence's novels perform no work (Mrs Morel is constantly at work within the home). It is rather the sense of achieved selfhood in and through the medium of handwork that Lawrence sees as something peculiarly belonging to the men in his narratives.

In *Sons and Lovers* Lawrence achieves a remarkable breakthrough in his aspiration to reach a certain truth through writing. His work is published at a key moment in the history of British literature and cultural history, just before the Great War and the High Modernism that will emerge in its wake. Stylistically, *Sons and Lovers* is a starkly realist novel in its depictions of northern working-class life. For all that, it is animated by anything other than a documentary impulse, being predominantly a coming-of-age narrative focused on the inner development of the central character, Paul Morel. Thus, its underlying intention is to articulate something of much more general significance in the nature of human relationships than would be striven for by a writer that was merely attempting to record his earlier life in a small Nottinghamshire town. While labour and landscape are key themes in his breakthrough work, it is the achievement of authentic selfhood through concrete relationships with others that constitutes the underlying concern of Lawrence's writing. Through the writing of *Sons and Lovers* this cardinal concern had become clear to the author. In his two subsequent novels, *The Rainbow* and *Women in Love*, Lawrence writes a veritable new testament to this concern.

THE RAINBOW: A SHORT HISTORY OF AUTHENTIC SELFHOOD

The gestation and realization of the two novels Lawrence published after *Sons and Lovers* is complicated and drawn out. Some of the complications stem directly from the immediate material conditions and exigencies of the author's life at the time. In April 1912 Lawrence met Frieda Weekley, the wife of one of his university professors whom he would go on to marry two years later after a protracted period spent together in continental Europe. Frieda was German and, following Britain's declaration of war with Germany, the Lawrences were obliged to abandon plans to return to Italy and to remain in England. They eventually settled in a remote rural cottage in Cornwall, where

Lawrence completed the final, published version of *The Rainbow*. Originally, Lawrence had written a draft novel entitled 'The Sisters' in 1913. Then, in early 1914, he completed a heavily revised second version of the narrative bearing the title *The Wedding Ring* (Lawrence 1997, ix). It was not until late that year that Lawrence began a third phase of revisions, now separating out the material that would become *The Rainbow* from the core of his original narrative, which would not be published until 1920 under the title *Women in Love*.

As noted, immediately prior to his drafting the final version of *The Rainbow* Lawrence worked intensively on his *Study of Thomas Hardy*. As we have seen, writing on Hardy gave Lawrence an opportunity for thinking through and articulating in detail a veritable metaphysic or theory of reality. Already, with the writing of *Sons and Lovers*, the struggle to achieve authentic selfhood was established as Lawrence's central literary concern. Couched in religious terms, this amounts to a motif of personal restitution and redemption. As with Eliot and Hardy before him, various modulations of Christian faith (Anglican, Methodist, and Evangelical) are interweaved into the text of Lawrence's early novels. The very title of *The Rainbow* is testimony to the centrality of religious imagery. The final passage of the novel, after Ursula Brangwen has come through a searing relationship and an unexpected pregnancy and stands at the threshold of an independent life, leaves the reader with a resonant example of Lawrence's use of religious language and motif:

> And the rainbow stood on the earth. She knew that the sordid people that crept hard-scaled and separate on the face of the world's corruption were living still, that the rainbow was arched in their blood and would quiver to life in their spirit, that they would cast off their horny covering of disintegration, that new, clean, naked bodies would issue to a new germination, to a new growth, rising to the light and the wind and the clean rain of heaven. She saw in the rainbow the earth's new architecture, the old, brittle corruption of houses and factories swept away, the world built up in a living fabric of Truth, fitting to the overarching heaven. (Lawrence 1997, pp. 493–94)

This final passage of the novel is a veritable apocalypse, in the original sense of a revealing vision of a prophetic future. While the image of the rainbow is, of course, taken from the story of the earth's flooding and Noah's task to begin life anew thanks to his saving of life on the ark, Lawrence's imagery of rebirth centres on organic growth, particularly that of plant life – 'a new growth, rising to the light and the wind and the clean rain of heaven'. Alternatively, we might take what is 'hard-scaled and separate', the ''horny covering of disintegration', as a snake's old skin to be sloughed off to reveal an integument that is incomparably more supple and sensitive to the natural elements. In other words, Lawrence takes the sublime language of Christian visionary experience and fuses it with his own first-hand experience of landscape and organic nature. His love of flowers has been alluded to before, as has his lived experience of the beauty of the Derbyshire countryside in juxtaposition to the ugliness of the Nottinghamshire milieu of industrialized coalmining.

Thus, Lawrence's vision as a writer involves the intertwining of various forces of opposition, but arguably the central dialectic for him is the one between life and death. If we consider the very beginning of *The Rainbow*, we immediately notice a similar, sublime Biblical tone (here, reminiscent of the opening book of Genesis), in this case even more evidently steeped in elements of the living landscape. The narrative centres on three generations of the Brangwen family, who have farmed the same area from time immemorial:

> They knew the intercourse between heaven and earth, sunshine drawn into the breast and bowels, the rain sucked up in the daytime, nakedness that comes under the wind in autumn, showing the birds' nests no longer worth hiding. Their life and interrelations were such; feeling the pulse and body of the soil, that opened to their furrow for the grain, and became smooth and supple after their ploughing, and clung to their feet with a weight that pulled like desire, lying hard and unresponsive when the crops were to be shorn away. The young corn waved and was silken, and the lustre slid along the limbs of the men who saw it. They took the udder of the cows, the cows yielded milk and pulse against the hands of the men, the pulse of the blood of the teats of the cows beat into the pulse of the hands of the men. (Lawrence 1997, p. 6)

The remarkable opening passage of *The Rainbow* combines not only religion and landscape, but also highly charged sexual imagery. The world described above is the world of the men who work the land. Lawrence juxtaposes this with the world of the women, 'who wanted another form of life than this, something that was not blood-intimacy' (p. 7). The Brangwen women look to those human elements in the vicinity that exist beyond the immediate locality and way of life known to the farmers: to the vicar with his religious and academic training and to the cities where new modes of existence and ideas are proliferating. Thus, Lawrence juxtaposes the settled attachment of the farming males to the restless desire for something more, something other in the farmers' wives and daughters. This opposition between male and female principles is far from being a dualistic opposition of opposed values; it is rather a matter of setting out what is for Lawrence a necessary dialectic that lies at the very heart of human existence and development. After all, the novel ends with Ursula, the elder grandchild of the first generation of Brangwens depicted, standing before a life that will take her far beyond her native land in

Lawrence's sequel, *Women in Love*. In fact, Lawrence's indexing of the male principle with the Brangwen men works against the traditional association of the feminine with the earth, with the natural, and with the human body.

While *Sons and Lovers* had depicted the limited development of one family, drawn from his own experience growing up in the working-class community of Eastwood, *The Rainbow* is far more expansive, both in terms of its linguistic diversity of registered but also, and more obviously, in its efforts to depict the development of three successive generations. This temporal expansion allows Lawrence to portray, in great personal detail, a certain dialectical development that occurs between generations. To a degree, this is presented as a matter of repetitions: for example, the inevitable breaking away from the parents to form one's own first intimate unions in maturity. But through the cyclical repeats of the individual's rites of passage Lawrence is able to trace out what is his central preoccupation, namely an ever-more pronounced coming to consciousness of the need for authentic selfhood. What is striking about the germination of *The Rainbow* in 1913–1914 is the fact that Lawrence began with the idea of depicting the lives of the two sisters, Ursula and Gudrun, but felt compelled to develop his narrative to describe the origins of the two women two generations earlier. This approach to the novel brings the author into line with a marked tendency of his own predecessors, Eliot and Hardy, who more often than not set their narratives a generation or two back in time.

While his predecessors tend to use distance of historic time to accentuate settled community customs, habits of mind and turns of phrase, Lawrence emphasizes, from the first, the singularity and isolation of the generations of Brangwens who have lived at the Marsh Farm. Certainly, the outward material changes that come to the area – the growth of coal mining and the canal system, along with the railway network – are described in basic outline; but it is the inner life of the family, viewed predominantly through one representative of each generation that clearly constitutes the real subject of interest for Lawrence. More specifically, the narrative endeavours to capture, in elaborate and sometimes almost suffocating detail, the manner in which the principal characters come into relationship with their respective intimate partner. Accordingly, the first chapter relates how Tom Brangwen, the youngest son who goes on to inherit and run the Marsh Farm, meets, courts, and marries Lydia Lensky, the widow of a Polish doctor and patriot who had died while still a relatively young man in exile in England. The scene where Tom Brangwen walks out to the vicarage to propose to the widow is a beautiful evocation of landscape that perfectly captures the emotionally surcharged moment:

> He went up the hill and on towards the vicarage, the wind roaring through the hedges, whilst he tried to shelter his bunch of daffodils by his side. He did not think of anything, only knew that the wind was blowing.

Night was falling, the bare trees drummed and whistled. The vicar, he knew, would be in his study, the Polish woman in the kitchen, a comfortable room, with her child. In the darkness of twilight, he went through the gate and down the path where a few daffodils stooped in the wind, and shattered crocuses made a pale, colourless ravel.

There was a light streaming on to the bushes at the back from the kitchen window. He began to hesitate. How could he do this? Looking through the window, he saw her seated in the rocking-chair with the child, already in its nightdress, sitting on her knee. The fair head with its wild, fierce hair was dropping towards the fire-warmth, which reflected on the bright cheeks and clear skin of the child, who seemed to be musing, almost like a grown-up person. (Lawrence 1997, pp. 40–41)

The literary effect of this description resembles the cinematic one of surveying a scene at a virtual distance that can never be traversed, or as space appears to us in dreams. The window Brangwen looks through is like a magic mirror that displays to him his future. His will falters as he realizes this is less a vision of a gifted time to be and ultimately an image created and maintained by his will and desire. This vertiginous moment, described as a kind of irreversible destiny and yet lived as a tarrying moment of decision, sets the tone for all other intimate encounters described in the novel. In this particular case, the struggle between Tom and Lydia turns on the widow's ability to wrench herself away from the ghosts of her past. She has already lived through a long and exhausting marriage with her former husband, in whose shadow she moved, subordinating all her heart's desires to his project of Polish independence. Tom's desire calls her away from this past, but it is only with a supreme effort that she opens, flower-like, to her new English lover. While Tom and Lydia go on to have several children together, it is Brangwen's stepdaughter Anna who, along with his nephew Will, constitutes the crux of the narrative relating to the second generation described in the novel.

In the intermediary passages between the marriages of Tom and later of Anna, Lawrence captures the relationship between father and stepdaughter in vivid and deeply moving ways. Like Eliot before him, Lawrence's writing exhibits an acute awareness of and sensibility for the thoughts and sufferings of childhood. Particularly in her portrayal of Maggie in *The Mill on the Floss*, Eliot was able to delineate in very striking ways how the nature of the adult is adumbrated in the already well-formed predispositions of the child. The first scene of note between Tom Brangwen and Anna as a young child comes on the night her mother gives birth to the first of her children to the English farmer. After a protracted period when the child insists on seeing her mother even though she is in the process of giving birth, Brangwen hits on the idea of bringing the child out to the barn with him when he gives the cows their last meal of the day. It is a dark, rainy night and the servant woman, Tilly, objects to what she considers an ill-conceived plan that threatens to give the young girl a cold. Brangwen, wracked with nerves due to his wife's condition, insists on taking Anna out to the barn to distract her from her insistence on seeing her mother. He proceeds to feed the cows their meal:

> The beast fed, he dropped the pan and sat down on a box, to arrange the child.
> 'Will the cows go to sleep now?' she said, catching her breath as she spoke.
> 'Yes.'
> 'Will they eat all their stuff up first?'
> 'Yes. Hark at them.'
> And the two sat still listening to the snuffing and breathing of cows feeding in the sheds communicating with this small barn. The lantern shed a soft, steady light from one wall. All outside was still in the rain. He looked down at the silky folds of the paisley shawl. It reminded him of his mother. She used to go to church in it. He was back again in the old irresponsibility and security, a boy at home.
> The two sat very quiet. His mind, in a sort of trance, seemed to become more and more vague. He held the child close to him. A quivering little shudder, re-echoing from her sobbing, went down her limbs. He held her closer. Gradually she relaxed, the eyelids began to sink over her dark, watchful eyes. As she sank to sleep, his mind became blank. (Lawrence 1997, pp. 77–78)

As the child's life at the Marsh Farm with her stepfather becomes established, she also relaxes her habituated grasp on her mother. The mother's attention now turned to the new baby, Anna looks to Brangwen for love and attention and he, united with the girl's mother, finds a further outlet for his care in the young girl. As will be even more pronounced in the two daughters she will go on to have, Ursula and Gundrun, Anna lives as a thing apart: 'Like a wild thing, she wanted her distance. She mistrusted intimacy' (p. 96). This isolation, drawing away from any open and free association with others in the village, is described as a deep sense of family culture at the Marsh Farm: 'They were a curious family, a law to themselves, separate from the world, isolated, a small republic set in invisible bounds' (p. 101).

There is no sense, in Lawrence's description of it, that this state of being unto itself of the family is to be regretted or deprecated. This marks an important difference when we consider the portrayal of rural community in Eliot and Hardy in comparison to Lawrence's depiction of the Brangwens. But this difference is not absolute. In the descriptions of Anna as a young girl, in particular, there is an affecting portrayal of the family's connections to the local community. For instance, Brangwen makes a habit of bringing his stepdaughter to the cattle-market at Derby each week, where she becomes a regular focus of attention at the George Inn where the father stops for a meal before returning home. The gentle teasing banter between the girl and the locals is evocative of the close-knit company:

> 'Well me little maid,' Braithwaite would say to her, 'an' how's th' lamb's wool?'
>
> He have a tug at a glistening, pale piece of her hair.
>
> 'It's not lamb's wool,' said Anna, indignantly putting back her offended lock.
>
> 'Why, what'st ca' it then?'
>
> 'It's hair.'
>
> 'Hair! Wheriver dun they rear that sort?'
>
> 'Wheriver dun they?' she asked, in dialect, her curiosity overcoming her.
>
> Instead of answering he shouted with joy. It was the triumph, to make her speak dialect. (Lawrence 1997, p. 87)

After two years of marriage, Tom and Lydia achieve an equilibrium. This condition does not abolish but rather establishes their respective singularity. This is how Lawrence describes a relationship that finds fruition rather than frustration. Lydia is able, initially after the birth of first son and then definitely in the settled union with her husband, to free herself from the ghosts of a dead and spectral past with her former spouse. She makes the demand of her second husband that he be, always and unquestioningly, there for her, a vital presence. But this demand is not a question of holding the other in a claustrophobic nearness, a kind of smothering. Rather, it is a matter of release. Lawrence sanctifies the union: 'Now He was declared to Brangwen and to Lydia Brangwen as they stood together. When at last they had joined hands, the house was finished, and the Lord took up his abode. And they were glad' (p. 94). This consummated union between the two parents reflects back on the child, and Anna stands supported in her being, rooted in her new ground firmly and permanently. Lawrence uses the same elevated Biblical language to express the constituting of this new stability in the child's existence:

> Anna's soul was put at peace between them. She looked from one to the other, and she saw them established to her safety, and she was free. She played between the pillar of fire and the pillar of cloud in confidence, having the assurance on her right hand and the assurance on her left. She was no longer called upon to uphold with her childish might the broken end of the arch. Her father and her mother now met to the span of the heavens, and she, the child, was free to play in the space beneath, between. (pp. 94–95)

In the union of Tom Brangwen and Lydia Lensky Lawrence acknowledges the higher-class status of the woman, but ultimately dismisses its relevance in the context of the man's lived sense of a kind of spiritual or even cosmic destiny to their pairing: 'There was an inner reality, a logic of the soul, which connected her with him' (p. 39). In this Lawrence as a writer shows his recognition of one of the stock contradictions of the novel, namely the difficulty differences in class background bring to a personally willed but socially resisted intimate relationship. His consummate expression of this problem is found in his final novel, *Lady Chatterley's Lover*. The male protagonist in that narrative, Mellors, is a character who, based on the outward description at least, bears comparison to a type of character found in Hardy. Examples of this character type would be Gabriel Oak, Giles Winterborne, and Diggory Venn. Their salient features include living in secluded contexts, with little concern for what others think of them, and possessing a rare and respected understanding of and affinity for the local environment. Tom Brangwen also belongs among this company and the heightened sensibility evoked in Lawrence's beautifully moving proposal scene is a sign that something of fundamental significance to the author's understanding of human relationships is being conveyed.

One aspect of this significance is derived from Lawrence's depiction of the farming work done by Brangwen and the solitude it involves. Lacking immediate human contact, there is a strong sense that the young farmer stands in connection with archaic cosmic forces. There is a level of blind and raw exposure to the natural elements of the scene that evokes an authenticity of unmediated relatedness to the landscape. Harking back to the opening description of the men's work at the beginning of the novel, with the farmer feeling the pulse of nature pass through his body, Lawrence now refers the working man to a further, heavenly principle of connection and exposure. What is expressed is the man's being referred to something undeniably other than the human domain of concerns in and through his connection to the natural elements:

> But during the long February nights with the ewes in labour, looking out from the shelter into the flashing stars, he knew he did not belong to himself. He must admit that he was only fragmentary, something incomplete and subject. There were the stars in the dark heaven travelling, the whole host passing by on some eternal voyage. So he sat small and submissive to the greater ordering. (p. 38)

In his earlier episodes of heavy drinking and occasional sexual liaisons with women, Tom has tried to burn out his oppressive sense of individualized self-presence. To Lawrence, however, this kind of obliteration of self is a dead-end and merely the symptom of a radical existential failure. To really rise to the challenge of authentic selfhood, Tom must admit his need to be referred to another in permanent union. His only genuine escape from the haunting self-presence of his own individuality is to find a grounded connection with a woman; and yet, there are seemingly none to hand who would furnish this self-consummating sense of connection. The moment he first sees Lydia there is an instant recognition for Tom that he has found his mate: 'That's her', he said involuntarily (p. 27). Something other than his conscious mind is speaking at this moment, something deeper and more primeval in him. In Lawrence's subsequent description, the farmer now finds himself in a wholly different dimension to the one he normally resides within in his everyday life:

> She had passed by. He felt as if he were walking again in a far world, not Cossethay, a far world, the fragile reality. He went on quiet, suspended, rarified. He could not bear to think or to speak, not to make any sound or sign, nor change his fixed motion. He could scarcely bear to think of her face. He moved within the knowledge of her, in the world that was beyond reality. (ibid.)

At the wedding celebration of Will Brangwen and Anna, Tom Brangwen, now well into staid and settled middle age, attempts to articulate to the gathered company of his brothers and their wives his thinking about the vital necessity for permanent union with another. His speech is taken as the incoherent ramblings of a man half way to drunkenness, but we see within it something of Lawrence's own thinking of human relatedness. The central image of the speech is the notion that a united man and woman constitute an angelic entity which surpasses in kind anything the constituent individuals could attain to alone. Compared with the transmogrification brought about in this way, any attempts to refine and perfect attributes of the isolated self are vain and essentially worthless:

> There's very little else, on earth, but marriage. You can talk about making money, or saving souls. You can save your own soul seven times over, and you may have a mint of money, but your soul goes gnawin', gnawin', grawin', and it says there's something it must have. In heaven there is no marriage. But on earth there is marriage, else heaven drops out, and there's no bottom to it. (Lawrence 1997, p. 136)

The farmer's speech about each marriage constituting 'one Angel' is quickly dissipated by the humorous heckling of the assembled company, but it still stands as a fitting tribute to the man who, having known the satisfaction of two decades with his wife, is soon to die at the hands of a night-time flood on the farm. He thereby bears witness, as representative of the first generation of Brangwens described in Lawrence's narrative, to the ineluctable task that will face all generations to come. Ostensibly, the author was led to write *The Rainbow* in order to establish more firmly the family history out of which the two sisters, Ursula and Gudrun, issue and in reference to which they live. While there is certainly a very different tone and register in his subsequent novel, *Women in Love*, what Lawrence relates of the two sisters in their efforts to become 'one Angel' in their relationships with Rupert and Gerald, gains huge depth and resonance when read in the context of the previous generations' struggles within marriage. There is, arguably, a true historical dialectic of love on display here, though the ultimate aim of this process is far from easy to identify and articulate.

The second generation depicted in *The Rainbow* centres on the marriage of Anna and Will. Vital elements in the portrayal relate to landscape and labour. On the first topic, the married couple remains in the village of Cossethay, living in a cottage next to the village church, in sight of the small churchyard and its lines of lugubrious yew-trees. Only in later life, when they have a large family and the two eldest daughters are already largely independent women, will this generation of Brangwens move to a larger neighbouring town whose landscape is more redolent of industry than the natural cycles associated with farming. Much of their courting is carried out in the stables, a natural refuge for the lovers out of sight of Anna's parents. Like the scene where her stepfather comforted her on the night when her mother was giving birth to her first son, there is an earthy comfort available to the young lovers amid the snuffling animals:

> Sometimes, when it was cold, they stood to be lovers in the stables, where the air was warm and sharp with ammonia. And during these dark vigils, he learned to know her, her body against his, they drew nearer and nearer together, the kisses came more subtly close and fitting. So when in the thick darkness a horse suddenly scrambled to its feet, with a dull, thunderous sound, they listened as one person listening, they knew as one person, they were conscious of the horse. (Lawrence 1997, p. 129)

As with the 'flashing stars' in the earlier scene describing Tom Brangwen's lonely night spent lambing in the fields, so too here the presence of the animals acts as a fusing agent to bring the lovers into profound connection with one another. The same can be said of the location of the couple more generally, namely the village of Cossethay where the Marsh Farm and later Anna and Will forge a family life. The process whereby one generation cedes space to the other is also addressed, in very harrowing yet touching ways, by Lawrence. It is only with great initial reluctance that Anna's stepfather agrees to sanction her marriage to Will. The young man is far from being established in his work and has no money with which to start a family and keep a home. Anna's father, by contrast, is materially well off and is respected as a solid farmer in the area. He is able to hand on a considerable sum to his stepdaughter in addition to securing their cottage on a twenty-one-year lease. And yet these worldly trappings do not count in the father's eyes as achievements carrying any spiritual worth:

> Was his life nothing? Had he nothing to show, no work? He did not count his work, anybody could have done it. What had he known, but the long, marital embrace with his wife! Curious, that thus was what his life amounted to! And any rate, it was something, it was eternal [. . .]. But the bitterness, underneath, that there still remained an unsatisfied Tom Brangwen, who suffered agony because a girl cared nothing for him. He loved his sons – he had them also. But it was the further, the creative life with the girl, he wanted as well. Oh, and he was ashamed. He trampled himself to extinguish himself. (p. 127)

There is an important contrast of work and creation here which is worth noting. During his courtship, Will works at a wooden sculpture of the Biblical account of God's creation of Eve out of Adam's rib. This creative work stops abruptly after the couple marry and a bitter rancour soon enters their relationship. The 'creative life' Lawrence appears to be alluding to in the passage cited is the authentic love relation thanks to which our everyday life and work become magnified through a sense of immeasurable connectedness. When Anna was growing up and her mother was turned to the boys she was rearing, she and her father enjoy a true union of souls. The father has held up the far end of the rainbow, bringing the young girl under the protection of heaven. He also grounds her in the farming country surrounding the Marsh Farm, thereby enabling Anna to strike roots in new earth. But now, in the presence of her budding relationship with his nephew, the father's calling is to relinquish the girl whose healthy spiritual growth he has ensured. His union is singular and relates solely and ultimately to Anna's mother. This difficult passage, from one generation to the next, at once building on but razing the foundations built up over time, reaches a definitive crisis as Lawrence's narrative nears the contemporary moment of writing. And so, as we turn to *Women in Love*, we find the author tackling that most intractable of literary challenges: how to capture the spirit of the times in the midst of a life the author is both living and attempted to depict in artistic terms.

WOMEN IN LOVE: THE CRISIS OF CREATIVE LIFE

Although it was published five years after *The Rainbow*, the original narrative of *Women in Love* was conceived earlier. Given the timing of his work on it in the autumn of 1914, it is not implausible that Lawrence's intense work on his *Study of Thomas Hardy* played a significant, perhaps pivotal role, in his decision to write a 'prequel' to the book originally titled *The Sisters*. There are many elements in *The Rainbow* that suggest parallels with Hardy's novels, for example, the presence of the male singers outside the cottage of Will and Anna Brangwen on their wedding night. Another would be the early scene when Tom Brangwen is tending to the lambing on a cold February night under the 'flashing stars', which brings to mind the opening passages of *Far from the Madding Crowd*. More generally, there is an evocation of local landscape in *The Rainbow* that marks it out from among Lawrence's novels, a sense of place as something elemental and sheltering, something veritably eternal in its psychological and spiritual significance. The village of Cossethay and the Marsh Farm themselves anchor the narrative as it traverses the generations of the Brangwen family depicted. This atmosphere of constancy, the thickness of place-bound time, is quite other than the underlying tone that pervades *Women in Love*. F. R. Leavis (1955) captures the difference between the two novels in the following way:

> *Women in Love* is wholly self-contained, and, for all the carryover of names of characters, has no organic connexion with *The Rainbow*. And, in a radical way, in fact, it refuses to be seen as establishing any continuity with the earlier-published novel: it represents, so decisively, a different phase in Lawrence's art. And, intimately related in conception and gestation as we can see the two books to have been, the order of publication puts them in their right places. *The Rainbow* is essentially a younger work, anterior in experience to *Women in Love*. Going back from *Women in Love* to *The Rainbow*, we can see that the later-published work, though not a sequel, does truly 'come after' and has *this* behind it: we can watch in the patently younger work Lawrence arriving at the themes and preoccupations and distinctive approaches to life in *Women in Love*. (p. 109)

The most obvious distinction between *The Rainbow* and *Women in Love* is the latter's contemporaneity. While conceived before the onset of the Great War, the latter novel was not published until after it. Cultural reception of the meaning of this conflict was generally focused, unsurprisingly, on the sense of collapse and dissolution. Lawrence was personally incensed by the war and consistently denounced its spiritual destructiveness. In common with others within what might be described as the intellectual class, he saw the war as a kind of inevitable conclusion of the mechanization of work and human society more generally. In stark terms, Lawrence sees the generative principle of love as opposed, in an elemental but ultimately dialectical manner, with the dissolving principle of death. His vision here is redolent of the earliest pre-Socratic thinkers in the ancient Greek philosophical tradition, for whom universal cosmic principles are the only means to capture the push and pull of observable natural phenomena. In a letter from 2 November 1915 Lawrence sets out his thinking at the time on the eternal opposition of love and war:

> If I love, then, I am in direct opposition to the principle of war. If war prevails, I do not love. If love prevails, there is no war. War is the great and necessary disintegrating autumnal process. Love is the great creative process, like spring, the making of an integral unity out of many disintegrated factors. We have had enough of the disintegrating process. If it goes on any further, we shall so thoroughly have destroyed the unifying force from among us, we shall have become each one of us so completely a separate entity, that the whole will be an amorphous heap, like sand, sterile, hopeless, useless, like a dead tree. This is true, and it is so great a danger, that one goes mad facing it. (Lawrence 1932, pp. 265–66)

While the descriptions and feel of *Women in Love* are clearly more or less contemporaneous with the point of writing, Lawrence consciously avoided affixing any explicit time indices to his narrative. He begins with the two sisters, Ursula and Gudrun Brangwen, at their family home discussing the merits of marriage. The spiritual meaning and necessity of marital union remains the abiding theme of the novel, focused as it is throughout on the two relationships: between Ursula and Rupert Birkin on the one hand and Gudrun and Gerald Crich on the other. While the former pair achieves a kind of resolution through marriage, the destructive and dissolving principle wins through in the depiction of the latter.

In terms of Lawrence's explicit understanding of the novel, what is striking is his ambivalence towards it being taken as an attempt to encapsulate the 'spirit of the times'. His short 'Foreword' to *Women in Love* at once avows engagement with the great ongoing events of the time and yet insists that the material stems from nothing more than ruminations on the deeply personal experiences of the author. Accordingly, on the one hand, he writes of his wish that 'the bitterness of the war be taken for granted in the characters', while insisting that the novel 'pretends only to be a record of the writer's own desires, aspirations, struggles; in a word, a record of the profoundest experiences in the self' (Warren and Moore 1968, pp. 275–76). This sentiment, however, does not prevent Lawrence from adopting a much more universal, veritably prophetic register later in the 'Foreword':

> We are now in a period of crisis. Every man who is acutely alive is acutely wrestling with his own soul. The people that can bring forth the new passion, the new idea, this people will endure. Those others, that fix themselves in the old idea, will perish with the new life strangled unborn within them. Men must speak out to one another. (p. 276)

For Lawrence, then, *Women in Love* is his earnest testimony to the 'passionate struggle into conscious being' (ibid.). It is a deeply philosophical work, in the sense that it constitutes an intense effort to understand the meaning of the historical moment in which Lawrence finds himself caught up. How do our overarching themes of labour and landscape permit us to articulate this struggle to articulate historical meaning in the novel? Beginning with the two sisters who form the nucleus of the original conception, Ursula continues to work as a local school teacher, in continuity with her position described in detail in *The Rainbow*. Her younger sister, Gudrun, has attended art college in London and consequently enjoys a wider social circle which includes members of the English upper class.

Of the male pair, Birkin holds the position of school inspector and Gerald Crich is the eldest son the most powerful local mine and landowner. Gerald's attitude towards mining and the local miners is portrayed as almost exclusively instrumental and emotionally detached. He is the new broom making a clean sweep of his father's antiquated ways of running the concern and his sympathetic, almost mawkish solicitude of the needy miners and their families. With the possible exception of Gudrun, all four characters' labour is regarded as a largely extraneous and non-essential factor in their lives. In this connection it is notable that the culminating chapters of the novel involve the two pairs of lovers leaving behind their country and their respective work-ties in order to put the meaning of their respective relationships to the test. In this test, Ursula and Rupert succeed while Gudrun and Gerald fail.

Given the world known to Lawrence as a child and a young man – the world of northern English mining country at the end of the nineteenth century – the descriptions of the working class in *Women in Love* have an unmistakable sense of psychological distance relative to those found in *Sons and Lovers*. Of course, even in the earlier novel the underlying pathos was one of emotional limitations and the stifling of spiritual growth for the principal character, Paul Morel. But there remained a sense of grounded and healthy intimacy within Lawrence's descriptions of everyday working-class life that gives way to an atmosphere of dispassionate separation, even radical incomprehensibility, in *Women in Love*. The scene of Birkin's botched and ultimately farcical proposal to Ursula can stand as a point of comparison with the moving scene of Tom Brangwen's proposal to her grandmother, Anna, in the opening chapters of *The Rainbow*. The character of Rupert Birkin, given to speeches about the metaphysics of love, is clearly a manner of self-portrait by Lawrence. The day after a pivotal scene, when Ursula discovers Birkin near the mill house obsessively attempting to obliterate the reflection of the moon on the surface of the water, the man decides: 'They must marry at once, and so make a definite pledge, enter into a definite communion' (Lawrence 1998, p. 264). The description of his walk to the Brangwen family home suggests Christ's self-sacrificial entry into Jerusalem or Jude's first face-to-face encounter with Christminster:

> He drifted on swiftly to Beldover, half-conscious of his own movement. He saw the town on the slope of the hill, not struggling, but as if walled-in with the straight, final streets of miners'-dwellings, making a great square, and it looked like Jerusalem to his fancy. The world was all strange and transcendent. (ibid.)

While Tom Brangwen looked through the rectory window at Lydia and the child Anna, marvelling at their self-containment in the quiet interior while the wind blew under the distant stars, Birkin is confronted by Ursula's father, Will Brangwen, as a basic nullity that feigns progeniture but has no essential connection to the daughter Birkin has come to seek permanent union with. This imputed emptiness of the working-class man and household is acerbic and disturbing in its directness:

> Birkin could see only a strange, inexplicable almost patternless collection of passions and desires and suppressions and traditions and mechanical ideas, all cast unfused and disunited into this slender, bright-faced man of nearly fifty years, who was as unresolved now as he was at twenty, and as uncreated. How could he be the parent of Ursula, when he was not created himself. He was not a parent. A slip of living flesh had been transmitted through him, but the spirit had not come from him. The spirit had not come from any ancestor, it had come out of the unknown. A child is a child of the mystery, or it is uncreated. (Lawrence 1998, p. 265)

On the simplest level, Lawrence is here mocking the social custom of the father's 'giving away' the bride. On a more profound level, Lawrence is alluding to his notion of true individuality that was articulated in his *Study of Thomas Hardy*. There is a mediating, third approach, one that refers back to social class. Lawrence was a child of working-class parents. He was intelligent, received high levels of formal education, and trained as a schoolteacher. Unlike Hardy's Jude, Lawrence was neither repulsed by the academy nor was he undone by social opprobrium on account of his unconventional marriage. From 1912 on Lawrence moved in social circles that were far above those of his working-class origins, and forged friendships with many of the leading British writers, artists, and thinkers of the day. He was horrified at the tawdry ugliness of the industrial landscape he had grown up in and managed to escape, and the radicality and relative rapidity of his separation from this milieu was bound to give rise to a profound reaction in his sensibility and thinking.

While the antagonism between a father and the one who comes to claim his daughter in marriage was amply displayed already in *The Rainbow*, it is the radical clash of worldviews that stands out in Birkin's encounter with Will Brangwen:

> There was a complete silence, because of the utter failure in mutual understanding. Birkin felt bored. The father was not a coherent human being, he was roomful of old echoes. The eyes of the younger man rested on the face of the elder. Brangwen looked up, and saw Birkin looking at him. His face was covered was inarticulate anger and humiliation and sense of inferiority in strength.
>
> 'And as for beliefs, that's one thing,' he said. 'But I'd rather see my daughters dead tomorrow than that they should be at the beck and call of the first man that likes to come and whistle for them.'
>
> A queer, painful light came into Birkin's eyes. (Lawrence 1998, p. 267)

Lawrence is here portraying, in a starkly candid manner, the gulf between the traditional working-class outlook of the Brangwens – intent as they are on protecting the good social standing of their children – and the sophisticated sense of social autonomy held by the formally educated middle class to which Birkin belongs. Admittedly, as he is described, Birkin does not readily accept any kind of group or class identity but insists on his sense of exceptional individuality. For all that, his desired union with Ursula possesses him, at this stage in the narrative, as a kind of necessity. His notion that the spirit of Ursula has come 'from the unknown' marks her, equally, as possessing this sense of inviolable autonomy. From the description of her late youth and early adulthood in *The Rainbow*, we know of Ursula's protracted but ultimately failed attempt at union with Anton Skrebensky. Her rejection of this lover is based on his failure to remain in contact with his individual self as expressed in his concern to meet conventional social expectations of him. As the main mouthpiece of his doctrine of freedom, however, it is important to note that Birkin seeks self-realization through profound communion. Birkin is driven by a sense of fate that is, despite all the differences of detail and tone, redolent of the proposal scene set two generations earlier:

> The two men sat in complete silence, Birkin almost completely unconscious of his own whereabouts. He had come to ask her to marry him – well, then, he would wait on, and ask her. As for what she said, whether she accepted or not, he did not think about it. He would say what he had come to say, and that was all he was conscious of. He accepted the complete insignificance of this household, for him. But everything now was as if fated. He could see one thing ahead, and no more. From the rest, he was absolved entirely for the time being. It had to be left to fate and chance to resolve the issues. (Lawrence 1998, pp. 268–69)

In a remarkable chapter of his *Study of Thomas Hardy* entitled 'Work and the Angel and the Unbegotten Hero', Lawrence writes in detail about his conception of true individuality. Here he writes of the essentially twofold nature of work: on the one hand, we work for sheer necessity in order to sustain biological life; on the other hand, it is a matter of 'the bringing of life into human consciousness' (Steele 1985, p. 41). It is this latter process that constitutes the specific work of becoming individual. Seen through this conception, we gain a compelling means of appreciating Lawrence's portrayal of character development in both *The Rainbow* and *Women in Love*. In the former, this process is charted over decades and generations, and this historic scope allows Lawrence to show a kind a slow evolutionary transformation. For all that, there is no real sense in *The Rainbow* that consciousness and individuality are more effectively realized through the work of each successive generation. Quite the contrary. When the gauge of success is the quality of genuine union in marriage, it is the initial pairing of Tom Brangwen and Lydia Lensky that seems the most profoundly achieved. The intermediary marriage of Anna and Will Bragwen is riven with initial hostility and then quiescence, Anna undergoing a seemingly endless series of pregnancies and Will finding solace in his civic roles of choir master and, later, craft teacher.

In the final section of *The Rainbow*, Ursula is unable to find any kind of lasting union with Skrebensky and the ending depicts her miscarriage and sense of bitter isolation, trapped in a meaningless and unrewarding life of home and work. All that remains to her is the metaphysical vision of the rainbow with its vague promise of resurrection and new life. In the language of the *Study of Thomas Hardy*, what is left to Ursula to do is the work of achieved conscious individuality:

> It seems as if the great aim and purpose in human life were to bring all life into human consciousness. And this is the final meaning of work: the extension of human consciousness. [. . .] But the bringing of life into human consciousness is not an aim in itself, it is only a necessary condition of the progress of life itself. Man is himself the vivid body of life, rolling glimmering against the void. In his fullest living he does not know what he does, his mind, his consciousness, unacquaint, hovers behind, full of extraneous gleams and glances. and altogether void of knowledge. Altogether devoid of knowledge and conscious motive is he when he is heaving into uncreated space, when he is actually living, becoming himself. (Steele 1985, p. 41)

This depiction of proper human work – the realization of authentic self – passes, then, beyond consciousness or self-consciousness and becomes a kind of post-conscious fate-like doing. It is truly a manner of consummation and self-realization. Most crucially, this achievement of self is clearly only possible for Lawrence – in his critical writings but also in his novels – in and through profound moments of encounter with others. Thus, we are faced with what is perhaps Lawrence's most significant and central paradox: that becoming oneself is only possible by overcoming oneself through radical connection to others.

It is here that we can return to the other principal theme in this book, namely to landscape. If there are two essential aspects or dimensions of work for Lawrence (work as the means to biological survival and work as bringing a person to authentic consciousness), can the same be said of the meaning of landscape for the author? Ursula's culminating Biblical vision of promise at the end of *The Rainbow* is set against the backdrop of desolation within the local mining country. The diction Lawrence employs here, as in other salient passages describing the industrialized landscape, centres on allusions to biological decay and degeneration. It is a veritable death in apparent life, a kind of putrescence at the heart of all the movement and change that characterizes restless modern existence:

> [. . .] she saw the hard, cutting edges of the new houses, which seemed to spread over the hillside in their insentient triumph of horrible, amorphous angles and straight lines, the expression of corruption triumphant and unopposed, corruption so pure that it is hard and brittle: she saw the dun atmosphere over the blackened hills opposite, the dark blotches of houses, slate roofed and amorphous, brittle, hard edged new houses advancing from Beldover to meet the corrupt new houses from Lethley, the houses of Lethley advancing to mix with the houses of Hainor, a dry, brittle, terrible corruption spreading over the face of the land, and she was sick with a nausea so deep that she perished as she sat. (Lawrence 1997, p. 493)

In reading this passage, I am reminded of a similar experience of my own childhood and early adulthood. I grew up not in Lawrence's Nottinghamshire but on the edge of Cheshire where it blends into Merseyside. My native landscape was flat, lacking the nearby hills and fells of Derbyshire onto which Lawrence could look when a child and young man. While there were the nearby picturesque villages of the Wirral, these were seldom visited and the landscape inhabited was one of endless houses, mostly built within the previous twenty to thirty years, with little to break up the stifling claustrophobia of this domestic milieu. There was an older part of my native town, Ellesmere Port, that consisted of the very type of terraced working-class housing described by Lawrence in his short, autobiographical essay 'Nottingham and the Mining Countryside'. As an adolescent I lived in such a house, with its concreted back yard and alleyway that skirted the facing 'back-to-back' terraced house. The town-centre did boast a few Depression-era civic buildings (a central library and civic centre), but mostly it was taken up by a badly designed outdoor shopping mall that was always seemingly threatened by terminal economic decay. As I came into consciousness of my native landscape, a growing sense of resentment and a desire to escape it grew with ever greater insistence in my mind. In Lawrence's essay, he rails against the industrialized landscape as a veritable crime against working-class humanity:

> The real tragedy of England, as I see it, is the tragedy of ugliness. The country is so lovely: the man-made England is so vile. I know that the ordinary collier, when I was a boy, had a peculiar sense of beauty, coming from his intuitive and instinctive consciousness, which was awakened down pit. And the fact that he met with just cold ugliness and raw materialism when he came up into daylight, and particularly when he came to the Square or the Breach, and to his own table, killed something in him, and in a sense spoiled him as a man. (McDonald 1968, p. 137)

Returning to *Women in Love*, this tone of repulsion at the ugliness and decay of the working-class milieu of the mining country found at the conclusion of *The Rainbow*, is picked up in the opening description of the sisters' walk to witness the local wedding. Gudrun has, by the age of twenty-three, attained a minor reputation as an artist in London. She is regarded with a kind of sneering respect by the local people with whom she grew up. Ursula, a broken engagement and miscarriage behind her, has remained on her vocational path as a teacher but is tortured by the sense of failing to find a way through to true development into self-realization: 'Her active living was suspended, but underneath, in the darkness, something was coming to pass' (Lawrence 1998, p. 7). At the same time, Gudrun is ruminating on the wisdom of her return to her hometown, having enjoyed an altogether more brilliant life in London and its environs. Over the three years of her absence, she has grown quite unused to and seemingly defenceless against the ugliness of her native landscape and its hardened working-class inhabitants:

> Gudrun, new from her life in Chelsea and Sussex, shrank cruelly from this amorphous ugliness of a small colliery town in the Midlands. Yet forward she went, through the whole sordid gamut of pettiness, the long amorphous, gritty street. She was exposed to every stare, she passed on through a stretch of torment. It was strange that she should have chosen to come back and test the full effect of this shapeless, barren ugliness on herself. Why had she wanted to submit herself to it, did she still want to submit herself to it, the insufferable torture of these mean, ugly, meaningless people, this defaced countryside? She felt like a beetle toiling in the dust. She was filled with repulsion. (p. 9)

While the bulk of the narrative in *Women in Love* is set in the refined context of country manor houses, amid the urban sophistication of London, or, in the culminating section, in a guest house in the snow-covered Alps, there are occasional encounters with the local urban landscape and its people. One notable example of this is the scene at the market where Ursula and Birkin purchase a chair, only to give it away to a young working-class couple. In Lawrence's description, Ursula experiences striking ambivalence towards the place and its inhabitants, finding herself 'superficially thrilled when she found herself out among the common people' (Lawrence 1998, p. 368). She observes the young couple: 'She excitedly watched a young woman, who was going to have a baby, and who was turning over a mattress and making a young man, down-at-heel and dejected, feel it also' (ibid.).

After Birkin and Ursula buy an antique chair they argue about the superiority of England's cultural past relative to their present moment and, as a consequence, Ursula decides to give the chair away to the young couple. There is a parallel between the two couples, poised as they both are on the brink of marriage. Yet there is also a gulf between them, the one bound to live out their lives in the local vicinity and the other intending to uproot themselves and travel the world. Amid the affinity and the distance between the two couples Lawrence captures the lines of attraction. Accordingly, the working-class woman feels a certain admiration for Ursula who, in turn, is strangely drawn to the young man:

> She was attracted by the young man. He was a still, mindless creature, hardly a man at all, a creature that the towns have produced, strangely purebred and fine in one sense, furtive, quick, subtle. His lashes were dark and long and fine over his eyes, that had no mind in them, only a dreadful kind of subject, inward consciousness, glazed and dark. His dark brows and all his lines were finely drawn. He would be a dreadful, but wonderful lover to a woman, so marvellously contributed. His legs would be marvellously subtle and alive, under the shapeless trousers, he had some of the fineness and stillness and silkiness of a dark-eyed, silent rat. (p. 372)

After they have gone their separate ways, Ursula and Birkin discuss how they differ from the young couple, and Birkin suggests the working-class pair are like the Biblical meek who shall inherit the earth while they, by contrast, 'want to be disinherited' (p. 376). This disinheritance refers to their imminent exile, when they will openly and gladly embrace a state of permanent homelessness. And here resides one of the great paradoxes of Lawrence: his passionate attachment to the landscapes he knew, in childhood and beyond, and yet his desire to remain unattached to it through an intentional state of exile. Not that this amounted to a paradox to the writer himself, who believed that to *see* a landscape for what it was he needed to refuse any kind of possessive, permanent habitation within in. The state of exile is also clearly a symptom of another element of Lawrence's sensibility, namely his intuition that his historical epoch was a period of inchoateness, a kind of lacuna between a past whose meaning was waning rapidly and a future whose contours were as yet unknown. Hence, Lawrence inhabited a kind of transitional space, a place where change is lived as such and a condition of exile is the price to be paid for remaining open to an unknown future.

This necessary state of exile runs through all three of Lawrence's novels that we have considered here: in *Sons and Lovers* it is Paul Morel's childhood and early adulthood that gives way to the move outwards to education; in *The Rainbow* there is the continuity of place as a foil to gradual spiritual exile; and in *Women in Love* there is the climactic move away from England to continental Europe. In more conventional literary terms, this trilogy marks the phases of a coming-of-age narrative or *Bildungsroman*. The key thing to acknowledge here is that Lawrence regarded these depictions of personal upheaval as microcosms pointing to the need for a universal process of humanity's spiritual renewal.

Throughout the last decade of his life (1921–1930), Lawrence wrote many essays on what his sense of such renewal amounted to. On the one hand, Lawrence recognized that the process of general education, together with political agitation, had brought the great masses of industrial working-class men to despise the work they did. On the other hand, he contends, working-class women have grown tired of the endless physical drudgery required of them to keep their homes and families 'decent'. The result, in Lawrence's terms, is that the working-class as a whole is in revolt against its body and is being rendered 'abstract': 'The vast majority of the lower classes – and this is most extraordinary – are even more grossly abstracted, if we may use the term, than the educated classes. The uglier sort of working man today truly has no body and no real feelings at all' (Roberts and Moore 1968, p. 590). In the short autobiographical sketch written shortly before and published shortly after his death, Lawrence left us with a final vision of a future of renewal and restitution in the face of this universal revulsion against the physical:

> Do away with it all, then. At no matter what cost, start in to alter it. Never mind about wages and industrial squabbling. Turn the attention elsewhere. Pull down my native village to the last brick. Plan a nucleus. Fix the focus. Make a handsome gesture of radiation from the focus. And then put up big buildings, handsome, that sweep to a civic centre. And furnish them with beauty. And make an absolute clean start. Do it place by place. Make a new England. Away with little homes! Away with scrabbling pettiness and paltriness. Look at the contours of the land, and build up from these, with a sufficient nobility. (McDonald 1968, p. 140)

Here we see Lawrence's childhood yearning long surviving into his adult years of exile. He is still, at the end of his life, filled with a desire to tear town and build up anew, to ennoble his native countryside with beautiful buildings to counter the industrial squalor and wreckage. In this final stage of his life, he remains possessed by a vision – like Jude's vision of a New Jerusalem – to construct a collective human relationship worthy of the natural landscape he had revered as a child and left as a grown man. He sees what the work might be that would resolve and heal an industrial civilization grown weary with its own 'progress'. It is, to the last, this crisis of civilization and his search for an adequate response to it that drives Lawrence's evocations of landscape and labour throughout his writing life.

Chapter 4

New Land, New Labour

WORKING THE LAND: THE ENGLISH WORKING CLASS AND THE STRUGGLE FOR SOCIAL VALUE

Throughout our examination of Eliot, Hardy, and Lawrence the experience of the local setting – of its climatic conditions, topography, cultural traditions, and ways of work – has been accentuated. While all three authors offer profound explorations of protagonists' connection to place, the drama of their narratives is almost invariably generated by movement: movement to a new place as is the case in *Silas Marner*, movement between places as is most prominent in *Jude the Obscure*, or movement quite beyond the known and familiar place as we found at the end of the last chapter when considering *Women in Love*. It is inevitable that these comings and goings represented in the novels studied represent signs of social and personal development.

Movement forwards is a readymade metaphor for such development, while movement backwards connotes some kind of regression or at least hesitancy. Clym Yeobright's return to Egdon Heath, in defiance of his aunt's expectation that he continue on his glorious path of self-improvement, is a powerful case in point. When Lawrence returned to England, towards the end of his life, his mindset of exile was so pronounced that he could see nothing other than a reality of despoliation and an ideal possibility of potential radical transformation. In *The Mill on the Floss*, Tom Tulliver's efforts to reclaim Dorlcote Mill and reinstall what remained of his family there ends with the tragedy of the flood and the death of the brother and sister, united in the final striking scene as they sink below the water in a last mortal embrace. The process of finding oneself, in childhood, in profound connection to a certain place, moving away from it in early adulthood, and returning to it after a series of mature experiences recapitulates and highlights certain elements of a much more general social process.

Towards the end of his sprawling and highly influential study, *The Making of the English Working Class,* Thompson (1968) charts the growth in self-consciousness of a body of workers whose formative experiences hinged on the transformations and dislocations that came with the advent of truly industrialized work from the 1770s on. The stresses placed on the labouring classes as the primary source of wealth passes from land to production made permanent changes to the social contours of England. The first novels considered in our study – Eliot's *Adam Bede* and *Silas Marner* – look back to the period of the early years of the Napoleonic Wars when the combination of a politically conservative milieu and a radically transformative economy placed the certainties of rural English culture very much in question.

This places Eliot, as author, in a strangely ambiguous position: not only does she live in the knowledge of the distance that separates her from the period described, but she also holds her own position in the class structure first coming into existence during the epoch portrayed. Certainly, there are the famous passages redolent of self-conscious nostalgia in Eliot, but these are more than offset by her descriptions of her protagonists' sense of personal development and often uneasy relationship with the set patterns of social standing. This latter element – the search for meaningful personal identity – reaches a pitch of permanent crisis by the time the author has attained to full maturity in her novel writing with *Middlemarch*. The historical setting of this novel amid the political turmoil surrounding the first Great Reform Act of 1832 is telling when we consider Thompson's (1968) sense of English working-class historical consciousness:

> To step over the threshold, from 1832 to 1833, is to step into a world in which the working-class presence can be felt in every county in England, and in most fields of life.
>
> The new class consciousness of working people may be viewed from two aspects. On the one hand, there is a consciousness of the identity of interests between working men of the most diverse occupations and levels of attainment, which was embodied in many institutional forms, and which was expressed on an unprecedented scale in the general unionism of 1830–34. This consciousness and these institutions were only to be found in fragmentary form in the England of 1780.
>
> On the other hand, there was a consciousness of the identity of the interests of the working class, or 'productive classes' as against those of other classes; and within this there was maturing the claim for an alternative *system*. (pp. 887–88)

As we saw in chapter 1, Eliot approaches this crucial period in which the class consciousness of the workers is forged in England by focusing on a particular type of worker – the skilled and autonomous craftsman – and accentuating individual moral characteristics over any depiction of overt political praxis. In other words, Eliot mirrors to her upper-middle-class readership their ideal image of a working-class man: someone who is deferential to upper-class authority, who defends the social status quo by preferring his allotted station in life, and who displays his virtues privately in his dealing with others rather than through the more general means of political action and social reform.

In Hardy the situation is essentially the same, though the centre of gravity of the author's sympathy has certainly shifted by the time he writes his final novel. Jude Fawley is unambiguously a man denied his natural rights by the social setting he encounters. His tragedy is not merely a personal tale of misfortune but unmistakably represents a more general caution against the unfairness of a social system that maintains the working class within a cage that stunts and eventually kills any native sense of initiative or free development. By the time we reach Lawrence and his early novels in the second decade of the twentieth century, Hardy's depictions of the working-class in the 1890s have been definitively surpassed and there is a world evidently available to Lawrence's workers that, if not generally attainable, is at least accessible in a limited manner. In sum, what our selected novelists' record is the first hundred years of social history following the making of the English working class.

In the period immediately following the Great Reform Act of 1832 it became clearer than ever to the English working class that the state did not work with their interests in mind. Voting rights had indeed been expanded and the demarcation of electoral districts reformed, but the vast majority of workers still lacked the franchise. While industrialization had brought rapid expansion in the population of the cities, the English countryside remained densely populated and agricultural labour remained vital to the everyday reality of the working class. One of the most notorious political elements that accompanied industrialization in England from the 1770s on were the numerous parliamentary enclosure acts which removed rights of commoning that were generally informal and customary rights to use land for grazing or gathering that passed from one generation to another. Pressures to produce more monetized yield from the land prompted landowners to enclose the commons for specific productive purposes. In tandem with this process, the lease-holding rights of local workers were generally limited in duration and homes could be seized and razed by local landowners at will.

In light of these forces and processes it becomes necessary to challenge the standard idea about industrialization in England that it was something concentrated, more or less exclusively, in the burgeoning industrial cities and towns. Instead, as Williams (1973) observes, it was rather a matter of a new economic and social order spreading into every country town and village, thereby linking city and country in a tight fabric of capitalist relations:

> The essential connections between town and country, which had been evident throughout, reached a new, more explicit and finally critical stage. It was characteristic of rural England, before and during the Industrial Revolution, that it was exposed to increasing penetration by capitalist social relations and the dominance of the market, just because these had been powerfully evolving within its own structures. By the late eighteenth century we can properly speak of an organised capitalist society, in which what happened in the market, anywhere, whether in industrial or agricultural production, worked its way through to town and country alike, as parts of a single crisis. (p. 98)

If we accept this observation as valid and reflect back on our discussion of the novels of Eliot and Hardy, we must acknowledge two things: first, that the typically rural settings do not merit the title 'rural backwaters', as though they were somehow secluded enclaves of land cut off from the revolutionizing impacts of capitalist production. Secondly, that the tendency on the authors' part to accentuate differences of kind between the city and the country is motivated by complex and often contradictory factors and impulses.

One such salient factor stems from the by then well-established Romantic belief that the countryside was a place where individual sensibility could more effectively and intensively develop. Intellectually speaking, this notion arguably stems from the influence of Rousseau (2007) who argued that sophisticated society taught children the value of affectations and inculcated dependence on others to meet basic needs. This idea became allied, through the work of Wordsworth (2008), with an anti-urban bias which insisted that rural innocence was doomed to be spoiled and corrupted by exposure to the degenerate social atmosphere of the city. In conjunction, these factors set the scene for the attitude of elegiac nostalgia often encountered in all three of the authors considered in this study.

At the same time, there is a distinct tension in the portrayals of rural life found in the novels of Eliot, Hardy, and Lawrence between the tendency to idealize country life and an impulse to record the actual social history. In the case of Eliot *Adam Bede* best illustrates this tension. First, we have the representation of the socially transformative impact of Methodism on English society as centred on Eliot's portrayal of Dinah Morris. As her psychological and social complement, Adam as a proudly independent artisan represents another dimension of the unfolding process of social transformation underway in England at the time. While the dramatic period of Eliot's narrative is the very end of the eighteenth century, the author writes in the knowledge of the ensuing sixty years of social history, years that were formative for her own childhood and subsequent adult experience. As Thompson (1968) makes clear, those years were radically transformative in the lived reality of the English artisan:

> What we can say with confidence is that the artisan *felt* that his status and standard-of-living were under threat or were deteriorating between 1815 and 1840. Technical innovation and the superabundance of cheap labour weakened his position. He had no political rights and the power of the State was used, if only fitfully, to destroy his trade unions. As Mayhew clearly showed, not only did under-pay (in the dishonourable trades) make for overwork; it also made for *less* work all round. It was this experience which underlay the political radicalization of the artisans and, more drastically, of the outworkers. Ideal and real grievances combined to shape their anger – lost prestige, direct economic degradation, loss of pride as craftsmanship was debased, lost aspirations to rise to being masters. (p. 289)

What is striking, then, is that Eliot is fully aware of this process that lies ahead in time for an artisan such as Adam. As represented, Adam is unsullied by any desire to politicize his position in the rural economy. Certainly, he pursues personal education in attending Bartle Massey's night school, but this desire for knowledge is limited to self-edification and the enhancement of practical skills. Most notably, Adam is content to accept the given social order and he suffers greatly when this order is violated not by himself but rather by the young squire, Arthur Donnithorne, when he seduces the milkmaid and Adam's love interest Hetty Sorel. Far from being a political radical, Adam is arguably the most socially conservative character in the novel, who displays throughout the narrative unwavering dedication to his work, great stoicism in the face of personal hardship, and assiduous attention to put right the wrongs done to Hetty.

There is, however, one aspect of Eliot's portrayal of Adam that does align him with the political radicalism of the artisans as captured by Thompson's political and social history: his desire for independence as a worker. Certainly, Adam is represented in the novel as strongly imbued by his staunch work ethic. The early scene when he discovers that his father, Thias Bede, has left undone the urgent task of completing a coffin needed first thing the following morning shows Adam willing and able to work through the night, impelled as he is by his pride as a conscientious worker. While Adam eschews his brother Seth's pious evangelicalism and adopts a much more humanistic blend of moderate faith, his commitment to hard work is uncompromising.

It is clear more generally from Eliot's depiction that Adam's character virtues are closely aligned with his strengths as a worker: diligence, endurance, perseverance, and a sense of duty towards the needs of others. In the context of the society in which he finds himself, it is also notable that Eliot more or less elides Adam's social class, granting him equal recognition by his social betters as much as his equals. The source of the almost universal regard in which Adam is held seems to stem from one conspicuous feature of the character: his independence. There is an implied connection here of great importance: independence of work allows for independence of thought. Thompson (1968) highlights this connection, while also pointing to its frustration in the subsequent history:

> If the agricultural labourers pined for land, the artisans aspired to an 'independence'. This aspiration colours much of the history of early working-class Radicalism. But in London the dream of becoming a small master (still strong in the 1790s – and still strong in Birmingham in the 1830s) could not stand up, in the 1820s and 30s, in face of the experiences of 'chamber' or 'garret' masters – an 'independence' which meant week-long slavery in warehouses or slop shops. This helps to explain the sudden surge of support towards Owenism at the end of the 1820s – trade union traditions and the yearning for independence were twisted together in the idea of social control over their own means of livelihood, a *collective* independence. (p. 290)

Thompson here alludes to the other leading passion of the emerging class of the time: the desire for land. It is his analysis of the popularity of the Chartist 'Land Plan' from the 1830s – partly realized through a lottery system that apportioned a certain number of acres to each working-class household for their own autonomous cultivation – that most directly bears on this class-based desire. There is an intergenerational process at work here: the generation that toiled on the land in the early decades of the 1800s transmits a collective memory to the generation of the 1830s–1840s who now increasingly work in the growing manufacturing cities of England. Thus, while the aspiration was first nurtured among the rural working class it became most overtly politicized in the context of the urban worker and a radicalized union movement:

> It is an historical irony that it was not the rural labourers but the urban workers who mounted the greatest coherent national agitation for the return of the land. Some of them were sons and grandsons of labourers, their wits sharpened by the political life of the towns, freed from the shadows of the squire. Some – the supports of the Land Plan – were weavers and artisans of rural descent: 'father, and grandfather and all folk belonging to I worked on land and it didn't kill them, and why should it kill me?' Faced with hard times and unemployment in the brick wastes of the growing towns, the memories of lost rights rose up with a new bitterness of deprivation. (Thompson 1968, pp. 255–56)

Independence in work and control over the land, then, are identified by Thompson as the great desiderata of the nineteenth-century English working class. And the seminal experience which underlies the attempts to satisfy these desires is that cooperation is necessary, that independence can only ever be realized through collective action. If we refer this point back to our previous chapter, what bearing does it have to Lawrence's depiction of the working-class culture of late nineteenth-century mining community in which he grew up?

In his late autobiographical essay 'Nottingham and the Mining Countryside' Lawrence looks back on his childhood milieu as to a 'life that was a curious cross between industrialism and the old agricultural England of Shakespeare and Milton and Fielding and George Eliot' (McDonald 1968, p. 135). He goes on to point out how the working conditions of the miners created an affective basis for the very collectivism that, according to Thompson, transformed the politics of the English working class in the early decades of the nineteenth century:

> Under the butty system, the miners worked underground as a sort of intimate community, they knew each other practically naked, and with curious close intimacy, and the darkness and the underground presence of danger, made the physical, instinctive, and intuitional contact between men highly developed, a contact almost as close as touch, very real and very powerful. This physical awareness and intimate *togetherness* was at its strongest down pit. They had, in a measure, to change their flow. Nevertheless, they brought with them above ground the curious dark intimacy of the mine, the naked sort of contact, and if I think of my childhood, it is always as if there was a lustrous sort if inner darkness, like the gloss of coal, in which we moved and had our real being. (p. 136)

In the opening passages of *The Rainbow* we clearly find something analogous to the close intimacy experienced by Lawrence in his childhood in his highly evocative portrayal of the agricultural labour of the generations of Brangwen men. In overtly sexualized terms, the men's rapport with the land is captured as something opening to the touch of the worker's hands and implements. For Lawrence, the key feature is the pervading intimacy that characterizes working-class lives. It is primarily but not exclusively in the context of work that this desire for intimacy is fulfilled. This intimacy involves the miners being absorbed within the immediate context of their lives, existing within their microcosm rather than tending to view themselves from this or that objectivizing perspective.

For Lawrence, the politicization of the miners and the growing self-consciousness of the working class more generally in the early twentieth century was not a development to be celebrated but rather something resulting in a spiritual diminishing of the kind of men he had grown up around. Collective improvement in working conditions was actually resulting, from Lawrence's perspective, in the vitiating of the miners' instinctual connection to beauty and the local natural and social environment:

> Now the colliers had also an instinct of beauty. The colliers' wives had not. The colliers were deeply alive, instinctively. But they had no daytime ambition, and no daytime intellect. They avoided, really, the rational aspect of life. They preferred to take life instinctively and intuitively. They didn't even care very profoundly about wages [. . .].
>
> The great fallacy is, to pity the man. He didn't dream of pitying himself, till agitators and sentimentalists taught him to. He was happy: or more than happy, he was fulfilled. Or he was fulfilled on the receptive side, not on the expressive. The collier went to the pub and drank in order to continue his intimacy with his mates. They talked endlessly, but it was rather of wonders and marvels, even in politics, than of facts. (McDonald 1968, p. 136)

I recognize this portrait of working-class men in my recollections of own grandfather. Born in the 1910s in Liverpool and having served for six years in the Navy during World War II, I remember his manners of speech and action during the times I stayed with my grandparents during the 1970s and 1980s. He loved to tell stories of his past life, but these narratives were always centred on his own sharp-tongued or humorous role. He never, to my recollection, had anything to say about the wider political events of the day. Both he and my grandmother lived more or less exclusively within the confines of the local social environment they inhabited, within a mile of the tower block in Childwall, Liverpool, where they spent the last twenty-five years of their lives.

I felt very content when with them, a feeling I enjoyed thanks to their satisfied and unambitious outlook on life. Their rented two-bedroom flat was modest but still a great improvement on the squalid terraced houses they had known before the war. 'The corporation' looked after all maintenance and improvements and, although in the 1980s there were perennial concerns about vandalism of the tower block's entrance and lifts, they knew most other residents of the block well and felt content to be there. I recall looking out from the concrete balcony to the swings, slide, and merry-go-round on the other side of the road; and to the pub, bowling green and betting shop lying just beyond, over the large grassy expanse. This encompassed the furthest extent of the lived world of my grandparents.

The intimacy and limitedness of working-class life, found in Lawrence's recollections of the mining community he grew up in and confirmed by my own childhood memories of my grandparents, are also identified and elaborated on by Richard Hoggart (2009) in his landmark study *The Uses of Literacy: Aspects of Working-Class Lives*. In the first part of the book, Hoggart draws extensively on his own experience of growing up in a working-class area of Leeds. One aspect of his descriptions that echoes Lawrence's earlier account of the colliery community he knew as a child is the accepted limitedness of the world inhabited by the working class:

> If we want to capture something of the essence of working-class life in a phrase, we must say that it is the 'dense and concrete life', a life whose main stress is on the intimate, the sensory, the detailed, and the personal [. . .].
>
> Working-class people are only rarely interested in theories or movements. They do not usually think of their lives as leading to an improvement in status or to some financial goal. They are enormously interested in people, they have the novelist's fascination with individual behaviour, with relationships – though not so as to put them into a pattern, but for their own sake. (Hoggart 2009, pp. 87–88)

One of the myths Hoggart sets out to debunk in his study is the sense that working-class people are, by and large, giving to political agitation to improve their lot. For Hoggart, quite the reverse is the case. Even at the individual level, he insists, a pronounced lack of ambition marks the outlook of working-class people: 'Once at work there is for most no sense of a career, of the possibilities of promotion. Jobs are spread around horizontally, not vertically, life is not seen as a climb, nor work as the main interest in it' (p. 66). Working-class life, for Hoggart as for Lawrence, is pervaded by a sense of stoical acceptance. For the political agitator or Marxist critic, of course, this attitude could be readily condemned as internalized oppression and a direct consequence of the working class being taught, from birth, to accept their lot within the rigid confines established and maintained by a capitalist social order.

What is common to Williams and Hoggart, as the two key founders of British cultural studies in the 1950s, is an effort to understand their own place and role as social theorists and academics relative to the working-class culture in which they grew up. Personally speaking, as Williams often writes about, there was the sense of displacement; of remaining, to some extent at least, in but not of the working class. But there is, also, the doubt and hesitation before the social verdict that they had risen above, or escaped, their working-class roots. Like Clym in *The Return of the Native* (a novel much loved by Williams), the two men return, in their key writings, to the working-class milieu in which they first learned to see and act in the world in an attempt both to understand and to pay homage to it A tension or contradiction is, however, intrinsic to this effort: for the very act of analysing working-class life presupposes gaining significant and irreversible distance from it.

In the case of Lawrence, as we have seen, there is a striking ambivalence towards the working-class world in which he came to consciousness. On the one hand, there is a pronounced revulsion at the sordidness of the built environment, at the way in which it despoils the beautiful landscape in which it is set. At the same time, there is an acutely sensitive environmental consciousness at work in the way Lawrence evokes the beauty of the natural environment of the English Midlands as a foil to the horrors of the industrial wasteland raised in its midst. This dual appreciation of local landscape is also apparent in his portrayal of the people. In his late autobiographical sketch, he very much genders this duality: praising the intimacy and appreciations of natural beauty among the colliers, as opposed to the worldly, materialistic ambition of the women.

What we find in these descriptions by Lawrence is a problem that haunts all three authors considered in this study: the extent to which there is a lived experience of solidarity between writer and subject, between the one who now writes at a distance and the child who lived among the places and people described in the novels. This is not merely a question of personal choices of attitude of a writer towards their past, but rather a matter of how to grapple with what Williams (1983) calls 'a divided culture, a form which includes an alienation' (p. 106):

> It is the more significant tension, of course with its awkwardnesses, its frequent uncertainties of tone, its spurts of bitterness and nostalgia, of the man caught by his personal history in the general crisis of the relation between education and class. What that crisis comes out as, in real terms, is the relation between intelligence and fellow-feeling, but this relation in the nineteenth and twentieth centuries had to be worked out at a time when education was consciously used to train members of a class and divide them from their passions as surely as from other men; the two processes, inevitably, are deeply connected. The writer moving through his history had to explore, as if on his own, the resources of what seemed to be and was not yet in fact a common language. In the novel, especially, this is the significant line of development. (Ibid.)

As we follow the line of development from Eliot to Lawrence, we find a pronounced sharpening of this struggle to find what Williams calls a 'common language'. While Eliot makes major breakthroughs in depicting the vernacular speech of her working-class characters, she ultimately remains most at ease with her educated, upper-middle-class protagonists who address others exclusively in the polite tones of received pronunciation. Hardy makes further strides, finding more effective focus on working-class characters, especially in the case of Tess and Jude in the final novels.

With Lawrence, the apologetic stance towards representing the lives of working-class characters, explicitly noted by Eliot and implied in many of Hardy's novels, has disappeared. Especially in his early short stories and novels, an authenticity of description and evocation is reached which makes his writing a permanent testimony to what Williams (1973) refers to as 'a cultural tradition much older and more central in Britain than the comparatively modern and deliberately exclusive circuit of what are called public schools' (p. 171). For Williams, however, it is vital to note that the achievements of Lawrence are ultimately long-range responses to a problem first made overt in Eliot's novels two generations earlier:

> It is a question of the relation between education – not the marks or degrees but the substance of a developed intelligence – and the actual lives of a continuing majority of our people: people who are not, by any formula, objects of record or study or concern, but who are specifically, literally, our own families. George Eliot is the first major novelist in whom this question is active. That is why we speak of her now with a connecting respect, and with a hardness – a sort of family plainness – that we have learned from our own and common experience.
>
> The problem of the knowable community is then, in a new way, a problem of language. (Ibid.)

Lawrence's development as a writer, his attempt to arrive at a new language of common experience, was tellingly shaped by his commitment to find, above all, a new way of living. Lawrence's self-imposed exile, which he sustained throughout most of the final two decades of his life, was chiefly motivated by a desire to find a more authentic mode of existence. It was a search for something elemental, something prior to the industrialized domestication he hated and feared from childhood. There was no resting place for Lawrence in terms of a permanent locale to which he remained attached for any length of time. His yearning for a native land was, instead, a desire conscious of the impossibility of its satisfaction. The ideal architectural scheme, sketched in his late autobiographical essay, for radical reconstruction of the country he knew from youth was deliberately utopian. It was not a plan to be realized, but rather a hope for a possible future. Equally, the schemes for alternative utopian communities are – as Birkin admits of his thwarted desire for brotherhood with Gerald – not anything Lawrence seriously intended to bring about. It was, in essence, a vision of a future the author felt he would not live to see. In the meantime, he would maintain his role as John the Baptist, looking ahead to a promised land with all the restless and sometimes almost fanatical zeal of a prophet unrecognized in his own country.

Chapter 4

THE CONTEMPORARY PROBLEM OF WORK UNDER NEOLIBERALISM

The underlying argument of this study is that the novels of Eliot, Hardy, and Lawrence offer invaluable insights into the British social history of work. Eliot's early novels centre on the working class and the various effects of work on character: it elevates Adam Bede and Dinah Morris, enervates Silas Marner, and offers an ambiguous redemption to Tom Tulliver. In Hardy, Tess suffers the hardships of hard agricultural work but also learns the social comforts of a supportive workplace. In Lawrence, by contrast, the entire edifice of twentieth-century capitalist work is rejected in favour of a vision of future community. In our own times, work has arguably reached a definitive point of crisis. This crisis can be captured in numerous different ways: most obviously, in terms of the precarity of paid work (the gig economy, zero-hours contracts, etc.); but also on the basis of the widespread sense of meaninglessness that comes with much contemporary employment (captured by David Graeber's [2019] notion of 'bullshit jobs'). Finally, there is the problem of a further wave of automation that threatens to reach into what have previously been considered highly skill professions (teachers, lawyers, or even doctors and surgeons). At the point of writing, all these factors impacting the current field of employment have been exacerbated by the dramatic impact of the coronavirus global pandemic.

The British novelists considered in this book all lived through different stages of capitalist economic and social development. They chose largely rural contexts for their settings and yet the social and psychological impacts of industrialization loom large, both in terms of the changes to the natural landscape and with regards to the patterns of work and social life. The current phase of global capitalism, however, is something none of these writers knew. The period of British social history covered in the novels examined in this book is the period between 1799 and 1913. *Adam Bede* and *Silas Marner* cover the early years of the Napoleonic Wars, while *Women in Love* stretches to the years immediately preceding World War I. Taken altogether, this was a period of unprecedented social upheaval, when the British working class agitated and organized to become the single most important factor in domestic political life. After suffering political persecution, military subjugation, and legal challenges, the principle of organized labour was finally allowed stable political and legal status in Britain with the Trade Union Act of 1871. As important as this was, however, it did little to stem the tide of growing working-class power in the decades that followed. Campaigns for reduced work hours, the eradication of child labour, and improved work conditions continued unabated. As the leading industrial nation in the nineteenth century, it was in Britain above all that Marx and Engel's proclaimed class struggle was being prosecuted and observed in all its twists and turns.

For the most part, however, the novels of Eliot, Hardy, and Lawrence are seldom read and studied for their depictions of work and class conflict. In the case of Eliot and Hardy, readers appreciate the charming depictions of English rural life with a fine sensitivity to antiquarian detail. While Lawrence's descriptions of the border country between Nottinghamshire and Derbyshire are invariably tinged by the author's ambivalence or even rancour with respect to English social life, still there are passages of astonishing pastoral beauty in a novel such as *The Rainbow*. Given this, it can be difficult to appreciate the novels in question for their depictions of the social realities of work. There is a further salient problem in this regard, namely the fact that we are living through a quite distinct phase of capitalism. The general accepted term for this is neoliberalism. Intellectually speaking, the origins of the neoliberal paradigm extend as far back as the Weimar Period in Germany, when economists and political scientists were concerned to chart a middle way between the perceived excesses of unregulated laissez-faire capitalism (which was seen as responsible for the post–World War I economic crisis in Germany) and the threat of totalitarian communism.

The realization of neoliberalism and a form of political governance, however, did not come about until the mid-1970s following the Oil Crisis of 1973. By that point, the unparalleled period of economic growth that followed the end of World War II had ground to a halt and some kind of major restructuring of the world economy was needed in order to stimulate further profits according to the terms of the capitalist economic model. For a Marxist thinker such as David Harvey (2005), the shift to neoliberalism was also principally impelled by a desire to re-establish capitalist class power in the face of the relative ascendency of working-class interests. By the time of the early 1970s, the distribution of wealth and income among the leading capitalist economies had never been some equitable.

In addition, the counter-cultural and student movements in places like the United States, France, and the United Kingdom had mounted an influential challenge to the ideological hegemony of capitalism. In the words of one famous slogan of the 1968 student and worker protests in France, the imperative amounted to a simple challenge: 'Never work!' This encapsulated the growing sense that the capitalist workplace was simply too soul-destroying and uncreative to be tolerated any more. Greater access to university education had also reached a broader swathe of the working class, opening horizons to an unprecedented degree. The widespread sense that the generation that was coming of age in the late 1960s and 1970s were lost to capitalism, combined with the falling profits of the leading capitalists, made the time ripe for a sudden and violent transition to neoliberalism. As Harvey (2005) relates:

Communist and socialist parties were gaining ground, if not taking power, across much of Europe and even in the United States popular forces were agitating for widespread reforms and state interventions. There was, in this, a clear *political* threat to economic elites and ruling classes everywhere, both in the advanced capitalist countries (such as Italy, France, Spain, and Portugal) and in many developing countries (such as Chile, Mexico, and Argentina). In Sweden, for example, what was known as the Rehn–Meidner plan literally offered to gradually buy out the owners' share in their own businesses and turn the country into a worker/share-owner democracy. But, beyond this, the *economic* threat to the position of ruling elites and classes was now becoming palpable. (p. 15)

The keyword of the neoliberal conception of the economy is flexibility. One explicit target in the wave of neoliberalization that swept the global economy from the 1970s on was the labour unions. Under collective bargaining, unions secure contracts for their workforce that set up fairly rigid boundaries around what an employer can and cannot do. The economic threat to elites highlighted by Harvey relates primarily to their share of wealth. In order to return a proportion of wealth more typical of other phases of capitalist development, union protections to workers more or less guaranteed through collectively bargained contracts had to be removed. In the case of Britain, high-profile direct confrontations with the coal miners' unions were crucially rationalized through an ideological argument concerning unproductive operations relative to the ability to source the commodity overseas at lower prices. The general argument employed here is simple: your work is worthless according to the logic of economic efficiency. One of the many things this argument ignores is the long-term community impacts of rendering the main source of employment null and void.

Throughout the 1980s in the United Kingdom, large swathes of northern England remained profoundly economically depressed. From my own childhood recollections of that period, I can remember the desolation of Liverpool – a city which still showed many visible signs of bombing from forty years earlier – with its ragged city centre and dilapidated housing. Growing up on the Wirral within the Merseyside area, I was told by a career counsellor in my final year of secondary school in 1986 that I should stay in education as 'there's nothing else out there for you'. Reactions to the situation in popular music expressed a mixture of ambivalence and defiance, Morrisey of the Smiths singing on *Still Ill*: 'I decree today that life is simply taking and not giving. England is mine, and it owes me a living.'

The sense of lacking a place in the job market and therefore facing a condition of economic and social uselessness is tackled extensively by the sociologist Richard Sennett. In his book *The Culture of the New Capitalism* Sennett

(2006) connects globalization and the endemic sense of uselessness among the workers of advanced capitalist economies since the 1980s:

> At home, the people who lose out would have to increase their human capital to compete, but few can do so; uncompetitive with these foreign peers, they face being no longer needed. The specter of uselessness here intersects with the fear of foreigners, which, beneath its crust of simple ethnic or race prejudice, is inflected with the anxiety that foreigners may be better armed for the tasks of survival. That anxiety has a certain basis in reality. Globalization names, among other things, a perception that the sources of human energy are shifting, and that those in the already developed world may be left out as a result. (Sennett 2006, pp. 89–90)

The connection made here between a widespread feeling among the domestic workforce that they have no meaningful place in the neoliberalized economy and the preference for cheaper foreign labour, creates a social psychological condition that has found pronounced expression in the wave of populism that has swept over US and UK politics in the last decade. As both Harvey and Sennett relate, one of the distinctive features of neoliberalism as a phase in capitalism's long history is the relentless and highly successful disciplining of the labour force. As we have seen in earlier chapters with reference to Thompson's (1968) exhaustive study, the emergence of the English working class was achieved through a series of collective actions and construction of collective institutions. These had the cumulative effect of constituting basic demands that the political and economic elite had to respond to and meet half-way. This certainly never precluded the direct use of state force and legislation to stymie the demands but the sense, between the 1840s and the 1950s, was that the arc of social history in Britain was bending in accord with the interests of the working class. This sense is precisely what was destroyed by neoliberalism which achieved, within a few short decades, a thorough demoralization of the British working class.

One of the intriguing ideas in Sennett's sociological diagnosis of the psychological impact of neoliberalism on the workforce is his notion that craftsmanship offers resources to overcome or at least mitigate the most corrosive effects. This idea is especially pertinent to this study, where we have noted how all three authors point to the positive effects of certain forms of autonomous, skilful work. Whether it is Adam Bede's pride in his woodworking skills, Giles Winterborne's knowledge of woodland crafts, or Will Brangwen's avocations of sculpture and organ playing, we are shown how pride in the work of the hand lends dignity and meaning in an individual's life. With these examples in mind, it is instructive to cite Sennett's account of the virtues of craftsmanship:

> *Craftsmanship* is a term most often applied to manual laborers and denotes the pursuit of quality in making a violin, watch, or pot. This is too narrow a view. Mental craftsmanship also exists, as in the effort to write clearly; social craftsmanship might lie in forging a viable marriage. An embracing definition of craftsmanship would be: doing something well for its own sake. Self-discipline and self-criticism adhere in all domains of craftsmanship; standards matter, and the pursuit of quality ideally becomes an end in itself. (Sennett 2008, pp. 103–4)

In this connection it is important to remember the craft of the writer who addresses us as reader. For novel writing is, of course, a meticulous mode of craft production. While Victorian-era writers such as Eliot and Hardy typically published novels in serial form distributed through periodicals that were subject to tight deadlines, Lawrence was freed from these terms of production. He appeared to overcompensate for this, however, at least in the earlier period of his novel writing, by composing multiple drafts of what was ostensibly the same story, *The Rainbow* and the *Women in Love* pairing being the most obvious case in point. Lawrence also dedicated much time to painting, gardening, and housework, all of which point to his felt need for skilful practice with his hands.

This illustrates another point that is central to Sennett's argument in *The Craftsman*, namely his critique of the time-honoured distinction in status between work of the head and work of the hand. Going back to Hannah Arendt's (2018 [1958]) hierarchy of value, as presented in her work *The Human Condition*, that understands manual labour as essentially worthless from a cultural perspective, Sennett questions why this denigration of the value expressed in skilful handwork arose in the first place and has remained so resistant to challenge. As he writes in the Prologue to *The Craftsman*:

> This division seems to me false because it slights the practical man or woman at work. The human animal who is *Animal laborans* is capable of thinking; the discussions the producer holds may be mentally with materials rather than with other people; people working together certainly talk to one another about what they are doing. For Arendt, the mind engages once labor is done. Another, more balanced view is that thinking and feeling are contained within the process of making. (Sennett 2008, p. 7)

This concern for the rigid cultural hierarchy between manual and mental work goes back to Sennett's much earlier ethnographic study, in the late 1960s and early 1970s, of Boston's white working-class. In *The Hidden Injuries of Class* (Sennett and Cobb 1993 [1972]), Sennett and his colleague Jonathan Cobb, reported on and analysed interviews with predominantly middle-aged male blue-collar workers. What he found was an extensively internalized sense of inferiority brought about by the limited scope his interviewees had to negotiate a meritocratic social system which increasingly hinged on specialized training and advanced formal education. While parents of working-class children wanted their offspring to 'get on' by attaining higher levels of education and formal qualifications to allow them to avoid their class fate of blue-collar employment, at the same time the older generation felt a certain scorn for the perceived frivolousness of white-collar professions.

The working class thereby get caught up in an established system of evaluation and prestige which operates, on the whole, to undermine the pride they make take from the work they do. This, as Sennett and Cobb (1993) see it, is the fundamental way in which the class system works to damage the self-image of workers:

> The use we see [of class] in general [. . .] is that society injures human dignity in order to weaken people's ability to fight against the limits class imposes on their freedom [. . .] the use of badges of ability or of sacrifices is to divert men from challenging the limits on their freedom by convincing them that they must *first* become legitimate, must achieve dignity on a class society's terms, in order to have the right to challenge the terms themselves. (153)

Returning to our authors, the line of thinking presented by Sennett here raises intriguing and fruitful thoughts. For what we encounter in the novels of Eliot, Hardy, and Lawrence are portraits of the English working class by a skilful cultural practitioner. The stigma against working-class subjects in the mid-Victorian period is such that Eliot felt obliged in her earlier novels, to apologize for their presentation. For his part, in his early novels Hardy obviates this concern by spinning out rather sensationalized plotlines, full of mystery, romance, and intrigue. But the four decades that span the divide between *Adam Bede* (1859) and *Tess of the D'Urbervilles* (1891) represent a huge leap in terms of the realistic literary rendering of working-class lives. This development seems to be significantly sped up when we compare the transition from *Tess* to *Sons and Lovers*.

In the hands of Lawrence as a writer the lives of working-class people are granted a self-standing dignity without the habitual recourse to using depictions of the middle and upper classes as a literary foil. In this sense, Lawrence's achievement hinges on an evocation of working-class existence that is in line with Hoggart's (2008) diagnosis of its fundamental characteristic:

> The more we look at working-class life, the more we try to reach the core of working-class attitudes, the more surely does it appear that the core is a sense of the personal, the concrete, the local: it is embodied in the idea of, first, the

family and, second, the neighbourhood. This remains, though much works against it, and partly because so much works against it. (22)

In my own childhood, I experienced this sense of tightly bound horizons and ingrained intimacy within a working-class cultural environment. There was very little economic and social diversity, so salient differences really hinged on matters of personal character. Knowledge was exchanged in the form of anecdotes and sharp, often caustically humorous portraits of others. The sense of narrow spatial limits was also highly pronounced. The closest city of Chester was a mere seven miles from where I grew up, but it might have been London for all it seemed to belong to our everyday reality. At an even finer-grained level, life went on at the scale of the street or neighbourhood, with childhood friends generally all within a half-mile walk; as were all other points of interest, such as shops, parks, and woods. This connection between the traditionally denigrated labour of the working class and the small-scale horizons of working-class culture offers a well-defined focus to draw some tentative conclusions about the relevance of the novels studied to contemporary political realities.

Thus far in this chapter, I have drawn attention to the paradigm of neoliberalism as something which has increasingly dominated everyday social realities over the past fifty years. At the time of its initial publication in 1957, *The Uses of Literacy* warned about the corrosive effects of advertising and popular entertainment on traditional British working-class culture. While Hoggart's personalized account of his upbringing in Leeds is open to the charge of nostalgic romanticizing, his sense that the authenticity of working-class lives was being degraded by a news and entertainment sector organized and directed by middle- and upper-class interests was well-founded. His book appeared amid the height of the 'kitchen-sink drama' phenomenon. John Osborne's *Look Back in Anger* was first performed a year earlier, Shelagh Delaney's *A Taste of Honey* premiered the same year, and the still-running TV series *Coronation Street* first aired in 1960. Film versions of both plays, along with other films such as Tony Richardson's *The Loneliness of the Long-Distance Runner*, appeared within a few years.

On the stage and on television, therefore, the British working class was literally and metaphorically under the spotlight as never before. For Hoggart, the essence of working-class culture is that it scorns the larger world of 'Them', that is, the cultural and political elite who organize the greater mechanisms of the economy and society. He accentuates, time and again, this tendency to defend oneself by rejecting the claims of social superiority by dismissing the desire that drives such claims, namely the will to 'get on' and improve oneself in the eyes of the world. As popular cultural production proliferated in post–World War II British society, the working class was increasingly under pressure to adopt the middle-class expectation of material and cultural betterment.

In *The Country and the City*, Williams (1973) highlights 'the critical problem of so much of English fiction, since the actual yet incomplete and ambiguous social mobility of the nineteenth century' (p. 200) in his chapter on Hardy. In this connection, he singles out the character of Clym Yeobright from *The Return of the Native* and emphasizes that the nature of the problem can be more precisely captured in terms of 'the more complicated and more urgent historical process in which education is tied to social advancement within a class society, so that it is difficult . . . to hold both to education and to social solidarity' (p. 202). The crucial juncture in the novel is reached at the point, shortly after his return to his native village, when Clym reveals to his mother that the underlying reason for his coming home is his wish to abandon what he considers the vain frivolousness of his life as a jewellery seller in Paris. His abandonment of personal ambition is not entertained out of stubbornness or a petty desire to thwart the expectations of others, but rather to attach the skills and enlightenment education has granted him to improving the lot of his local community. Hardy tackles this mental bent directly in the mode of authorial commentary before he allows Clym the opportunity to articulate it in direct speech:

> Yeobright loved his kind. He had a conviction that the want of most men was knowledge of a sort which brings wisdom rather than affluence. He wished to raise the class at the expense of individuals rather than individuals at the expense of the class. What was more, he was ready at once to be the first unit sacrificed.
>
> In passing from the bucolic to the intellectual life the intermediate stages are usually two at least, frequently many more; and one of these stages is almost sure to be worldly advance. We can hardly imagine bucolic placidity quickening to intellectual aims without imagining social aims as the transitional phase. Yeobright's local peculiarity was that in striving at high thinking he still cleaved to plain living – nay, wild and meagre living in many respects and brotherliness with clowns. (Hardy 2008, p. 170)

Williams (1973) praises this passage for the 'subtlety and intelligence of this argument from the late 1870s' (p. 202). In the course of development within Hardy's novel writing the depiction of Clym most obviously points ahead to the figure of Jude. It is striking that, in both cases, the character who seeks a greater wisdom through learning ultimately ends up on the margins of society: Clym becomes a solitary itinerant preacher, while Jude dies a young man from illness, sorrow, and self-neglect. As we have seen, Lawrence was exasperated at Hardy's treatment of those characters who show independence of will vis-à-vis the expected current of their lives within the community. As

Williams notes of Lawrence, however, the later writer pointedly rejected the idea, articulated by Hardy through the character of Clym, of education being used to elevate one's native community:

> He pushed beyond it to ideas of natural independence and renewal, and he saw quite clearly as an enemy a materialist and capitalist industrial system. But it is characteristic and significant that he aligned the ideas of human independence and renewal – the ideas of nature itself – with an opposition to democracy, to education, to the labour movement. (Williams 1973, p. 271)

In fact, it is fair to say that all three of our authors display ambivalence towards the currents of the working-class labour movement: Eliot representing a vague kind of ameliorative reformism, Hardy a sense of the futility of progressive sentiments in the face of a tendency towards tragic misfortune, and Lawrence in the consciousness that he was living through a transitional phase whose future could not yet be discerned. Their representations of labour and landscape are, for all that, of utmost value as they showcase the dilemmas of personal development under the weight of a deeply alienating and socially corrosive capitalist class system. By the time we arrive at Lawrence's *Women in Love* all the contradictions and tensions of this system seem to have been boiled down to one overwhelmingly urgent question: are authentic human relations even possible?

For David Harvey (2005), neoliberalism hinges on an ideology and series of practices that elevates personal liberty and, most crucially, the realization of this liberty within a context of market transactions. The transition to neoliberal governance is for Harvey, equally, a reassertion of ruling class power in the face of a trend towards improved economic equality in the west following the end of World War II. When neoliberalism became a tangible reality in the United Kingdom and United States in the early 1980s under Thatcher and Reagan, a key element of the transition was the effort to erase the legacy of worker solidarity from the preceding century. For Raymond Williams, when he published early books such as *Culture and Society* (1958) and *The Long Revolution* (1961) it seemed that the economic, social, and cultural ascent of the working class evident in recent British history would almost certainly continue. He didn't doubt that the traditional establishment and its aristocratic penumbra remained active and potent, but the presumption was that the process of democratization that had begun with the Great Reform Bill of 1832 would continue indefinitely. Looking back to that point in time of British political history, sixty years ago, allows us to gauge in more precise terms what neoliberalization has brought about. One salient feature of the neoliberal transition is the virtual erasure of work as a radical social question. Such questioning allows for a consideration of work not so much as an imponderable necessity, the nature of which is no more remarkable than the need to eat to sustain life, but rather as something whose social reality leaves open multiple complex articulations and expressions.

What help is a consideration of the novels of Eliot, Hardy, and Lawrence to an analysis of the contemporary realities and potentialities of work under neoliberalism? One of the salient features of neoliberalism is that it naturalizes and normalizes both the primacy of individual liberty and its particular articulation under advanced commodity capitalism. In doing so, it constructs and renders hegemonic a certain conception of the human condition and what count as desirable and viable possible futures of human society and political community. This has the effect of distorting or even erasing the history of working-class struggle for social justice. In an Orwellian fashion, once it reaches a mature state neoliberal governance not only counters the formally potent discourse of worker-led projects to achieve a fairer and more just society, it actually renders them all but invisible.

As Harvey (2005) notes: 'Neoliberal rhetoric, with its foundational emphasis upon individual freedoms, has the power to split off libertarianism, identity politics, multiculturalism, and eventually narcissistic consumerism from the social forces ranged in pursuit of social justice through the conquest of state power' (p. 41). In this regard, the novels of Eliot, Hardy, and Lawrence offer valuable documentation of earlier phases of capitalism when the class conflict inherent to the paradigm was readily apparent and the oppositional discourse founded on struggles for social and worker justice was very vibrant and political consequential. Central characters in these novels – Adam Bede and Felix Holt in Eliot, Clym Yeobright and Jude Fawley in Hardy, and Ursula Brangwen and Rupert Birkin in Lawrence – exemplify alternative visions of the individual and collective meaning of labour.

Inherent to its structure is a tendency of the novel to filter experience through the consciousness of one or more protagonists. Accordingly, the dramatization of labour often looks like the struggle of the individual against a more or less well-defined mass society. This struggle between the individual and the enveloping society sharpens as we pass from the high Victorian period into the early decades of the twentieth century; so that by the time we reach the early novels of Lawrence the central characters often register a total rejection of societal mores and values. But it should always be borne in mind that a certain, highly specialized mode of work is making possible this dramatization, namely the work of literary writing itself. The novelist is a specialist producer and, as such, a worker producing social value like any other. Further, the novelist is embedded – through his or her immediate lived experience, recollections of childhood, or aspirations for the future – in a social web to not less degree than other workers. The key difference is the relative autonomy that the literary producer enjoys. To the extent that a writer lives by their writing this constitutes in itself an act of relative emancipation in a capitalist context where control over workers and conditions of work is a central concern. As Harvey remarks:

> Control over the labour process and the labourer has always been central to capital's ability to sustain profitability and capital accumulation. Throughout its history, capital has invented, innovated and adopted technological forms whose dominant aim has been to enhance capital's control over labour in both the labour process and the labour market. This attempted control encompasses not only physical efficiency but also the self-discipline of the labourers employed, the qualities of labour supplied in the marketplace, the cultural habits and mentalities of workers in relationship to the work they are expected to do and the wages they expect to receive. (Harvey 2014, pp. 102–3)

As we saw at the beginning of this study when we began with Eliot's presentation of the artisan Adam Bede, worker autonomy proves attractive to novelists precisely because it portrays a condition that they themselves have striven to attain. However, novels do not exist simply to project wish symbols of authors onto their literary subjects. Rather, in the works of Eliot, Hardy, and Lawrence we encounter a highly involved and nuanced meditation on the social conditions of the worker and on the places – the landscape – where labouring communities exist. The novels we have studied constitute historical microcosms or monads which may be extrapolated to reveal hidden possible futures of work beyond the confines of capitalist determination. Precisely because neoliberalism operates with a 'there is no alternative' monovalent logic, we need such literary works to explode the closed confines of the neoliberal template of work.

Along with this mental emancipation from the ideological confines of the neoliberal schema of work, engagement with the novel allows for alternative 'productions of nature'. All the authors examined in this book exhibit a profound sensitivity to place, constructed as a natural but also psychologically charged, affective landscape. Whether it is the trysts of Maggie and Philip in the Red Deeps, the assignations of Wildeve and Eustacia on Egdon Heath, or the ambivalence of Ursula and Gudrun towards the mining town of Beldover, the novels we have considered offer profound meditations on the construction of landscape in the lifeworld of their respective protagonists. Regarded holistically, therefore, these novels allow us to grasp with greater focus and sensitivity the profound imbrication of labour and landscape, a connection shaken to the point of virtual disintegration in the stage of neoliberal governance we are presently living through.

VISIONARY LANDSCAPES OF THE FUTURE

In the previous section, I expanded on and summed up the significance of depictions of work and workers in the novels studied. In this section, I turn to the other key theme of the book, namely landscape. As outlined in the Introduction, the word 'landscape' is employed to name a literary evocation of place. The connotations of artificiality and spectacle are deliberate and acknowledged. After all, literary landscapes are, no less than the genre of painting from which the English term is derived, conscious constructions meant for aesthetic consumption and appreciation. But such landscapes portrayed in a novel are equally evocations of a lifeworld where a common existence is taking place. To take an example, much of the pathos of the scene in *The Rainbow* when Tom Brangwen proposes to Lydia Lensky is derived from Lawrence's deft summoning of the elemental forces at work in the local landscape: the dark, windy, early spring night at once situating and amplifying the veritably unconscious resolve of the young man captured in this moment of personal crisis. Equally, Hardy's depiction of Gabriel Oak staring out at the stars from his solitary sheep hut places the man in the enfolding landscape in a manner than is both intimate in its feel and vast in its reach. All of this is of crucial importance in light of the fact that neoliberal capitalism brings about an unparalleled and accelerating process of what Harvey calls 'space-time compression':

> The increasing speed of transport and communications reduces the friction and barrier of geographical distance, making the spatiality and temporality of capital a dynamic rather than a fixed feature of the social order. Capital literally creates its own space and time as well as its own distinctive nature. The mobility of the different forms of capital (production, commodities, money) and of labour power is also perpetually subject to revolutionary transformation. (Harvey 2014, p. 99)

This is Harvey's contemporary rendition of Marx and Engels's famous dictum, from *The Communist Manifesto* of 1848, that under capitalism 'all that is solid melts into air'. While the novels of Eliot and Hardy undoubtedly contain elements of conservative nostalgia that lead them to lend certain timelessness to their depictions of local landscape, this should not blind us to the fact that traces of the material processes of constant transformation under capitalism are everywhere present. Part of the parallax effect at work here relates to the fact that these two authors have a tendency to situate the action of their novels a generation or so in the past. This places the action within living memory, but generally in a typical reader's time of youth. Childhood memories are apt to have a sense of timelessness attached to them, something made into a leitmotif of English literature by Wordsworth from the time of *Lyrical Ballads* (1798) on.

As we have seen, Lawrence completed *The Rainbow* in close conjunction with his *Study of Thomas Hardy*. His decision to recontextualize the original narrative of the two sisters, Ursula and Gundrun, by constructing the history of the two earlier generations of the Brangwen family is a remarkable one. From our consideration of his critical essays, we know that Lawrence found abhorrent the impact of industrial capitalism on his native English countryside and its people. In the opening chapters of *The Rainbow* Lawrence sketches the early changes wrought on the landscape within close proximity to the Brangwens' home:

> About 1840, a canal was constructed across the meadows of the Marsh Farm, connecting the newly-opened collieries of the Erewash Valley. A high embankment travelled along the fields to carry the canal, which passed close to the homestead, and, reaching the road, went over a heavy bridge.
>
> Then, a short time afterwards, a colliery was sunk on the other side of the canal, and in a while the Midland Railway came down the valley at the foot of the Ilkeston hill, and the invasion was complete. The town grew rapidly, the Brangwens were kept busy producing supplies, they became richer, they were almost tradesmen. (Lawrence 2008, pp. 9–10)

This terse description of rapid material change stands in opposition to the sensibility of the exhilarating initial paragraphs of novel which relate the timeless work done by the preceding generations of Brangwens who have tended the earth: 'But heaven and earth were teeming around them, and how should this cease?' (p. 5). In *Women in Love*, considered as a problematic sequel to *The Rainbow*, the full effect of the revolutionizing social impact of such material transformations is made apparent as Ursula and Gundrun drift further away from their original locale. The final chapters of the book relate their flight to continental Europe and eventually to the snowed-in desert of the high Alps. As Gerald's climactic death on a dark mountainside starkly illustrates, the contemporary social condition of restless uprootedness threatens at any moment to become mortally wounding.

Based on his directly biographical writings, we know in great detail the lengths Lawrence went to, in the two short decades of his mature adult life, to experience landscapes free of the deathly carapace he felt covered his native landscape. Intellectually speaking, Lawrence was profoundly drawn to the vitalism that featured strongly in such thinkers as Nietzsche and equally to the celebration of 'primitivism' that saw in non-Western cultures something more authentic and elemental to counter the effete decadence of occidental arts and letters. None of this ultimately expunged Lawrence's connection to his native landscape, however, as we have shown in our earlier exploration of his late critical essays.

What we are left with, then, at the end of this investigation of Eliot, Hardy, and Lawrence is a profound meditation on the nature and meaning of landscape for human welfare. While the word 'landscape' may suggest a setting to human action that is ultimately separable from the actors, this is emphatically not the case in the novels discussed. In fact, the underlying sense of literary landscape made apparent in the novels indicates something like a common context of social action. Whether it be the uncanny resonances of the absent scaffold near the Red House from where Jude descries Christminster, the nearby fields where Maggie and Tom play as young children, or the cowsheds of the Marsh Farm where Brangwen calms the young Anna while her mother gives birth in the farmstead, all these depictions of place are redolent of a sense of essential emplacement. It is quite possible, in fact, that literary writing is the only context in which the most profound experiences of lived space can be socially recorded and shared.

Of all the places evoked in the novels we have considered in this study it is Hardy's depiction of Egdon Heath in *The Return of the Native* that is perhaps the most striking in terms of its presence in the action. From the beginning of the narrative, Hardy has the heath play a crucial role and attributes human-like characteristics to it. The underlying feature of Egdon Heath is its obscurity and immemorial antiquity: it exists as though outside of time and beyond direct human comprehension. In a way, it would be most apt to say that it does not function as a landscape at all, in the sense that it is not a bounded backdrop to human action but rather a boundless sense of ancient presence. As such it exists beyond the processes of human history and, therefore, remains untouched by progress. It is a waste that has escaped enclosure precisely because it resists subordination to intensive human cultivation:

> Here at least were intelligible facts regarding landscape – far-reaching proofs productive of genuine satisfaction. The untameable, Ishmaelitish thing that Edgon now was it always had been. Civilization was its enemy. Ever since the beginning of vegetation its soil had worn the same antique brown dress, the natural and invariable garment of the formation. In its venerable one coat lay a certain vein of satire on human vanity in clothes. (Hardy 2005, p. 11)

In his *Study of Thomas Hardy,* Lawrence registers his admiration for and profound attraction to the depiction of Egdon Heath in *The Return of the Native*. This is unsurprising, given Lawrence's own sense of natural landscape as something persisting, in a state of indifference, amid the tumult and change of human society. Throughout his novels, short stories and poems Lawrence attempted to invoke a sense of this permanence of landscape. In his initial survey of Hardy's books in the *Study*, Lawrence notes that *The Return of the Native* is 'the first tragic and important novel' (Steele 1985, p. 23). Lawrence's description of Hardy's heath is closely akin to the early passages of the life lived by the succeeding generations of the Brangwen family in *The Rainbow* and points to the essential affinity between Hardy's attraction to the immemorial history of the landscape and Lawrence's yearning to make contact with something that antedates all human civilization:

> What is the real stuff of tragedy in the book? It is the Heath. It is the primitive, primal earth, where the instinctive life heaves up. There, in the deep, rude stirring of the instincts, there was the reality that worked the tragedy. Close to the body of things, there can be heard the stir that makes us and destroys us. The [earth] heaved with raw instinct, Egdon whose dark soil was strong and crude and organic as the body of a beast. Out of the body of this crude earth are born Eustacia, Wildeve, Mistress Yeobright, Clym, and all the others. [. . .] The Heath persists. Its body is strong and fecund, it will bear many more crops besides this. Here is the sombre, latent power that will go on producing, no matter what happens to the product. Here is the deep, black source from whence all these little contents of lives are drawn. (Steele 1985, p. 25)

It would be easy to diagnose a certain misanthropic scorn for the pettiness of human life from such a description. However, I believe hatred of humanity is no more present in Lawrence than it is in Hardy. Quite the reverse. The sense of tragedy invoked by both is in fact shot through with sympathy and pathos: for their writings tap into the inevitable pain and sufferings of individual life, the struggles for meaning and fulfilment that almost inevitably go awry due to the perversities of circumstance and the recalcitrance or insensitivity of others. Nor is it possible here to discount the sense of landscape in play as a matter of sentimentalized nostalgia. The sublime depiction of Egdon Heath places it beyond the confines of individual childhood recollection. Clym, the returning native, does not fully understand what binds him to the heath such that he throws away a materially successful life in Paris. Certainly, he returns filled with a sense of reverence, service, and self-sacrifice to his native place, but Hardy makes clear in his portrait of Clym that his mission is borne of a deep-seated sense of the ultimate vanity of human ambition. Hence, we can concur with Lawrence when he observes of *The Return of the Native*: 'The real sense of tragedy is got from the setting' (Steele 1985, p. 25).

The value of our novelists' depictions of place and landscape can be appreciated from quite a different perspective than a purely literary one. On a biographical level a novelist draws on their direct experience of certain locales, often from childhood. At the same time, as we have repeatedly shown, the life of the writer is caught up more generally in the social-material processes that transform the places they inhabit. It is striking that there is a conspicuous attraction – at least in the case of Hardy and Lawrence – towards an appreciation of natural landscape as something that can repel and resist the abilities of human activity to transform it. For a writer such as Neil Smith (2008), positioning 'Nature' outside of the material processes of capitalist production is an ideologically motivated obfuscation: it strives to present Nature as something inviolably other than human society. Working in the Marxist tradition of Henri Lefebvre and his conception of the 'production of space', Smith calls for a quite different appreciation of the relationship between space and society:

> A fundamental change of perspective is demanded here. For while we as theorists may have drastic conceptual problems in achieving an integration of space and society, capital seems to achieve it in practice on a daily basis. What it achieves in fact is the production of space in its own image, and exploration of this idea will lead to a more complete integration of space and society in the theory of uneven development. For not only does capital produce space in general, it produces the real spatial scales that give uneven development its coherence. (Smith 2008, p. 7)

What Smith's theory of 'uneven development' sets out is an account of the fact that capitalist development necessarily takes place at different speeds according to the place in question. On the global level, we articulate this in terms of a 'developed' as opposed to a 'developing' world. On the level of a nation state such as the United Kingdom, there is the notion of a centre (London and its immediate surroundings) and a periphery. It is striking, in this context, that all three of the novelists considered in this study are distinctly provincial rather than metropolitan with respect to their origins and to the settings of their narratives. In the case of Eliot, for the most part action takes place in the rural Midlands; for Hardy, of course, it is the villages and towns of 'Wessex'; and in the early novels and short stories of Lawrence, it is the mining communities of his native Nottinghamshire. In all three cases, however, there is a profound sense in which the novels powerfully invoke the intertwining of place and society.

As was pointed out earlier in this chapter, the sense of intimate shared space might be considered a particular characteristic of working-class community. More recently, this has been expressed in political terms by referring to the working class as citizens of somewhere as opposed the globally mobile more affluent classes who exist as citizens of nowhere. This distinction was made newsworthy when in 2016, in the context of the post-Brexit political landscape in the United Kingdom, the then British prime minister Theresa May remarked: 'If you believe you are a citizen of the world, you are a citizen of nowhere' (The Guardian 2016). It was pointed out at the time, by the left-leaning newspaper *Guardian* that May's sentiments were redolent of Hitler's strident hatred of non-natives and racial minorities and of the contemporary strains of neo-Nazism to be found in Germany and elsewhere. This connection seems fair, on one level at least, but it should not be allowed to obscure other important aspects of the society-space relation.

Communities of place are not by any means necessarily reactionary and exclusionary in nature. To recur to Hardy's depiction of Egdon Heath, it is clear that the underlying sense of the evocation is precisely that this place radically resists overt attempts to claim it as one's own. It has resisted integration into the nexus of capitalist commodification and production and thereby acts as an embodiment of a recalcitrant 'outside' or 'beyond' of these processes. Of course, this cannot be asserted in any absolute sense. As the history of capitalist production teaches us time and again, there is virtually nowhere on the earth than remains in principle out of reach for potential profit extraction. But it is the novelist's delineation of a place that resists conversion, at least for the time being, that points towards a profound experience of landscape that has crucially emancipatory potential.

For all its strengths, the Marxian analysis of the materialist dialectic that characterizes historical development tends to neglect the variegation of capitalism as a global regime. This involves both spatial and temporal differentiation. As Hardy's evocative description of Egdon Heath makes clear, there is an experience of immemorial antiquity available to us thanks to the quality of certain places. Certainly, it is possible to dismiss such descriptions as mere residues of a Romantic idealization of nature that act as a social palliative in the face of rampant capitalist exploitation of natural resources. On the other hand, the experience of landscape as an affective anchor to place is not reducible to a variant of reactionary 'blood and soil' politics. Lawrence's constant references to blood and his appreciation of the fashionable artistic trend for primitivism can be readily presented in this light. Ultimately, however, I believe this is a crude and fruitless interpretation of the role of landscape in his writings and in those of his predecessors.

Eliot, Hardy, and Lawrence were not merely capturing their own idiosyncratic experiences in their novels but were instead trying to make sense of the common world in which they were caught up. In this sense, their writings involve what we might call an inner dialectic between estrangement and connection, a dialectic that plays out in the dramatization of places featured in their narratives. Raymond Williams captures this point beautifully towards the end of *The Country and the City*:

> For we have to look, in country and city alike, at the real social processes of alienation, separation, externality, abstraction. And we have to do this not only

critically, in the necessary history of rural and urban capitalism, but substantially, by affirming the experiences which in many millions of lives are discovered and rediscovered, very often under pressure: experiences of directness, connection, mutuality, sharing, which alone can define, in the end, what the real deformation may be. (Williams 1973, p. 298)

In Eliot's early novels such as *Adam Bede* and *The Mill on the Floss* she weaves together the different strands of small-scale rural life to produce a fabric of compelling density and complexity. In her juxtaposition of Loamshire and Stonyshire in the earlier novel, Eliot draws attention to how the relative richness of the land directly affects the characteristics of the people and their way of life. Stonyshire with its industrialized urban settings renders people harder, more fixed and fervent in their religious sensibilities, whereas Loamshire allows for a salutary laxness in religious observation and an altogether more generous disposition towards others. Above all, Eliot uses the compact scale of small-scale community to highlight the mutual reliance of individuals, such that their personal growth is only possible through the work done to cultivate difficult relationships of authentic care and reciprocity. Certainly, it is true to say that a constant appeal for moderation, faith in the benign effects of ruling class authority, and deference towards the existing class structure are salient features of Eliot's authorial presentation. These features are always undergirded, however, by the persistence of place. Those who find themselves cast out into unfamiliar territory are generally individuals beyond redemption, whereas those who come into the main site of narrative – such as Silas Marner – are found to be ripe for restitution. Above all, then, the narrated landscape for Eliot is a site of healing.

In Hardy we find a similar pattern at work. In *The Woodlanders* Giles Winterbourne and Marty South represent the natives whose knowledge of localized sylvan lore grants them a conspicuous dignity despite the fact both of them lack much in the way of social and economic status. Contrariwise, Edred Fitzpiers is cast as a restless outsider and the local landowner Felice Charmond possesses no genuine affection for the village of Little Hintock she presides over. Opposites come together in *The Return of the Native* when Clym Yeobright's determination to find meaning by reattaching himself to Egdon collides with Eustacia Vye's yearning for Clym to cleave to his former life in Paris. In the case of Egdon Heath, as we have discussed at length, there is a certain antiquity and tragedy attached to the place and landscape such that it seems to predestine Clym's mother to early death and Clym himself to becoming the ragged figure of a solitary itinerant preacher. Much the same can be said of Diggory Venn, who wanders the landscape alone, nursing his hopeless love of Thomasin Yeobright. This marks a key distinction between Hardy and Eliot, in that Hardy depicts characters' relationship to place often as something informed by a kind of immemorial tragedy. This features most obviously and starkly in the case of Tess and Jude, whose early attachments to place are marked by deprivation and sadness, but whose subsequent relocations never manage to lift them out of the groove of this incipient tragedy.

Finally, in Lawrence, following the rite of passage narrative set out in *Sons and Lovers*, *The Rainbow* offers a supreme evocation of place in its depiction of the three generations of the Brangwen family in the environs of the Marsh Farm. The rural locale and its agricultural activities form the indispensable context for Lawrence's presentation of characters and relationships. While the patent focus on the novel is the struggle for authenticity on the part of the protagonists, key elements of the natural landscape are invoked time and again to present this struggle. In Lawrence, as we have seen, there is a clear appeal to some putatively timeless element in the natural world, to something that ultimately grounds an individual's search for authentic being. The artificiality and rootlessness of upper-class life, whether in rural landed estates or in the sophistication of city life, are on ample display in *Women in Love*. In that novel, the Brangwen sisters are placed in a precarious situation, feeling disdain for their native community of working-class colliers but disaffection with the vanities of upper-class aristocratic existence. Ursula eventually fights through to form a lasting union with the Lawrence-like figure of Rupert Birkin, but Gundrun is unable to achieve the same with Gerald Crich, whose attachment to death is shown to stem from his involuntary killing of his brother in childhood. Thus, by the time we get to the novels of Lawrence, achieving restitution and fulfilment in one's native place no longer seems a viable option for the principal characters.

Just over sixty years spans the divide between the publication of *Adam Bede* and *Women in Love*, a period in which the 'structure of feeling' captured in these novels exhibits a remarkable transformation. A century has now passed since the appearance of *Women in Love* and it would be plausible to argue that social-material conditions have changed so much in the intervening period that there is little affinity between Lawrence's evocation of the times and the current historical juncture. This conclusion, however, could only be reached by mistaking the nature of literary presentation. For Lawrence was not, any more than Eliot or Hardy, shaping his narratives with a view to verisimilitude. Certainly, all three authors embrace a realist aesthetic of a kind; but their respective approach to the novel is, at the same time, deeply imbued with ethical and metaphysical perspectives that critically inform their representations of people and places.

In this study, the primary focus has been on depictions of work and workers and the underlying thesis has been that the social reality of working-class lives has been brought into more effective focus in the process. This achievement is of crucial importance to us in present times, in light of four decades of sustained neoliberal erasure of working-class realities. As Owen Jones (2011) demonstrated in detail in his widely read book *Chavs: The Demonization of the Working Class*, popular media and entertainment alike have worked in concert in recent decades to offer a denigrating picture of working-class people as feckless, loutish individuals who are largely responsible for any deprivations and sufferings they endure. In light of this, the novels of Eliot, Hardy, and Lawrence offer resources for reclaiming a collective history of working-class struggle and dignity to counter the neoliberal construction.

At the same time, in the third decade of the twenty-first century we stand at what may prove to be a definitive crisis in the neoliberal construction of space. This is a grand claim to make, but much academic work has been done by critical geographers to bear out the point. The novels we have explored in this study make evident an intimate and effective coupling of people and place. Certainly, the literary worlds depicted are deeply imbued with a class structure that turns on degrees of ownership and control over one's material conditions. But the manner in which people and their activities are in vital connection to place is everywhere in evidence. By contrast, the current era of neoliberal capitalism has been rapidly rendering lived space irreal through processes of intensive marketization and commodification. Under neoliberal urbanism, whole neighbourhoods and districts, if not whole cities, are increasingly objects to be sold as lifestyle choices. To cite Guy Debord's (2014 [1967]) famous words at the beginning of his seminal work *The Society of the Spectacle*: 'Everything that was directly lived has receded into a representation' (p. 10). David Harvey, who has written on the transformation of urban experience throughout the neoliberal period, offers this encapsulation of the contemporary stakes in his book *The Enigma of Capital*:

> So, are our cities designed for people or for profits? The fact that this question is so often asked takes us immediately on to the terrain of the vast array of class and social struggles over place formation. These are the landscapes within which daily life has to be lived, where affective relations and social solidarities are established and where political subjectivities and symbolic meanings are constructed. Capitalist class and developer interests are all too well aware of this dimension and seek to mobilise it through community or city boosterism and the deliberate fostering of a sense of local or regional identity, sometimes successfully preying upon popular sensitivities derived from strong relations to the land and to place. (Harvey 2010, p. 193)

Harvey is unusual as an urban theorist, insofar as he resolutely insists that the fundamentals of Marx's class-based analysis of capitalism have never been more pertinent when attempting to understanding the contemporary condition of cities. Nowhere more than in such iconic cities as London and New

York has neoliberalism brought about a materialized place befitting its condition. The centres of such cities have essentially become gated communities for wealthy elites, as real estate speculation makes more and more evident that profit trumps immediate human need in the functioning of the urban environment. Within the richest countries, finance has long since dominated manufacturing in terms of social and political clout. Governments almost invariably appeal to the inevitable processes of capitalism competition and innovation when manufacturing companies fold and lay off thousands of workers, whereas financial giants are propped up by huge injections of public money and declared 'too big to fail'. The shadow of the 2008 financial crisis brought to a head economic developments and social tensions that had been mounting ever since the neoliberal Washington Consensus became inviolable political common-sense in the late 1980s. At the point of writing, we stand in the current of a further global economic crisis, this time precipitated by the coronavirus pandemic. Given the already threadbare conditions of state-funded welfare provision, unparalleled levels of income and wealth inequality and a hegemonic neoliberal political order it is now credible to ask: will our cities even exist in a recognizable form once the dust has settled following the current global health crisis?

As the previous quote from Harvey indicates, the drive to forge communities of place is ruthlessly exploited by the agents of neoliberal urbanism. Human action has an indissoluble tie to place; it requires a landscape in which to make sense of itself. On one level, this simply amounts to recognizing that human social organization is intrinsically material and spatial in character. The virtualization of our everyday lives since the beginnings of the computer age may have made recognition of this basic fact more difficult to arrive at, but it remains true. An important part of the ebb and flow of urban development and experience over the last forty years has been the reclaiming of cities following flight to car-centred suburbs in the post–World War II decades. The homogeneity and lack of density in suburban contexts have been displaced in favour of the density and potential for random encounter that the central city offers. However, this 'urban renaissance' has been meticulously curated by the forces of capitalist real-estate speculation and stage-managed so as to offer a kind of sanitized pastiche of once-gritty urban experience. But amid this reengineered urban landscape the original drive for connection and community abides and struggles, as it always has, to find authentic articulation within the context of capitalist spectacle. This perennial struggle, as Williams notes, makes the literature marked by the beginnings of the capitalist transformation a permanent point of reference: 'But as we gain perspective, from the literature of country and city, we see how much, at different times and in different places, it is a connecting process, in what has to be seen ultimately as a common history' (Williams 1973, p. 288).

Conclusion

Neoliberalism and a New Working-Class Politics

LABOUR LOSES ITS VOICE

In the previous chapter the relevance of the novels examined in this study to the subsequent social history of labour and landscape in Britain was delineated. In this conclusion, I wish to indicate how the observations and insights achieved here can help us to construct a future path for progressive working-class politics in the United Kingdom and elsewhere. This task is vitally important given the widespread and deeply rooted phenomenon of contemporary populism. In a recently published book (Elliott 2021), I examine this phenomenon in light of the long history of British working-class politics from the 1780s on. My basic argument there is that populism should not simply be written off as a matter of demagoguery and nativism, but rather viewed as something that articulates a fundamental tension between bureaucratic managerialism and appeals to popular sovereignty. As explained in the previous chapter, the shift to neoliberal governance in Britain in the late 1970s and early 1980s brought with it a thoroughgoing erasure and denigration of the working class as a political and social agent. Systematic attacks on labour unions also ensured that these key institutions of working-class self-representation became marginalized and increasingly irrelevant within British party politics.

In the case of the British Labour Party this process involved a gradual severing of the intimate historical ties between the party and key union organizations. By the time Tony Blair became leader of the Labour Party in 1995 a 'New Labour' movement was poised to bring a brand of 'Third Way' politics to Britain that would unapologetically espouse a 'beyond left and right' centrism. Not only did this amount to subjugating what was meant to be a party of the British working class to middle-class and business interests, it also a signalled a wholesale collapse into the neoliberal orthodoxy established in the

1980s under Margaret Thatcher. While it would be true to say that New Labour did redirect funding into the public education and health systems, equally it was under Blair's watch that public-private initiatives became the norm, university fees were introduced, and a relentless fetishizing of the innovative and entrepreneurial became a settled political ideology. As a contemporary exponent of British cultural studies, Angela McRobbie (2016), points out in a review essay, there is an entire ideological field to come to terms with here:

> We need to better understand the precise ways and means by which leftism in all of its many varieties has been so relentlessly disavowed, demonised, and judged irrelevant, by an ever-present infrastructure of media and popular culture. We need to understand the scale of the undoing: this is one outcome of what Mrs Thatcher used to refer as the 'there is no alternative' logic. We also need to pay more attention to the means by which contemporary neoliberalism is able to harness the power of feel-goodness and optimism – indeed fashionability – particularly in relation to the rise of the Google-type start-up or 'new economy', which partly accounts for its special attraction to young people. (McRobbie 2016, p. 120)

The key point raised here by McRobbie that I wish to take up is the centrality of entrepreneurialism to the neoliberal image of society. This image has been long in the making, but it has also borne particular fruit in the current phase of British populism. Since 2015 Britain has gone through what is arguably one of the most tumultuous and destabilizing political periods in its post-war history. The June 2016 referendum on the UK's membership of the European Union produced the narrow Brexit result and a cascading set of consequences that led to the resignation of two Prime Ministers (David Cameron in 2016 and Theresa May in 2019), two snap elections (in 2017 and 2019), Britain's exit from the EU at the beginning of 2020 and finally a trade agreement at the end of the same year. The confounding impact of a global pandemic in 2020 also precipitated Britain into an economic crisis which is generally believed to be the most profound in its modern history. In electoral terms, the UK Labour Party suffered its worst defeat in generations, with scores of northern English constituencies shifting allegiance to Boris Johnson's Conservative Party under the slogan 'Get Brexit Done!' The soul-searching conducted by the Labour Party goes on, but it is reasonably clear that its defiance of the popular mandate to withdraw from the European Union played a decisive role in its defeat. A longer-term cause of Labour's electoral losses, however, is undoubtedly its presiding over more than a decade (between 1997 and 2007) when significant economic growth was accompanied by ever-widening disparities in income and wealth. This naturally raised the question for many: what is the Labour Party for?

While middle-class voters were arguably more disaffected by Blair's strident support for the American-led invasion of Iraq, it was the growing sense of being abandoned by its traditional party-political representatives that more than anything caused working-class voter disenchantment with the political establishment more generally. Ideologically, neoliberalism tends to elide class differences and constitute the social-political domain as a matter of coordinating individuals according to their capacity for rational choice. As Foucault (2008) sets out in his celebrated lectures on the origins of neoliberal theory of governance from the late 1970s, human nature is constituted as *Homo economicus* and choices become trade-offs to maximize personal benefit in accord with investments made. In our private as in our public lives, the overriding norm is profit maximization. This makes clear the stark divide with traditional working-class politics, which turns largely on solidarity and self-sacrifice. When neoliberal governance and its attendant ideology become hegemonic, the image of society as intimate community becomes highly problematic and, above all, shared experiences and institutionalized articulations of work and the workplace become anathema.

As Foucault's incisive analysis makes clear, neoliberal governance brings with it two key social impacts: on the one hand, the principal task of government becomes the regulation and safeguarding of frictionless market transactions; on the other, work and the economy more generally become a matter of maximized individual return on investment. In Foucault's (2008) famous phrase, under neoliberalism we are conditioned to be 'entrepreneurs of ourselves'. As Thatcher and Reagan worked in the 1980s to weaken the collective bargaining powers of labour unions, the commodification of everyday life reached new heights. While local councils, especially those that were left leaning, were deprived of economic resources and decision-making power by central government, the relentless message doled out to unemployed workers was that it was down to them to reskill and seek alternative employment. At the same time, a wholesale ideological attack on any form of 'welfare dependency' was waged on both sides of the Atlantic. Under neoliberalism, we therefore encounter a virulent recrudescence of Malthusian economics as individuals are thrust back onto their own resources in a pitiless fight for survival. In his book *Together: The Rituals, Pleasures, and Politics of Cooperation*, Richard Sennett (2012) ties together these changed realities of work with the dangers of a new populism:

> The new forms of capitalism emphasize short-term labour and institutional fragmentation; the effect of this economic system has been that workers cannot sustain supportive social relations with one another. In the West, the distance between the elite and the mass is increasing, as inequality grows more pronounced in neo-liberal regimes like those of Britain and the United States;

members of these societies have less and less a fate to share in common. The new capitalism permits power to detach itself from authority, the elite living in global detachment from responsibilities to others on the ground, especially during times of economic crisis. Under these conditions, as ordinary people are driven back on themselves, it's no wonder they crave solidarity of some sort – which the destructive solidarity of us-against-them is tailor-made to provide. (Sennett 2012, p. 279)

As the book title indicates, Sennett advocates cooperation and social ritual as a salve to the social and psychological ills of neoliberalism. By contrast, solidarity – the traditional value and goal of leftist politics – risks precipitating the working class into jingoistic populism that makes scapegoats out of minority groups as a compensation for generalized economic deprivation and political impotence. According to Sennett's analysis, over the last five decades the neoliberal transformation has acted as a potent solvent undoing ritualized connections of mutual dependency and trust in the workplace. The decades following World War II saw unprecedented economic growth in the West and a relatively stable form of governance sometimes referred to as 'embedded liberalism'. This involved a series of trade-offs between government, business, and trade unions, amid a sense that everyone was, more or less, getting what they wanted out of the situation.

Of course, many social issues connected to race, gender and sexuality, were far from resolved during those post-war decades. The 1973 Oil Crisis, along with a plethora of structural tensions which had mounted during the 1960s, led to a protracted stand-off between government and labour unions. By the mid-1980s labour had been effectively disciplined and the vestiges of union power all but destroyed as a political force to be reckoned with. In the ensuing decades, as the neoliberal regime matured and colonized ever-greater swathes of our public and private lives, worker precarity and in-work poverty become the rule rather than the exception. On the far side of the neoliberal transformation, it is useful to recall what has been lost along the way. As Sennett (2012) points out, not least of these losses are the 'informal relations' that were habitually forged in the workplace prior to the advent of neoliberal governance:

These informal relations consisted of three elements composing a social triangle. On one side, workers extended grudging respect to decent bosses, who returned equally grudging respect to reliable employees. On a second side, workers talked freely about significant mutual problems, and also covered in the shop for co-workers in trouble, whether the trouble was a hangover or a divorce. On the third side, people pitched in, doing extra hours or other people's jobs, when something went temporarily and drastically wrong in the shop. The three sides of the social triangle consisted of earned authority, mutual respect and cooperation during a crisis. (Sennett 2012, p. 148)

Just as work has largely ceased to provide resources for cooperation and mutual trust, so has the urban landscape become progressively more spectacularized and commodified under neoliberal governance. On the surface, many Western cities enjoyed a post-industrial rebirth from the 1980s on: former industrial building being repurposed as upscale flats and condos, nimble and attractive start-ups being founded by young entrepreneurs, and a whole plethora of urban greening initiatives coming into play to make our cities and towns more 'liveable' and walkable. As Marxist geographers such as David Harvey have recorded in detail, however, the spectacle of the green, progressive, and liveable city masks a readily apparent landscape of material depravation and rampant economic inequality. Rough sleeping, homeless shelters, and food banks are now all too familiar sites in urban centres across the United Kingdom and the United States. In-work poverty is now a baseline reality for people who, in previous decades, would have been more than able to meet their basic needs thanks to a wage. The withdrawal of government from the everyday lives of the working class may look like liberation through the lens of neoliberal ideology but, in reality, it amounts to abandonment to the feral forces of capitalism's relentless 'creative destruction'.

None of this should be surprising when we reflect on the fundamental fact that the logical conclusion of capitalism, particularly in its current neoliberal iteration, is the dissolution of society into its constituent individual parts. We are better able to gauge the progress of this dissolution by reflecting on the way landscape and labour are presented in the novels of Eliot, Hardy, and Lawrence. As we have striven to show in the central chapters of this book, landscape and labour can be seen to operate as key elements of narrative that demonstrate the imbricated lives lived in community. Literary landscapes make evident inter-generational memory and custom, creating thereby a shared cultural horizon. This horizon allows for the articulation of difference and conflict, thereby making sense of broader historical conditions and changes through the prism of individual lives. Labour, simply put, is purposive human activity that involves material transformation of the surrounding environment. In other words, landscape and labour are positioned as terms in a necessary dialectic that is central to human existence. While novels may be seen as highly idiosyncratic and personal renderings of particular, largely fictional human lives, the presumption of this study is that they are vital repositories of historical meaning. It is my hope to have made a convincing case for this claim in this book.

So far, in this conclusion I have mostly focused on the theme of labour. The key point has been that work under the conditions of neoliberal capitalism has become largely emptied of its capacity to shape meaning and give direction to workers. Let me now turn to the second key theme of this book, namely landscape. As mentioned in the Introduction, I have chosen to use the word landscape in order to make clear the artifice involved. The term 'landscape' entered English through Dutch. As Simon Shama (1995) points out in his commanding work of cultural history *Landscape and Memory*, '*landschap*, like its Germanic root, *Landschaft*, signified a unit of human occupation, indeed a jurisdiction, as much as anything that might be a pleasing object of depiction' (p. 10). Building on this observation, the argument of Shama's investigation is that we should recognize, indeed celebrate, the fact that landscapes are culturally created spaces rather than pristine wildernesses devoid of essential human activity. Similarly, the literary landscapes that appear in the novels of Eliot, Hardy, and Lawrence are dramatic sites, that is, spaces of meaningful human action rather than decorative backdrops. Even if we say that they frame such action it is then necessary to add that they are, in their own right, agents within the narrative.

The novels studied offer landscapes both as verisimilitudes of historically existing human communities but also ones that construct images of ideal human connection. Eliot's habit of narrative commentary on the actions of her protagonists and her constant allusions to the superiority of the rural culture of the near past bodies forth a kind of moralizing utopia. In Hardy's novels, protagonists such as Clym, Tess, and Jude represent for him types of person who presage a more liberated and enlightened future for which the times are not yet ripe. Similarly, in *Women in Love* Rupert Birkin seeks manners of human connection thwarted by conventional morality and societal conceptions of propriety. There is, therefore, a more or less latent act of imaginative utopian construction involved in the novels studied in this book. Drawing out elements of this construction can be useful to gain better purchase on contemporary modes of place-based idealization to be found under the aegis of neoliberal governance. To consider this point, we can turn again to the work of David Harvey. In *The Enigma of Capital*, Harvey (2010) points to the neoliberal tendency to advertise to wealthy investors whole cities through the creation of iconic landmarks:

> The selling and branding of place, and the burnishing of the image of a place (including states), becomes integral to how capitalist competition works. The production of geographical difference, building upon those given by history, culture and so-called natural advantages, is internalised within the reproduction of capitalism. Bring a signature architect to town and create something like Frank Gehry's Guggenheim Museum in Bilbao. This helps put that city on the map of attractors for mobile capital. If geographical differences between territories and states did not exist, then they would be created by both differential

investment strategies and the quest for spatial monopoly power given by uniqueness of location and of environmental and cultural qualities. The idea that capitalism promotes geographical homogeneity is totally wrong. It thrives on heterogeneity and difference. (Harvey 2010, p. 203)

Harvey is making this point in opposition to a familiar line of cultural critique, found in such works as Howard Kunstler's (1993) *The Geography of Nowhere*, according to which twentieth-century capitalism spawned lifeless homogeneous suburbs devoid of character or any authentic sense of place. While Harvey is perfectly aware of the role played by the growth of the suburbs in post–World War II America, he rejects the underlying thesis that capitalism has an inherent tendency to homogenize the built environment. In fact, if neoliberal capitalism works on one particular formula it would be the proliferation of customized difference in every field of consumer choice. Certainly, when we recall the sentiments of abhorrence expressed by Lawrence in his novels and essays about the industrialized landscape he knew in his native Nottinghamshire, we can see a direct lineage leading to the kind of critique offered by Kunstler in the 1990s. The key difference, however, is that Lawrence also recognized the living lineaments of working-class communities that were able to thrive despite the aesthetic deficits of the material landscapes in which these lives went on. Despite desultory remarks to the contrary, it is not plausible to derive from the writings and thought of Lawrence a kind of environmental meliorism found in proponents of urban design such as Kunstler.

MAKING SPACE FOR A FUTURE POLITICS

While it is important to recognize that literary landscapes are caught up in processes of cultural construction, it is equally significant to observe that they are nothing more than products of an individual writer's imaginary projections. Above all, the landscapes we encounter in the novels of Eliot, Hardy, and Lawrence are common spaces. The commonality in question has several dimensions to it; first, it relates protagonists by providing a shared space of action; second, it allows for collective cultural memory in the present; third, and most problematically, it intimates access to some 'outside' of human action and history. This third dimension of landscape is the most difficult to articulate but it is crucial to recognize it. There also seems to be a dialectical intensification of the presence of what we might call *the alterity of landscape* as we pass from Eliot through Hardy to Lawrence. In this book, we have touched on this theme many times without naming it as such. It is present in Hardy's depiction of Egdon Heath as a kind of living spirit of place, whose origins go back into immemorial history and inform the fate of the characters who reside there. It is also present, in a more explicit and sustained way, in Lawrence's use of the presence of the stars and moon in *The Rainbow*.

In alluding to this aspect of landscape we are entering into difficult territory. Referring to a kind of transcendence of nature in this way leaves us open to the criticism that this is yet another instance of Romantic idealization. This would directly contradict the previous claim that landscape is culturally constructed, a product of collective human action and consciousness. If we are to do justice to the evocation of landscape in the novelists studied, however, this cannot be the final word. For there is clearly something else at work in their narratives, something that recognizes landscape as beyond human history and action, something radically intractable to human influence, yet that works on and in human experience. To say this is to recognize nothing more startling than the agency of landscape itself. This does not, to be clear, amount to some kind of environmental determinism according to which a certain topography and climate necessarily produce a certain set of human characteristics. Rather, it is a matter of the necessity of commonplace or landscape to the act of writing itself. Without it, the protagonists and their actions would appear as so many disembodied ghosts floating in the ether. Both metaphorically and literally, then, landscape grounds narrated action, thereby granted it shareable meaning. For Lawrence, most of all, it is this grounding function of natural landscape that strikes him as essential in the novel. In his *Study of Hardy* he singles out *The Return of the Native* as exemplary in this regard:

> The [earth] heaved with raw instinct, Egdon whose dark soil was strong and crude and organic as the body of the beast. Out of the body of this crude earth are born Eustacia, Wildeve, Mistress Yeobright, Clym, and all the others. They are one year's accidental crop. What matter if some are drowned or dead, and others preaching or married: what matter, any more than the withering heath, the reddening berries, the seedy furze and the dead fern of one autumn of Egdon. The Heath persists. Its body is strong and fecund, it will bear many more crops beside this. Here is the sombre, latent power that will go on producing, no matter what happens to the product. Here is the dark, black source from whence all these little contents of lives are drawn [. . .] It is very good. Not Egdon is futile, sending forth life on the powerful heave of passion. It cannot be futile, for it is eternal. What is futile in the purpose of man. (Steele 1985, p. 25)

Here Lawrence enunciates a metaphysical and veritably cosmological vision that animates all his writing. It is eminently susceptible to deconstruction and critique as proto-fascist or straightforwardly mystifying in its fusion of religious and antihumanist language. In face of the more recent consensus that we are now living in the 'anthropocene' – the historical epoch marked by the pervasive and undeniable impact of human activity on all the earth's natural systems – Lawrence's insistence on the transcendent otherness of landscape seems more objectionable than ever. However, as inconvenient as it is, I believe it is essential to acknowledge this experience, for without doing so something essential animating the evocation of landscape in Eliot, Hardy, and Lawrence will be passed over or negated. And it is not merely a question of accepting Lawrence's highly idiosyncratic take on nature and its relation to human existence, steeped as his language is with a kind of religiously heightened organicism. The impulse is readily recognizable as a psychological inclination: the compensatory rewards of identifying a radical 'outside' for a man born into the extremely limited vista of working-class life in industrialized England in the late nineteenth century. Something similar could also be said of Eliot and Hardy.

But this psychologistic reductivism would also constitute an evasion, for the experience of natural landscape as something grounding yet beyond human action is actually common enough in everyday life. There is also something key here to contemporary environmental sensibility. In the *Dark Mountain Manifesto*, Paul Kingsnorth and Dougald Hine (2009) announced a project of what they call 'uncivilized writing' and describe it in the following manner:

> It sets out to paint a picture of homo sapiens which a being from another world or, better, a being from our own – a blue whale, an albatross, a mountain hare – might recognise as something approaching a truth. It sets out to tug our attention away from ourselves and turn it outwards; to uncentre our minds. It is writing, in short, which puts civilisation – and us – into perspective. Writing that comes not, as most writing still does, from the self-absorbed and self-congratulatory metropolitan centres of civilisation but from somewhere on its wilder fringes. Somewhere woody and weedy and largely avoided, from where insistent, uncomfortable truths about ourselves drift in; truths which we're not keen on hearing. Writing which unflinchingly stares us down, however uncomfortable this may prove.

The project of 'uncivilized writing' is something inspired by earlier literary encounters with the natural environment. The American poet and friend of Lawrence, Robinson Jeffers, is credited in the Manifesto as a significant precursor. Jeffers' notion of 'inhumanism' turns on the idea that there is a vital need, in the life of both the individual and the collective, to shift away from an increasing tendency to be caught up in self-regard. It is not difficult to see the affinities with how Lawrence, in *The Rainbow*, avoids the psychological introspection and narrative self-reflection typical of Eliot and instead grants a broader significance to the action of his protagonists by anchoring them in the seemingly timeless and cyclical processes of the earth. While Jeffers' star waned in the 1940s and 1950s, he is still revered as a founder of a certain strain of environmentalism, as the authors of the Dark Mountain Manifesto attest.

As lived and expressed by Lawrence, 'inhumanism' is anything but a denial of the importance of human relations. It is not – any more than it is for Jeffers – a misanthropic perspective that seeks to rid the earth of humanity as a kind of sickness or superfluity. In fact, for Lawrence an appreciation of our embeddedness in natural and cosmological processes is precisely the key for understanding and appreciating what is at stake in human relationships. The latter are locked into, as a microcosm, the surrounding and grounding forces of the greater world. In this light, Lawrence's keenly experienced revulsion in the face of the squalid industrial landscape he knew as a child and young man did not spawn a rejection of human endeavours and values more generally. Rather, it was the covered over and blocked access to a greater sense of connection against which he revolted in the midst of the closed circle of working-class life he knew. Although even here he found grandeur and freedom, as when he described the lives of the colliers he had known as a boy:

> The collier fled out of the house as soon as he could, away from the nagging materialism of the woman. With the women it was always: This is broken, now you've got to mend it! or else: We want this, that and the other; and where is the money coming from? The collier didn't know and didn't care very deeply – his life was otherwise. So he escaped. He loved the countryside, just the undiscriminating feel of it. Or he loved just to sit on his heels and watch – anything or nothing. He was not intellectually interested. Life for him did not consist in facts, but in a flow. Very often, he loved his garden. And very often he had a genuine love of the beauty of flowers. I have known it often and often, in colliers. (Lawrence 1964, pp. 136–37)

A profound, but unreflective relatedness to the natural landscape, characterized by receptiveness rather than possessiveness is the experience Lawrence describes here. And it is here that the practice of novel writing enters in for Lawrence, for it is the novel that represents 'the perfect medium for revealing to us the changing rainbow of our living relationships' (Lawrence 1964, p. 532). Lawrence's great literary breakthrough, in writing and rewriting what would eventually become *The Rainbow*, was his realization that human relationships contained, as a microcosm, vital connections to all the forces of the earth and cosmos. It is the relatedness that stands at the heart of human life, a relatedness that is constant and yet constantly evanescent in its modulations, that constitutes for Lawrence the perennial and, in fact, the only true theme of the novel:

Conclusion

> The great relationship, for humanity, will always be the relation between man and woman. The relation between man and man, woman and woman, parent and child, will always be subsidiary.
>
> And the relation between man and woman will change for ever, and will for ever be the new central clue to human life. It is the *relation itself* which is the quick and the central clue to life, not the man, nor the woman, nor the children that result from the relationship, as a contingency.
>
> It is no use thinking you can put a stamp on the relation between man and woman, to keep it in the *status quo*. You can't. You might as well try to put a stamp on a rainbow or the rain. (McDonald 1968, p. 531)

The relationship to natural landscape is, for Lawrence, the greater context within which relations between human beings go on. As such, landscape is profoundly related to but not subsumed by such relations. To the extent that natural systems and the whole ecological context that sustains life are subject to exploitation and commodification by capitalist modes of production, the vital connections between human life and landscape are attenuated or even entirely lost from view. In more contemporary language we can say that Lawrence experienced ecological crisis as a human existential crisis. He was not alone in this, as a whole lineage of ecological thought ranging from Thoreau and Emerson to Muir, Leopold, and Naess has given voice to this experience.

More broadly, the current of literature that has been traced in this book through Eliot, Hardy, and Lawrence represents an alternative heritage of this variety of ecological sensibility and experience. While in Eliot and Hardy it often wears the conservative garb of nostalgic yearning for a more honest and simpler rural England of the past, we should not fail to see the latent utopian dimension of their writing. While relations between principal characters are largely foregrounded by these writers, the landscapes in which these relations are located are in no way reducible to mere artificial stage sets. For what the novels of Eliot, Hardy, and Lawrence ultimately and most profoundly have in common is the effort to represent ways of maintaining and discovering authentic human relatedness in the midst of convulsive and radical social-material transformation. While the changes they document are not those we as readers now face, there is nevertheless a vital chain of experience that still binds us to their efforts. In their various attempts to tie together vital labour and living landscape we can find our own resources of hope and visions of the future.

Index

anthropocene, 142–43
Arendt, Hannah, 118
Arnold, Matthew, ix–x, xiv–xv; *Culture and Anarchy,* ix, 5

Benjamin, Walter, ix
Blair, Tony, 135, 137
Brexit, 129, 136
British Labour Party, x, 135–36

Cameron, David, 136
capitalism: ending, xii; Marxist critique, xviii
Chartism, 108
Cobb, Jonathan, viii, xi, xix, 118–19
Corbyn, Jeremy, x–xi
cultural studies, vii

Debord, Guy, 133
Delaney, Shelagh, 120
democracy, xvii
Dickens, Charles, xiii, 26

education, xvi
Eliot, George: Anglicanism, 14; class, 4, 24, 27–30, 105, 108, 112; Evangelicalism, 9, 13–14, 16; Methodism, 2–3, 106; Radicalism, 25–26, 107; Romanticism, 16–17
Emerson, Ralph Waldo, 145

enclosure, 105
Engels, Friedrich, 27, 114, 125

Foucault, Michel, viii, 137
Freud, Sigmund, 67

Gaskell, Elizabeth, xiii, 15
Graeber, David, 114
Gramsci, Antonio, 26

Hardy, Thomas: industrialization, 42, 63–64; landscape painting, 35, 62; rural *vs.* urban life, 41–42, 48, 66; social standing of women, 38–39; the working class, 105, 112–13
Harvey, David, 115–17, 122–25, 133–34, 139–41
Hine, Dougald, 143
Hoggart, Richard, vii–viii; *The Uses of Literacy,* ix, 111, 119–20

Jameson, Fredric, xii
Jeffers, Robinson, 143–44
Johnson, Boris, 136
Jones, Owen, 133

Kempis, Thomas à: *Imitation of Christ,* 21, 23
Kingsnorth, Paul, 143
Kunstler, Howard, 141

Lawrence, D. H.: Christianity, 82–83; class, 88; landscape, 98–102, 113; *Study of Thomas Hardy,* 45, 82, 91, 95, 97, 126–28, 142–43; War, 92–93; work, 91, 94, 97–98, 109–10, 115; the working class, 94–96, 100–101, 110, 112–13, 144
Lawrence, Frieda, 81
Leavis, F. R., 74, 92
Leopold, Aldo, 145
localism, xviii

Marx, Karl, 27, 114, 125, 133
May, Theresa, xi, 129–30
McRobbie, Angela, xi, 136
Mill, John Stuart, 5
Muir, John, 145

Naess, Arne, 145
neoliberalism: cities, 133–34, 139–41; creativity, xi–xii; entrepreneurialism, viii, 137; origins of, 115; work, 114, 116, 123–24, 139–40
New Labour, 135
Nietzsche, Friedrich, 126
Novalis, 19

Osborne, John, 120

Piketty, Thomas, xii
populism, xvii, 135

Reagan, Ronald, 122, 137
Reform Act: of 1832, 24, 28, 104–5, 122; of 1867, 5, 23
Richardson, Tony, 120

Rousseau, Jean-Jacques, 106
Ruskin, John, 16

Schiller, Friedrich, 10
Scuton, Roger, xiv
Sennett, Richard, viii, xi, xviii–xix, 118–19; *The Culture of the New Capitalism,* 116–18; *Together: The Rituals, Pleasures, and Politics of Cooperation,* 137–39
Shakespeare, William, 35
Smith, Neil, 129
Starmer, Keir, xi

Thatcher, Margaret, 122, 136–37
Third Way, xi
Thompson, E. P.: class, xvi; *The Making of the English Working Class,* xiii, xv, 5, 24, 104, 107–8, 117
Thoreau, Henry David, 145
Trotter, David, 74

unions, 114, 137

Williams, Raymond, vii, ix, xii–xiii, 14, 26–27, 33–34, 52, 57–58, 71, 74, 106, 111–12; *Border Country,* xiv; *The Country and the City,* 46, 66–67, 113, 121–22, 130–31, 134; *Culture and Society,* xiv, 122; *The Long Revolution,* xiv, 122; *Second Generation,* xiv
Wordsworth, William, xviii, 13, 21, 106, 126
working class: culture, vii, x, xiii; disappearance, x; education, vii–ix, xiii, 121; media representation, 120, 136; politics, xii

www.ingramcontent.com/pod-product-compliance
Lightning Source LLC
Chambersburg PA
CBHW021851300426
44115CB00005B/110